Zend Framework 3: Developer's guide

ADAM OMELAK

First Edition – February 2018

ISBN: 1983514640
ISBN-13: 978-1983514647

Table of contents

About the author

Adam Omelak has developed applications and websites for the needs of the Internet for over 11 years, using different languages like PHP, JavaScript, JAVA and ActionScript. In 2011, he graduated and acquired an Internet Computing degree at the University of Wales in Aberystwyth, Great Britain. Two years later at the same university, he completed a title of Masters of Science in Software Engineering, by writing a dissertation based on Zend Framework 1.

Creator of portals and on-line applications like: Funkcje.net, ZaplanujTransport.pl, GazetkiSklepowe.pl, Polish Shopping List Android and ChangeTires.net with Android app. One of his biggest applications is a web e-learning platform within Frog Education Ltd. made for the education sector in the United Kingdom, Denmark, Australia and Malaysia. The platform is used currently by over 12 million users worldwide.

For two years he worked in London for a company called Portal Technology Ltd. where he created from scratch a new e-commerce application: QuickLive, based on the biggest commercial technology on the market: hybris. He lived in Halifax and worked for Frog Education Ltd. for another 2 years, and he has been working there to the present day (another 4 years) remotely from Wrocław, Poland.

At the moment, he runs his own consultancy company in which he designs complex websites based on the latest technologies. He follows new trends and seeks for new solutions, mainly those which are popular in the United States of America.

More information about the projects and author's work experience can be found in the following links:

http://www.goldenline.pl/adam-omelak/

https://www.linkedin.com/in/adam-omelak-673134107

Direct email contact: *adam.omelak@gmail.com.*

Thanks

To my lovely parents, sister and my fiancé, without whom I would not have written this book. Additionally, I would like to thank the people with whom I was working and from whom I have learnt particular single Zend's components and the whole framework, these people are: Enrico Zimuel, Matthew Weier O'Phinney, Lee Mills (currently working at the biggest UK on-line shop), Steve Holt (Frog's Product Manager), Simon Marshall, Igor Pochyły, Simon Law, James Wilson and Tom Chapman. At the very end I would like to say a big thanks to Frog Education Ltd., the company for which I still work with, for the opportunity to discover and implement new technologies and solutions during my work on their main application.

CHAPTER 1.

Introduction

1.1. What is Zend Framework?

It is a complex work environment for PHP programmers that offers a range of facilities and amenities to improve and speed up the process of writing applications for the Internet. ZF initially created by Zend Technologies consists of, among others, components like: Zend Form to generate and handle forms, Zend Session to control user's sessions or Zend DB to communicate with different data bases. Each component handles a separate code folder so we can easily embed single components into our applications without the need for embedding and using the whole framework. However, only the whole Zend package offers us the full integration of all components along with another module called MVC, which defines how we should use Zend Framework in order to create full on-line websites.

Undoubtedly, what will be of interest to you, is the fact, that the authors of Zend Framework (Matthew Weier O'Phinney – team lead and Enrico Zimuel – core developer) are also the open source contributors of the PHP language. Thanks to this we are sure that the support for Zend will be long lasting and popular among other developers. Currently, ZF has over 220 million installations (*https://framework.zend.com/about*) and it runs on the PHP versions 5.6 and higher. That kind of support for the previous PHP versions improves the newly released version of the framework even more. Another positive is the New BSD license, which grants an ability to use this tool without any unnecessary fees both in private and commercial projects. Zend Framework uses a Composer package, which organizes the import of dependencies and third-party libraries. More about that can be found in chapter 2.1. Zend Framework is currently used by the biggest market players, through created on the basis of Zend commercial platform called Magento or BBC.

1.2. Components

Zend, like a majority of frameworks, is based on design patterns, which we will cover later in this book. To be able to move smoothly in the framework and implement new things, we should know at least the basics of patterns on which Zend uses its default plugins. As we have already mentioned, Zend consists of modular components, which are the biggest strength of the framework. Apart from main components (Session, Form or DB) the other essential fundaments are:

- `Authentication` — a plugin responsible for authorization and logging in of users;

- `Config` — a package allowing read and write access to configuration files;

- `Crypt` — a powerful tool for various types of password cryptography and hashing mechanisms;

- `DOM` — plugin responsible for querying and selecting elements in `DOM/HTML` via `CSS` selectors;

- `Event Manager` — an implementation for managing events according to the design pattern of the same name;

- `File` —a full service of local files on the server;

- `Mail` — a tool for sending e-mail messages with attachments in various formats HTML/PDF etc.;

- `MVC` — a lightweight Model View Controller package for handling requests from the browser;

- `MVC-i18n` integration — an international integration of multi languages for MVC packages;

- `Service Manager` — a tool for managing dependencies based off the Factory Pattern;

- `Validator` — a refreshed version of the validator designed to check the inputted data, available to use in any part of the code (not just the forms);

- `View` — an elastic view layer, supporting helpers, layouts and offering additional support for extra view types;

- `Toolbar` — a helpful debugging and profiling bar at the bottom of the page, which displays useful information around the executed piece of code.

The components mentioned above are just a small part of all available components in Zend Framework 3. In order to discover a full list of plugins you need to visit: *https://docs.zendframework.com*.

1.3. Why choose version 3.x?

The main argument for using ZF is the dissemination of good practices and design patterns among the web developers. Thanks to them the "self-learning programmer's" code is more readable and easy to understand. Why then should we use the 3.x version? The primary reason is the addition of new functionality and improvements over the previous version. Version 1.12.19 is no longer supported and 2.4.9 is only supported by bug fixes and crucial patches for errors in the codebase. Zend in version 1.0 is an initial part of what we can see now in 3.0, whereas it doesn't have any standalone components to manage overall as Service Manager does. This aspect has given developers a free hand to figure out their own way of handling project dependencies, such as passing objects via constructors (Dependency Injections) or creating one primary file (Façade), which returns already created objects and saves their copy in the cache memory, by using for instance: MemCached. MemCached is a tool for storing data on the server side in a machine's RAM memory. It is the quickest way to read/write objects. However, in the case of restarting the server machine the cache memory is also be wiped out.

Version 2.0 created a Module Manager service and other configuration facilities, which unfortunately looked very bad due to the fact that all the references of class names and others have been written in strings, which caused the issue that none of IDE has supported autocompleting in those cases. That along with the lack of backwards compatibility resulted in the discouragement of developers who used previous versions of ZF1 to move toward later versions. Of course, ZF3 version is not (same as 2.0) compatible with its precursor, however, thanks to ZF3 and the support from PHP 5.6, the initial problems with ZF2 have vanished for good, and additional solutions have been improved so that the new Zend Framework 3 developers could finally convince themselves to upgrade to the later version. The most important advantage of the new Zend is its speed, or rather the complete usage of the new available functions of PHP 7 language. The authors themselves are declaring that Zend Framework 3.x is almost 4 times faster than version 2.0. It was easy to predict after the previews of the new Zend Engine which powers PHP 7 and is profiled so that the new ZF would be the most efficient and effective framework.

1.4. What's new in ZF3?

- Compatibility. Zend Framework 3 is completely compatible with the 2.0 versions. A full list of migrations from 2.0 into 3.0 is available at: *https://docs.zendframework.com/tutorials/migration/to-v3/overview/*.

- Compositionality. Each of the components is now in a different GIT repository. Thanks to that change every component has its own separate development cycle, which improves modularity of each functionality and it speeds up releasing new versions to the clients.

- Full support of PHP 7. As the only one from the ZF3 family is supported in the latest available version of PHP.

- Speed. An efficiency of the new Zend is much higher. ZF3 is almost 4 times quicker on PHP 5 and another 4 times quicker on PHP 7 when compared to Zend Framework 2 – it speaks for itself.

- Documentation. Much better documentation together with full examples, maintained on GitHub. Fixes and improvements of docs can be done by any GIT users by reporting issues on GIT page for the given component, or by forking of the branch and creating pull requests.

- PSR-15. PHP Standard Recommendations 15 (PSR-15) is a set of standards defining the heading interfaces of HTTP protocol. All other languages, like Ruby, Python and Node.js already have standards like these, hence their application in ZF3 will only improve compatibility of the components in one library and their usage in other work environments.

- Middleware. Zend Framework provides a middleware architecture to execute PHP code using a pipeline of actions based on PSR-7 request and response.

- Fewer dependencies. Even further reduction of dependencies between the modules and their enhanced self-reliance allow the efficient responsibility spreading for components and enable the multiple use of these components in different situations. More information: *https://mwop.net/blog/2015-05-15-splitting-components-with-git.html*.

1.5. Community

At present, the community of new Zend Framework rapidly shares its knowledge in the GIT repositories, that's why we should begin looking for the issues and changes there. Obviously we can become the authors of Zend Framework – we just need to write a custom component or improve an existing one and share it on GitHub. If we search for a tag `zf3` on StackOverflow, we will see all questions related to Zend Framework 3 together with the potential answers. We could also notice that the number of queries is still growing and, currently, after a year from the release we have over 430 questions. Zend Framework also offers its own Forum platform, available at: *http://forums.zend.com*. On that website we can ask questions and request for help in fixing our code. Of course Zend also organizes meetings, courses and workshops in the whole world. Some of the more popular USA events are: ZendCon in Las Vegas or MidWest PHP in Bloomington. In addition, Zend offers an opportunity to get a certificate of Zend Certified Engineer, which requires passing one of the paper tests. The test on its own costs $195, while a course with one test attempt can be bought by $995. It will raise the qualifications and help in negotiating a better salary, when we apply to a new company for the Zend developer position.

1.6. Examples

All code samples used in this book can found and downloaded at the page: *http://divix.home.pl/zend3/zf3_chapters.zip* or via GitHub: *https://github.com/divix1988/zf3dg_chapters*. Inside there will be a list of chapters in which you will find folders like: *module*, *config* and *vendor*, which needs to be copied into the root directory of your own Zend Framework 3.0 installation folder. To unzip the examples, you will need a program like 7zip or WinRAR. Both are free and globally accessible tools to download.

Warning: the examples from this book can be only run on Zend Framework versions 3.1 or higher and PHP 5.7+. If another stable versions of Zend Framework comes out, I will try to systematically update the code in the samples. Can I please ask you – the readers, to give me a feedback on any potential issues that you can spot to the address: *adam.omelak@gmail.com* or by GitHub issues channel: *https://github.com/divix1988/zf3dg_chapters/* ↪*issues* .

CHAPTER 2.

Installation

2.1. Required applications

In order to start working with Zend Framework, we would need a work environment setup and suitable programs. The work environment is a local or remote server that handles services like Apache, PHP, databases and .htaccess. All the things related to the code environment will be outlined in the next subsection of this chapter. Here, however, I will focus on the selection of applications and tools helping to write our code.

Let's start with a basic tool, which is undoubtedly IDE - the programmer's code editor. Every experienced developer for sure knows more than one IDE from among the most popular ones. These are for example: Eclipse, Netbeans, Komodo, Sublime or PHPStorm, which offer support not only for PHP and HTML with CSS, but also for native languages, like JAVA or C++ (of course apart from PHPStorm, which is primarily designed for the PHP development). I have already used all of the above tools and the best choices were: Komodo Edit for very big projects, NetBeans for the smaller ones and PHPStorm for medium size projects. For the purpose of this book and for projects based on Zend Framework I would definitely recommend NetBeans, most of all due to the native and full support for ZF2 and ZF3, Symfony and because it is extremely quick with these projects. My version 8.1 is available to download from the link: *https://netbeans.org/downloads/index.html*, column PHP. If you have a 64-bit version of an operating system, I would recommend you download the Download x64, for any others there is of course a x86 version. After downloading and installing the IDE we can move to the application which will design and build the database. One of the most known tool of this type is MySQL Workbench, which we can get from here: *https://www.mysql.com/products/workbench/*.

2.2. Setup of work environment

Now, when we have all the required applications, we can begin setting up the work environment, that is the server. To do that we will use a free package called XAMPP, made by Apache Friends. This is a self-configuring set, thanks to which we won't have to do much (apart from the installation) to set it up on Windows machines types. For this book we will be using XMAPP in version 5.6.3, which has the following specifications:

- Apache 2.4.4,

- MySQL 5.5.32 (Community Server),

- PHP 5.6.3 (VC11 X86 32bit thread safe) + PEAR,

- phpMyAdmin 4.0.4

We are not using the latest version of XAMPP on purpose, because 5.6.3 is the last available stable version available for Windows XP, 2003, Vista and 7. The later versions support only Windows 7 SP1, Windows 8 and Windows 10. Although nothing stands in your way to update XAMPP with a more recent version of PHP 7, however I will be using the stable 5.6 one.

If during the installation process of XAMPP or after running a file from the main folder *xampp-control.exe* and clicking *Start* next to Apache we get an error with the following message:

> The program can't start because api-ms-win-crt-runtime-l1-1.0.dll is missing from your computer

then we would need to install additional C++ libraries: Redistribution package 2008 and Redistribution package 2015. Both of these libraries are available here: *http://www.microsoft.com/en-us/download/details.aspx*

↳?id=5582 and *https://www.microsoft.com/pl-pl/download/details.aspx* ↳?id=48145 .

After the installation of these C++ libraries we need to open once more the admin panel *xampp-control.exe* and click the buttons Start next to Apache and MySQL. We should get result shown on the image 2.1.

If we notice an error with the following message:

1:14:33 PM [apache] Possible problem detected!
1:14:33 PM [apache] Port 80 in use by "c:\program files
(x86)\skype\phone\skype.exe"!

in such case we would need to go into Skype settings: *Tools/Advanced/Connections* where we can uncheck the option: Use 80 and 443 ports for additional incoming calls.

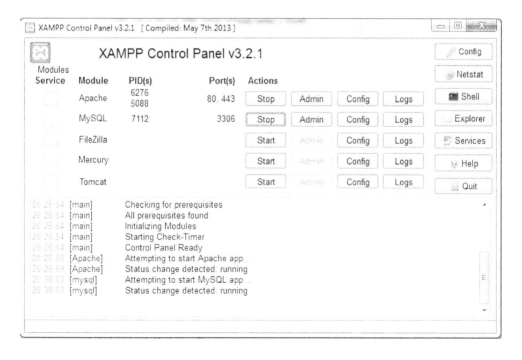

Image 2.1.

For starters we need to double check if our freshly configured server works correctly. We would need to open our web browser and type in: *http://localhost/*. If that doesn't work, then we should try: *http://localhost/xampp/*. The starting page of XAMPP should appear – see image 2.2.

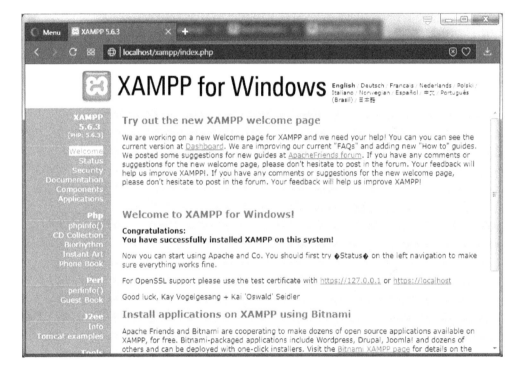

Image 2.2.

The one last check is to verify if our database is also working as expected. To do that we need to click the *phpMyAdmin* link, which should display a list of the available databases and modifications options.

Once we would finally setup our XMAPP instance correctly, we need to install a Composer. It is a tool in the command line, which manages all dependencies of other projects by integrating them with our codebase. The installation of the Composer is done through the command line; the best option is Shell, which is available in the control panel of XAMPP. On the right-hand side there is a Shell button - click it and then navigate to the folder *php/* by typing:

```
cd php/
```

Now we can paste the following code, which will organize the installation on its own (you can copy it from: *https://getcomposer.org/download/*):

```
php -r "copy('https://getcomposer.org/installer', 'composer-setup.php');"
php -r "if (hash_file('SHA384', 'composer-setup.php') ===
'e115a8dc7871f15d853148a7fbac7da27d6c0030b848d9b3dc09e2a0388afed865e6a3d6b3c
0fad45c48e2b5fc1196ae')
{ echo 'Installer verified'; } else { echo 'Installer corrupt';
unlink('composer-↪setup.php'); } echo PHP_EOL;"
php composer-setup.php
php -r "unlink('composer-setup.php');"
```

If we get an information complaining about the old version:

```
Composer: Warning: This development build of composer is over 60 days
old. It is recommended to update it by running
"C:\ProgramData\ComposerSetup\bin\composer.phar ↪self-update" to get the latest
version. hp
```

then we are required to type and run:

```
php composer.phar self-update
```

Like you have already noticed, the Composer is available by calling *composer.phar*, which is quite long and unfortunately local. In order to make it easier to use, we need to go to the folder *php/* in XAMPP and create a file in there with the name *composer.bar* with the following contents:

```
@ECHO OFF
php "% ~dp0composer.phar" %*
```

Thanks to the lines above, we can use our new tool without any issues, wherever we are, by simply executing the command *composer*.

The last thing to finish setting-up the Composer is changing to a development mode:

composer development-enable

This gives us the option to update all the related dependencies to our local project, even these designed to be injected when in dev mode. In order to verify if our installation was successful, we should type:

composer

by that we should get a window with contents similar to the following:

Image 2.3.

Optionally we can install and setup an application that controls the version of a code, like GIT or SVN, however this dependency goes beyond the subjects of this book. Using the version control, we can safely change the code and go back to the previous versions of the old code by using the history of changes and logs of these revisions and branches.

2.3. Downloading application skeleton

There are two ways to get an application skeleton of ZF3: by the Composer or by downloading a ZIP file. Here, we will download the Zend Framework 3 skeleton via Composer tool. To do that, we need to follow the instructions from: *https://docs.zendframework.com/tutorials/getting-started/skeleton-application/*. This can be done in 2 ways as well. By default Zend 3 installs itself with only two built-in components: `zend-mvc` – for handling the views and controllers, and `zend-component-install` – for managing additional dependencies and configurations. Let's create an empty folder with the name *zend3* in *htdocs/*, then type in a first command to get Zend via SHELL (of course we are still running this inside the *htdocs/* folder):

```
composer create-project -s dev zendframework/skeleton-application zend3
```

The given command creates a default project of a Zend 3 structure and the development type. Straight after running this line we will get a set of questions asking about extra tools. To the first question: `Do you want a minimal install?` we answer `N`, then `Y` for the following: `toolbar`, `caching`, `database`, `forms`, `json`, `logging`, `mvc`, `i18n`, `mvc plugins`, `psr-7`, `session`, `testing` and `zend-di`. We are going to use these components in the next chapters of this book, so we may as well get them now, all in one go. In the middle of this creation process, we will be also asked about:

```
Please select which config file you wish to inject 'ZendDeveloperTools' into:
```

For the answer we type `1`, as we want to have the Zend configuration just in one file*: modules.config.php*. To the next question:

```
Remember this option for other packages of the same type? (y/N)
```

we answer `y`, in order to remember our configuration choice for the other components which might be added later in this paper.

2.4. Zend Configuration

Finally, in order to display a welcome page of Zend Framework 3, we need to configure our fresh skeleton for the XAMPP purposes.

We could use a composer to start a server, if you are a Mac or Linux user, by running: `php -S localhost:8000` in the console, but this approach is obsolete since we use a XAMPP approach.

By default main Front Controller file, by which every request is handled, is located in the folder *public/index.php*. However, we want to call this file from the main directory of file like: *http://localhost/zend3*. In order to do that, we can either modify a vhosts file in: *xampp\apache\conf\extra\httpd-vhosts.conf* and add these lines:

```
DocumentRoot "[xampp_location]/htdocs/zf3/public"
ServerName localhost/zend3
```

That way we don't have to do anything to the Zend Skeleton Application as its designed to be ready to run without any code change.

Or we can avoid changing any apache configuration files (for instance when we have a hosted and shared server and we don't have an access to edit config), by creating a file: *index.php* (with the content shown below) in the folder *zend3/*:

```
<?php include 'public/index.php';
```

It is the same approach as in Zend 1 and it has no effect on the efficiency of the new Zend. Next, in the same directory as new file *index.php*, we have to create another new file called *.htaccess* with below data:

```
SetEnv APPLICATION_ENV development
RewriteEngine On
RewriteRule .* index.php
```

The first line sets the global environment variable `APPLICATION_ENV` with the development value, thanks to which we will output more information about the errors and see the toolbar console on the site.

The second line enables for us, a rewrite function, which will handle setting and translating URL addresses. The last line redirects all of the requests to the *index.php* file.

Now we just need to set our base URL at the *public/* folder so that the images or JavaScript files can be properly referenced to the right location. The base URL is a relative address to our project. In the file *zend3/module/Application ↪/config/module.config.php* we need to add the following lines to the 'view_manager' key:

```
'template_path_stack' => [
    __DIR__ . '/../view',
],
'base_path' => '/zend3/public/'
```

We have to remember to add a coma before `'base_path'`. The last thing in the initial configuration of the skeleton is enabling a display of all errors reporting, warnings and debug information on the development machine. Let's add the code below to the file *zend3/public/index.php* at the very beginning:

```
/**
 * Display all errors when APPLICATION_ENV is development.
 */
if ($_SERVER['APPLICATION_ENV'] === 'development') {
    error_reporting(E_ALL);
    ini_set("display_errors", 1);
}
```

Finally, when we visit *http://localhost/zend3/*, we should see a full welcome page similar to the one below – image 2.4.

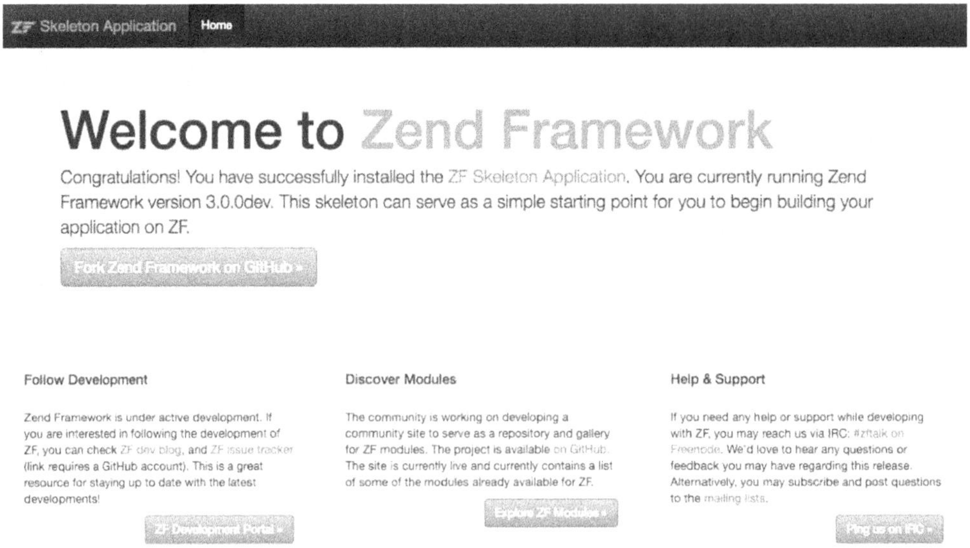

Welcome to Zend Framework

Congratulations! You have successfully installed the ZF Skeleton Application. You are currently running Zend Framework version 3.0.0dev. This skeleton can serve as a simple starting point for you to begin building your application on ZF.

Fork Zend Framework on GitHub »

Follow Development

Zend Framework is under active development. If you are interested in following the development of ZF, you can check ZF dev blog, and ZF issue tracker (link requires a GitHub account). This is a great resource for staying up to date with the latest developments!

ZF Development Portal »

Discover Modules

The community is working on developing a community site to serve as a repository and gallery for ZF modules. The project is available on GitHub. The site is currently live and currently contains a list of some of the modules already available for ZF.

Explore ZF Modules »

Help & Support

If you need any help or support while developing with ZF, you may reach us via IRC: #zftalk on Freenode. We'd love to hear any questions or feedback you may have regarding this release. Alternatively, you may subscribe and post questions to the mailing lists.

Ping us on IRC »

Image 2.4.

The final database configuration are in the files: *config/autoload/global.php* and *local.php.dist*. First of all, we need to start by changing the second file. This type of file has an additional extension called .dist, since it's just a distributed file. Because the distribution files are used as placeholders, that item has only a structure without any optional elements. For now, we have done everything which is necessary to setup the sample Zend application. For more information about the connection with database, please check a section called "Initial configuration" 4.1.

We are now ready to analyze the structure of the freshly added Zend Framework 3 skeleton in the next chapter :)

CHAPTER 3.

Structure of Application Skeleton

3.1. Configuration files

Main configuration files like *global.php* or *local.php* are located (same as in Zend 1) in the root folder *config/*. What has changed is the way the configuration files are stored. Instead of INI files, we have regular PHP files, which return an associative array, thanks to which the new Zend 2 and 3 are much quicker. All the other configuration settings dependent on the development environment mode are entered into *development.local.php*. This file clones itself into *development.local.php* after changing into developer's mode by:

```
composer development-enable
```

We can turn it off by typing:

```
composer development-disable
```

If we want to check environment status, we have to call:

```
composer development-status
```

It is worth mentioning that compared with Zend Framework 1, version 3 does not support the reading of specific sections in the file nor its inheritance anymore. The component responsible for handling config files is still called `Zend\Config`; it supports reading, writing and parsing the following formats: `INI`, `PHP arrays`, `JSON`, `YAML` and `XML`.

The easiest usage example of `Zend\Config` will be a separate file with a PHP array, called *debug_config.php*

```
return [
    'display_errors' => true,
    'styling' => [
        'headings' => true,
        'theme' => 'aqua'
    ],
];
```

which we will then include for reading in another PHP file:

```
$config = new Zend\Config\Config(include 'debug_config.php');

//line below will return: true
echo $config->display_errors;
```

Thanks to the line above we will get a configuration in `Zend\Config` format. What if we have an `INI` file and we want to use it in another form, for instance an `Array`? There is nothing simpler: instead of passing the `INI` to the constructor, we will use a factory from the `Config` class.

```
$config = Zend\Config\Factory::fromFile(__DIR__ . '/config.ini');

//will return a PHP array from ini file
$print_r($config);
```

If, however, we again need an instance of `Zend/Config`, then we can pass a second argument `boolean` set as `true` and we will be able to operate on the instance of object `Zend/Config`.

Another possibility is updating or adding a new property to the already existing configuration. The `Zend/Config/Writer` package, because that class supports all the already mentioned file types for reading. Let's have a look at a simple example, in which we will create two configuration files, one in XML format and another in JSON.

```
//create empty configuration object
$config = new Zend\Config\Config([], true);
$config->debug = true;
//set two arrays
$config->db = [];
$config->db->debug = true;
$config->db->params = [];

$config->db->params->host = 'localhost';
$config->db->params->user = 'root';
$config->db->params->password = 'abc';
$config->db->params->dbname = 'users';
```

In order to display a configuration in XML format, we only need two lines of code:

```
$writer = new Zend\Config\Writer\Xml();
echo $writer->toString($config);
```

which will result in output:

```
<?xml version="1.0" encoding="UTF-8"?>
<zend-config>
    <db>
        <debug>true</debug>
        <params>
            <host>localhost</host>
            <user>root</user>
            <password>abc</password>
            <dbname>users</dbname>
        </params>
    </db>
</zend-config>
```

In a very similar way we can also get a result in JSON; the only difference is to use another class for creation:

```
$writer = new Zend\Config\Writer\Json();
echo $writer->toString($config);

//will return:
```

```json
{
    "db": {
        "debug": true,
        "params": {
            "host": "localhost",
            "username": "root",
            "password": "abc",
            "dbname": "users"
        }
    }
}
```

The configuration files generated in a such way can then of course write into a specific file by using a static method from factory `toFile()`, which takes two arguments: a file path to file and an object of `Zend\Config` or PHP array.

```php
$config = new Zend\Config\Config([], true);
$config->request = [];
$config->request->url = 'http://funkcje.net';
$config->request->method = 'get';
```

```php
//save to file
Zend\Config\Factory::toFile(__DIR__ . '/custom_config.php', $config);
```

There is yet another useful function of `Zend\Config` package – merging many configuration files into one. Obviously, those types of formats can be different - we can easily merge INI, JSON or YAML files. We will illustrate that by the method `fromFiles()` in the code below:

```php
$config = Zend\Config\Factory::fromFiles([
    __DIR__.'/first_config.ini',
    __DIR__.'/second_config.json',
    __DIR__.'/third_config.yaml'
]);
```

3.2. Third-party libraries

All dependencies in new Zend Framework 3, along with a whole autoloader, are now managed by the Composer. We can easily check that by opening a file *public/index.php* and analyzing two lines:

```
// Composer autoloading
include __DIR__ . '/../vendor/autoload.php';
```

What does it mean for developers? It means that whatever changes in dependencies, like for instance adding/removing libraries or modules, have to be performed accordingly to the guidelines of Composer itself. In order to do that, we have to first edit a file named: *composer.json*, which defines new libraries, and later execute a command `composer update [packaged_name]`, to add our dependency. By default *composer.json* is defined according to the following schema:

```
{
    "name": "zendframework/skeleton-application",
    "description": "Sample application in Zend Framework 3",
    "license": "BSD-3-Clause",
    "keywords": [
        "zend framework",
        "zf3"
    ],
    "homepage": "http://funkcje.net/",
    "repositories": [
        {
        "type": "vcs",
        "url": "https://github.com/... "
        }
    ],
    "require": {
        "php": "^5.6 || ^7.0",
        "zendframework/zend-mvc": "^3.0.1",
    },
    "autoload": {
        "psr-4": {},
        "include": {}
    },
    "autoload-dev": {},
    "extra": [],
```

```
    "scripts": {},
    "require-dev": {}
}
```

- name – defines of course the project name on github (if its published in there);

- description – a brief piece of information about the project;

- keywords – used for describing a project by tags followed by the coma;

- license – the type of the license of the released project;

- homepage – the project's home page URL or author's website;

- repositories – a list of linked GIT repositories;

- require – a list describing required applications and their dependencies; it contains records such as: author/name: version;

- autoload – defines the way of loading other libraries;

- autoload-dev – same as autoload, but for development mode;

- extra – an optional key, which might contain the data available for scripts;

- scripts – listener scripts for appropriate Composer actions, for example: Class::postUpdate() in a class, or command from SHELL. An event list is available here: *https://getcomposer.org/doc/articles/scripts.md#command-events* ;

- `require-dev` – a list describing requirements of an application in development mode;

The most important and frequently edited sections are `require` and `autoload`. If we will be attaching other libraries, then of course our table require will get much bigger. On the other hand, not all external libraries have the same architecture and autoloader method. That is why a key `autoload` offers different variants we can use. The easiest one is files, used mainly in very old and small libraries, which did not profit from the standard `autloaders`. Thanks to files we can specify which files need to be available straight away when using the library.

```
"autoload": {
    "files": [
        "somelibrary/folder/file1.php",
        "somelibrary/inny_folder/file2.php"
    ]
}
```

Another option is using a `Classmap`. It requires passing an array of the folders only, in which the Composer will be searching PHP and INC files. Currently, the `Classmap` is used for all incompatible libraries with PSR-4 and PSR-0 which we will mention in a moment.

```
"autoload": {
    "classmap": [
        "src/",
        "lib/",
        "inny_plik.php"
    ]
}
```

The most advanced examples are based on a PSR-4/0. They both are also recommended structures of new libraries. Depending on which format we choose, they will be slightly different in the *folder/files* structures. Zend Framework 3 uses a PSR-4 format, which we will describe below:

```
"autoload": {
    "psr-4": {
```

```
        "Monolog\\": "src/",
        "Vendor\\Namespace\\": ""
    }
}
```

In the same configuration, the autoloader is trying to read, for example, class: `Monolog\Main` in folder *src/Monolog/Main.php*, if that file does exist. Do not forget about the double backslashes in the record names; they are used to avoid name conflicts like `Monologer` in another library.

3.3. Modules configuration

Our whole configuration concerning the single module we place in a file *config/Module.config.php*, which can contain various keys, available below:

Key name	Method name	Manager name
controller_plug ins	getControllerPluginCon fig()	ControllerPluginMana ger
controllers	getControllerConfig()	ControllerManager
filters	getFilterConfig()	FilterManager
form_elements	getFormElementConfig()	FormElementManager
hydrators	getHydratorConfig()	HydratorManager
input_filters	getInputFilterConfig()	InputFilterManager
route_manager	geRoutetConfig()	RoutePluginManager
serilizers	getSerializerConfig()	SerializerAdapterMan ager
service_manager	getServiceConfig()	ServiceLocator
validators	getValidatorConfig()	ValidatorManager

view_helpers	getViewHelperConfig()	ViewHelperManager
log_processors	getLogProcessorConfig( )	LogProcessorManager
log_writers	getLogWriterConfig()	LogWriterManager

Instead of defining the keys in the configuration file we can define the above methods that will return either the same or a custom configuration array in the file *Module.php*, for example:

```
public function getControllerConfig()
{
    return array('factories' => array(...));
)
```

Obviously, the methods are overriding the configuration from the configuration files, so they have a bigger priority.

A key service_manager and method getServiceConfig(), which we will use the most, will be explained in the section 7.3. Setting a view_manager, which is responsible for the view files configurations, is important as well. Here you can see an example of that key from the Zend Framework 3 skeleton:

```
'view_manager' => [
    'display_not_found_reason' => false,
    'display_exceptions' => false,
    'doctype' => 'HTML5',
    'not_found_template' => 'error/404',
    'exception_template' => 'error/index',
    'template_map' => [
        'layout/layout' => __DIR__ . '/../view/layout/layout.phtml',
        'application/index/index' => __DIR__ . '/../view/
↪application/index/index.phtml',
        'error/404' => __DIR__ . '/../view/error/404.phtml',
        'error/index' => __DIR__ . '/../view/error/index.phtml',
```

```
    ],
    'template_path_stack' => [
        __DIR__ . '/../view',
    ],
    'base_path' => '/zend3/public/'
],
```

- `display_not_found_reason` – defines if the system should display the reason why the user is seeing a 404 error – page not found;

- `display_exceptions` – used to control the display of exceptions;

- `doctype` – a standard HTML document type, which will be attached to every generated website;

- `not_found_template` – a file path to the view for error 404;

- `exception_template` – a file path to the view for 500 errors;

- `template_map` – an array of file paths to a template of a home page, 404 error and a general error on the main page;

- `template_path_stack` – a list of directories, in which Zend will be looking for adequate views;

- `base_path` – main path to application (previously called: "base URL");

Let's have a look at the simpler configuration keys like `filters`, `input_filters` or `form_elements`; the latter will be used in the example soon. All these keys are describing: regular filters, validator filters and elements of forms like `Password` or `Capctha`. In the following example we illustrate how we can override an existing element type `Email` with a custom class `MyEmail`, when using a `getFormElementConfig()` method. A key `invokable` is the easiest configuration service. It takes a format `name => class` and it does not allow embedding extra parameters.

```php
public function getFormElementConfig()
{
    return array(
        'invokables' => array(
            'Email' => 'Application\Form\Element\MyEmail'
        )
    );
}
```

3.4. How Zend 3 works?

Zend Framework 3 is obviously based on the previous Zend 2 version, while the MVC approach has been established in the very first version of Zend. The MVC is based on one main file *public/index.php* that functions like Front Controller - the first point of contact. Next, `Zend Router` (or other registered router component) recognizes an address and redirects to the right controller. A controller's class then executes an appropriate action method, which also defines the variables needed to generate a view with the same path as the action name. For example, if we try to open a link *localhost/users/add*, our router will locate a controller with name `UsersController` and will call the method `addAction()` and display the contents of the view from the location *view/users/add.phtml*. At the same time, before displaying the view, Zend checks if there is a declared view template, and then it attaches it by pasting the generated contents of action into an already defined placeholder in that template file.

In this version, however, Zend gives us the ability to choose between the standard MVC and the new MOVE. The MOVE is a shorthand for Models, Operations, Views and Events. So, as the name suggests, it's an ideology based on the events architecture. The events themselves are detailed in section 7.1, that is why I will only outline some differences between these two architectures. First off, the modules stay the same, and all the knowledge about the single object's logic is kept in here. The MVC allows the "fat model, skinny controller" approach, however, the MOVE forbids declaring events in models. Operations in our models are moved into a new layer, called Operations. Views in these two implementations are exactly the same. In place of a controller in the MOVE we have events that link all 3 layers together. Of course, it is a dynamic linkage, thanks to which all modules or operations are independent and can be used in any situation. The communication principles are easy: the views listen to events from models and operations, operations can change models, but models cannot interfere with operations or views.

On the other hand, the process of configurations has changed massively (especially the Service Manager is a main guy here) and because of that it became a wall which most of the programmers could not jump over. Reviews were like: "I don't know what is going on there. Why I cannot just pass my own dependencies the way I want to? Alright, I am moving back to Zend 1." In reality, creators of Zend have confessed that they had created a system based on too innovative and complex configuration which had no transitional phase. Zend Framework 3 tries to make it up and improve a process of acclimatization for new developers. In a nutshell, the process of configuration looks like below:

- A load of system configuration, defined in *config/application.config.php*.

- An optional config manipulation via class methods.

- Sending the configuration to the instance of Application and `ModuleManager` objects, to begin a process of running the components.

- Loading the configuration of an application module. `ModuleManager` gets all configurations from components and/or class methods.

- Merging of configuration with method `getConfig()`.

- Setting and full merging of additional files with service configurations `config_global_path`. Next run of event `EVENT_MERGE_CONFIG`, after which configuration is linked by `ConfigListener`.

- At the end, the final configuration is passed to the `ServiceManager` object.

## CHAPTER 4

Simple application and workflow

4.1. Initial configuration

By default Zend comes with a first module named Application. It is designed mainly to display the static informative site with links to the module documentation or help pages. We are going to use exactly that module to edit the code and to enter changes, so we can learn how the new Zend Framework works.

Our goal in this chapter is to implement a connection with MySQL database and then get values from a specific record.

We will start by creating a sample table called users in MySQL, which will contain 3 columns: id, username and password. We can create it via phpMyAdmin which comes with XAMPP package, or directly by SQL query in MySQL command line prompt.

```
CREATE TABLE IF NOT EXISTS `users` (
    `id` int(11) NOT NULL,
    `username` varchar(100) NOT NULL,
    `password` char(128) NOT NULL
```

```
) ENGINE=InnoDB
ALTER TABLE `users`
ADD PRIMARY KEY (`id`);
ALTER TABLE `users`
MODIFY `id` int(11) NOT NULL AUTO_INCREMENT;
```

Next we will begin with the modification of the configuration of our application in the main folder. To *config/global.php* we will add the code below:

```
'db' => array(
    'driver' => 'Pdo',
    'dsn' => 'mysql:dbname=zend3;host=localhost',
    'driver_options' => array(
        PDO::MYSQL_ATTR_INIT_COMMAND => 'SET NAMES \'UTF8\''
    )
),
'service_manager' => array(
    'factories' => array(
        'Zend\Db\Adapter\Adapter' => 'Zend\Db\Adapter\AdapterServiceFactory',
    ),
)
```

and to *config/local.php.dist*, which we will later change to *local.php*:

```
'db' => array(
    'username' => 'root',
    'password' => ''
)
```

Now we just turn on the development mode in the command line, so our `.dist` files will clone into their native `.php` form:

```
composer development-enable
```

Everything we did above results in setting a password and user name for our default MySQL database. A default XAMPP name of our main user is root, the password, however, is not set at all.

The same as in the previous Zend version, in order to connect to any database, we need to provide access information. A default host in XAMPP is *localhost*, while a name of a database can be anything (in our example it is "zend3"), in which we already have a new table users. Next, in a key `driver` we describe a type of database; MySQL default value is `Pdo`. Additionally, we define a type of character encoding for our database, that is `UTF-8`; if we don't set it up properly here, then instead of for instance Polish chars we will get funny characters like ??. Take a close look, *global.php* does not contain information about the username and password. All related configuration data should be placed in *local.php*. This results from the version control system where *global.php* is sent to repository, while *local.php* is added to ignored files by GIT or SVN. Thanks to that you will never "share" your private passwords with other people, if you send by mistake send something over on the public version control server.

Apart from adding the data to database we also add a record called `service_manager`, which determines dependencies of our module on other classes. An option `factories` means that we will be creating a new instance of class `Zend\Db\Adapter\Adapter` (so practically the same class as in Zend 1). It will be created with a driver parameter `Zend\Db\Adapter\` ↪`AdapterServiceFactory`. As a result we will not have to worry about creating any new Zend objects in our controllers or models. The class will be already available to use in other configuration files, which we will mention in a moment.

Next step is to configure, this time the module itself, by adding the code below to the *modules/Application/config/module.config.php*

```
'controllers' => [
    'factories' => [
        Controller\IndexController::class => function($sm) {
            $usersService = $sm->get('Application\Model\UsersTable');
            return new Controller\IndexController($usersService);
        }
    ],
],
```

A key named controllers, like the name suggests, sets all the controllers available in a module. Because we would have to get and display a record from a table `users`, we also need to have an access to the new module (named `UsersTable`). We are passing an object out of the module `$usersService` by a constructor `Application\src\Controller\`

↪`IndexController.php`. The only "magic" here is to get `UsersTable` by `$sm`, that is Service Manager, which is always available as a first argument, by using a method `get()`. Obviously, currently the Service Manager does not have our model, because it doesn't exist yet. In order to add our class into SM, we need an additional code in the file *module/Applcation/src/* ↪*Module.php*:

```
public function getServiceConfig()
{
    return array(
        'factories' => array(
            'UsersTableGateway' => function ($sm) {
                $dbAdapter = $sm->get('Zend\Db\Adapter\Adapter');
                $resultSetPrototype = new ResultSet();
                $resultSetPrototype->setArrayObjectPrototype(new User());
                return new TableGateway('users', $dbAdapter, null,
↪$resultSetPrototype);
            },
            'Application\Model\UsersTable' => function($sm) {
                $tableGateway = $sm->get('UsersTableGateway');
                $table = new UsersTable($tableGateway);
                return $table;
            }
        );
    }
```

As you can see, we have added to the file *Module.php* a new method `getServiceConfig()`, which determines extra configuration of our internal components like models, forms or regular objects.

In order to make the above method work as expected, we also need to add links to classes (just under the namespace definition in file), the classes which we link to are:

```
use Application\Model\User;
use Application\Model\UsersTable;
use Zend\Db\ResultSet\ResultSet;
use Zend\Db\TableGateway\TableGateway;
```

At the very start we define `UsersTableGateway` which will be inherited from Zend object `TableGateway` directed towards the table called users. That class will be returning objects of type *Application/src/Model/User.php* where we will put methods such as `getId()` or `getUsername()`. Notice that thanks to the earlier `Zend\Db\Adapter\Adapter` class declaration in *config/global.php*, we already have access to the instance of that class by Service Manager.

Afterwards, we configure `Application\Model\UsersTable` by grabbing the just defined `UsersTableGateway` and returning the object of `UsersTable` class. Now we just need to create the appropriate files and modify a controller.

4.2. Modifications in controller and view

Let's maybe start from two new classes, `User` and `UsersTable`.

First of them represents a single record in a table/database. So if our table has 3 columns, we need to have at least 3 methods like: `getId()`, `getUsername()`, `getPassword()`, plus an additional method `exchangeArray($row)`, which will convert a returned associative array into class properties. The class `User` from *Application/src/Model/User.php* file looks like below:

```
namespace Application\Model;
class User
{
    protected $id;
    protected $username;
    protected $password;
    public function exchangeArray($row)
    {
        $this->id = (!empty($row['id'])) ? $row['id'] : null;
        $this->username = (!empty($row['username'])) ? $row['username'] : null;
        $this->password = (!empty($row['password'])) ? $row['password'] : null;
    }
    public function getId() {
        return $this->id;
    }
    public function getUsername() {
```

```
        return $this->username;
    }
    public function getPassword() {
        return $this->password;
    }
}
```

Let's make another class `UsersTable`, which we will store in the same place as *User.php*.

```
namespace Application\Model;
use Zend\Db\TableGateway\TableGateway;
class UsersTable
{
    public function __construct(TableGateway $tableGateway)
    {
        $this->tableGateway = $tableGateway;
    }
    public function getById($id)
    {
        $id = (int) $id;
        $rowset = $this->tableGateway->select(array('id' => $id));
        $row = $rowset->current();
        if (!$row) {
            throw new \Exception('user not found with id: '.$id);
        }
        return $row;
    }
}
```

`UsersTable` is our model, which will responsible for the communication with the database. In this class we can have standard CRUD operations, like: `create()`, `replace()`, `update()` or `delete()` and – just like in the above example – `getById()`, `getByUsername()` and so on. If you remember the *Module.php* file, you probably know that the constructor of that class requires an object of `TableGateway` type. As a reminder:

```
$table = new UsersTable($tableGateway);
```

In such a way we created an object which will be received in `__constructor()`. We could also create a new and specific exception to our case when user is not found, called: `NotFoundException` which would be place into *src/Exception/* folder.

Inside of the only method `getById()` we pass an `id` number of a record we are searching for. The rest is just a regular usage of Zend Db, which we call method `select()` with an `$id` argument. Thanks to `$rowset->current()` we grab a first result of the query. If it's empty, we throw an exception; otherwise we return a single object of `Application\Model\User` type.

Let's move into controller `IndexController`. We should link it with a module and view where we would display the data about the user; it should look like:

```
namespace Application\Controller;
use Zend\Mvc\Controller\AbstractActionController;
use Zend\View\Model\ViewModel;
use Application\Model\UsersTable;
class IndexController extends AbstractActionController
{
    private $usersTable = null;
    public function __construct(UsersTable $usersTable)
    {
        $this->usersTable = $usersTable;
    }
    public function indexAction()
    {
        $view = new ViewModel();
        $model = $this->usersTable;
        $row = $model->getById(1);
        $view->setVariable('id', $row->getId());
        $view->setVariable('username', $row->getUsername());
        $view->setVariable('password', $row->getPassword());
        return $view;
    }
}
```

The first thing we do is a definition of class variable of our model `$usersTable`, which is received from the controller's constructor. Later we modify a method `indexAction()`, which now calls a method `getById()` from the `usersTable` with parameter 1. At the same time we should add a single record to the table of MySQL database called users with `ID = 1` and some other dummy data. In my example a dump of the table users looks like:

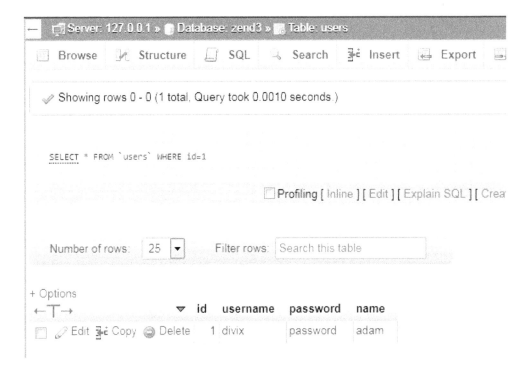

Image 4.1.

Back to the controller, we call a function `setVariable()` from the object `new ViewModel()`, which will send us one variable to the view file *index.phtml*. This method takes the first argument as the name of the variable in a view, and then a value. Variable `$row`, which is returned by `getById()` is our object of `Application\Model\User`. Due to this fact we are able to call its methods such as: `getId()` or `getUsername()`. We repeat analogically first line with the `id` for `username` and `password` fields.

The last task is to display the user's data in the *Application/view/application/↪index/index.phtml* view:

```
<div class="jumbotron">
    <h1><span class="zf-green">Zend Framework 3</span></h1>
    <p>
        Found user:<br /><br />
        Id: <?php echo $id; ?><br />
        Username: <?php echo $username; ?><br />
        Password: <?php echo $password; ?>
```

```
            </p>
        </div>
```

In here you can freely ignore any HTML tags; we are only interested in the chunks of `<?php echo $username; ?>`. These are the key names, which we have passed in the controller.

If you have done everything right, to your eyes there should be presented an index page without any errors.

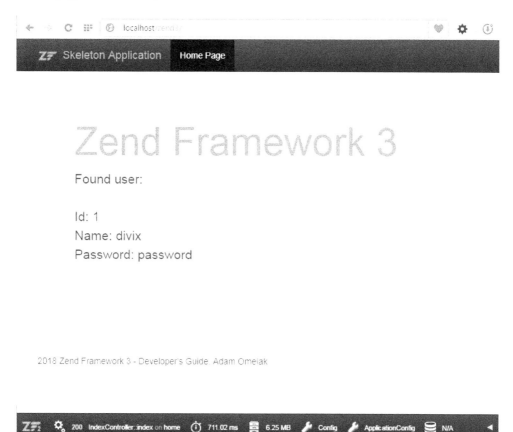

Image 4.2.

## CHAPTER 5

Create a new component

In this chapter we are going to create a new component called `users`, which will be responsible for simple operations, helping us to manage our data in the database. We will write a handle to display a list of all records from a given table, add a new record, edit an already existing row and remove it with an extra screen asking for a delete confirmation. We will describe a straightforward usage example of a form with validations in a model file in order to illustrate the new usage of `Zend\Form` in Zend Framework 3 better.

In chapter 10, "Forms", we will show how to use more advanced examples of using forms and how they can be decorated with the use of Bootstrap CSS framework along with their own validations in the form object itself.

5.1. Adding a sample component

We will start with creating a new controller named `UsersController` in *module/Application/src/Controller*.

```
namespace Application\Controller;
use Zend\Mvc\Controller\AbstractActionController;
```

```
use Zend\View\Model\ViewModel;
use Application\Model\UsersTable;
use Application\Model\User;
use Application\Form\UserForm;
class UsersController extends AbstractActionController
{
    private $usersTable = null;
    public function __construct(UsersTable $usersTable)
    {
        $this->usersTable = $usersTable;
    }
    public function indexAction()
    {
        $view = new ViewModel();
        $rows = $this->usersTable->getBy();
        $view->setVariable('userRows', $rows);
        return $view;
    }
}
```

Same as in the previous example, our new controller has only one method - `indexAction` and a constructor. The only difference is the execution of a `getBy()` method without any parameters instead of `getById()` in `IndexController`. With that the model will return us all available rows in the table users.

To register our newly created controller, we have to add a record into routes in *modules.config.php* file:

```
'users' => [
    'type' => Segment::class,
    'options' => [
    'route' => '/users[/:action[/:id]]',
    'defaults' => [
        'controller' => Controller\UsersController::class,
        'action' => 'index',
    ],
    ],
],
```

It looks almost identical as the application, except for the added parameter `[/:id]`, which from now will be intercepted by the controller as a parameter `id`. Thanks to that we are able to pass an identification user number in the URL address, to for instance change its details. The characters: `[]` indicate that the parameter inside is optional and can be `NULL`.

Let's not forget to also add a `UsersController` definition in the same configuration file below in the controllers key:

```
Controller\UsersController::class => function($sm) {
    $postService = $sm->get('Application\Model\UsersTable');

    return new Controller\UsersController($postService);
}
```

Let's now modify a template file *module/Application/view/layout/* ↪*layout.phtml*, by adding a new option in navigation.

```
<div class="collapse navbar-collapse">
    <ul class="nav navbar-nav">
        <li><a href="<?= $this->url('home') ?>">Home Page</a></li>
        <li><a href="<?= $this->url('users') ?>">Users</a></li>
    </ul>
</div>
```

Now we will add an example view file *index.phtml* in the new folder *module/Application/view/users*, to display all records from the database and links to modify each user.

```
<div class="jumbotron">
    <h1><span class="zf-green">Users</span></h1>
    <a href="<?= $this->url('users', ['action' => 'add']) ?>">Add User</a>
    <table class="table">
        <tr>
        <th>Id</th><th>Name</th><th>Actions</th>
        </tr>
        <?php foreach ($userRows as $user): ?>
        <tr>
            <td><?= $user->getId() ?></td>
            <td><?= $user->getUsername() ?></td>
            <td>
                <a href="<?= $this->url('users', ['action' => 'edit', 'id' =>
↪$user->getId()]) ?>">Edit</a> |
                <a href="<?= $this->url('users', ['action' => 'delete', 'id' =>
↪$user->getId()]) ?>">Remove</a>
```

```
            </td>
        </tr>
        <?php endforeach; ?>
    </table>
</div>
```

From the very first lines we can illustrate the usage of URL helper. You are probably wondering what these "magical helpers" are. Well, they are objects available in each view file. Thanks to them we do not have to worry about things like importing JS or CSS files into meta tags, generating HTML code for forms or – as in our example – display relative links to other subpages. Let's come back to line:

```
<?= $this->url('users', ['action' => 'add']) ?>
```

It is very easy to assume that the result of this line will return the following address: `[baseURL]/users/add`, where `baseURL` is the main root folder in which Zend Framework is installed. In my example, on XAMPP it will be *http://localhost/zend3/users/add.*

Next step is to iterate results from the array and generate a HTML table with the records, by using `foreach()`: loop. Notice that we are not using curly brackets here like in controllers or models, but a semicolon. Due to that we are able to declare more easily where our loop is ending by typing a key `endforeach`. The last thing worth mentioning in this file is another use of the method `url()`; this time to display the links to update: `[baseURL]/users/edit/[userId]` and, similarly, to remove: `[baseUrl]/users/delete/[userId]`.

The next important element is the use of short PHP tags `<?= $variable ?>`. They are a shortcut version of writing: `<?php echo $variable ?>`, which is still supported. New short tags have been added in the new version of PHP 5.4 and they are a recommended format to display variables in templates, especially due to the old format of short tags: `<% %>` has been deprecated and completely removed in version PHP 7.

5.2. A new form

The correct way to manage forms using Zend Framework 3 is to use objects that extend `Zend\Form\Form`. Let's write a form which contains 2 elements (1 hidden and 1 input text) and a button to submit. First, we will create a new folder named `Form` in *module/Application/src/Form*, then we would create a new file in there *UserForm.php*:

```
class UserForm extends \Zend\Form\Form
{
    public function __construct($name = 'user')
    {
        parent::__construct($name);
        $this->add([
            'name' => 'id',
            'type' => 'hidden'
        ]);
        $this->add([
            'name' => 'username',
            'type' => 'text',
            'options' => [
                'label' => 'Username'
            ]
        ]);
        $this->add([
            'name' => 'submit',
            'type' => 'submit',
            'attributes' => [
                'value' => 'Save',
                'id' => 'saveUserForm'
            ]
        ]);
        //by default it's also POST
        $this->setAttribute('method', 'POST');
    }
}
```

Each element of the form is added via method `add()`, which takes an array of parameters like type, name or attributes. The last line, `setAttribute()`, is optional, as ZF3 currently defaults each form into a method POST anyway. I have left it here just in case a newer version of framework might change its behavior. By using `setAttribute()` we can change any HTML attribute of our form, like class, id or encode.

5.3. Adding records

Let's now cover adding the user feature into the database. Since our address is of course: `[baseUrl]/users/add`, we need to start with creating a new action in the controller.

```
public function addAction()
{
    $request = $this->getRequest();
    $userForm = new UserForm();
    $userForm->get('submit')->setValue('Add');
    if (!$request->isPost()) {
        return ['userForm' => $userForm];
    }
    $userModel = new User();
    $userForm->setInputFilter($userModel->getInputFilter());
    $userForm->setData($request->getPost());
    if (!$userForm->isValid()) {
        return ['userForm' => $userForm];
    }
    $userModel->exchangeArray($userForm->getData());
    $this->usersTable->save($userModel);
    return $this->redirect()->toRoute('users');
}
```

As we can notice, our function uses `UserForm`, which we have just created, then it changes a default text of the submit button to `Add`. Checking `if (!$request->isPost())` { determines if the request was sent in a POST mode. If it is true, we end the execution of the method and return the form to the view. If however the form was submitted correctly, then we validate the input fields of that form to check their results. A method `setInputFilters()` sets the new rules of the object data validations; after that line we execute passing the data from a form into the model: `$userForm->setData($request->getPost());`. At the end, we call `isValid()`, to verify whether the data from the form meets all the `User` model requirements. If it is not, then we need to go back to the view where the form would handle a display of all form error messages.

At the very end of the `addAction()` method we store the data from the form into the `User` object, so that during a call of `usersTable->save()` we could pass a whole model as an argument. The last line is using the `redirect()` helper, which – like the name suggests – handles various request redirects. In our example we redirect to the main controller (`UserController`) action.

The difference between `setData()` method and `exchangeArray()` is that the first one sets the data for validations and input filters, while `exchangeArray()` sets permanently sent values without any validations.

Our new view file for `addAction()`, called *add.phtml*, should contain the following lines:

```
<div class="jumbotron">
    <h1><span class="zf-green">New User</span></h1>
    <?php
        $userForm->setAttribute('action', $this->url('users', ['action' => 'add']));
        $userForm->prepare();
        echo $this->form()->openTag($userForm);
        echo $this->formHidden($userForm->get('id'));
        echo $this->formRow($userForm->get('username'));
        echo $this->formSubmit($userForm->get('submit'));
        echo $this->form()->closeTag();
    ?>
</div>
```

As I already mentioned, `setAttribute()` establishes any form attribute, hence we also set an action to *users/add*, then with `prepare()` we set a status of the form to active; thanks to that, potential validation errors will be visible in the view.

The next lines are displaying the whole form in HTML. This time, the helper `form()` simplifies rendering of open and close tags of `<form>`. To display another elements of the form we have to call `formHidden()` for the hidden elements, `formSubmit()` for buttons and `formRow()` for any other form element. Each method displaying an element has to receive an appropriate value from our model; we do that with `$userForm->get([elementName])`.

The last task which has left to do is to add new validation rules to our model `User`. First step is to add an interface of `InputFilterAwareInterface` and a few new imports:

```
use DomainException;
use Zend\Filter\StringTrim;
use Zend\Filter\StripTags;
use Zend\Filter\ToInt;
use Zend\InputFilter\InputFilter;
use Zend\InputFilter\InputFilterAwareInterface;
use Zend\InputFilter\InputFilterInterface;
use Zend\Validator\StringLength;

class User implements InputFilterAwareInterface
{
    private $inputFilter;
```

Because we will be using a "hydrator", we have to implement `InputFilter`
↪`AwareInterface` in this class.

Next, we should add new methods like `getArrayCopy()`,
`setInputFilter()` and `getInputFilter()`, which are all required by the
added interface:

```
public function getArrayCopy()
{
    return [
        'id' => $this->getId(),
        'username' => $this->getUsername()
    ];
}
public function setInputFilter(InputFilterInterface $inputFilter)
{
    throw new DomainException('This class does not support adding of extra input
↪filters');
}
public function getInputFilter()
{
    if ($this->inputFilter) {
        return $this->inputFilter;
    }
    $inputFilter = new InputFilter();
    $inputFilter->add([
        'name' => 'id',
        'required' => true,
        'filters' => [
```

```
                    ['name' => ToInt::class],
            ],
    ]);
    $inputFilter->add([
        'name' => 'username',
        'required' => true,
        'filters' => [
            ['name' => StripTags::class],
            ['name' => StringTrim::class],
        ],
        'validators' => [
            [
            'name' => StringLength::class,
            'options' => [
                'encoding' => 'UTF-8',
                'min' => 1,
                'max' => 100,
                ],
            ],
        ],
    ]);
    $this->inputFilter = $inputFilter;
    return $this->inputFilter;
}
```

The most important method is `getInputFilter()`, defining rules on the basis of which the form decides whether or not the value inputted by the user is correct. For instance, an element `id` accepts numbers only and has to be typed, while `name` must be an alphanumeric string of `UTF-8` characters ranged from 1 to 100. To speed up the operation of this function, we set class variable to `$inputFilter`. Thanks to that, another call will not cause a duplicated creation of the same rules.

5.4. Editing a record

Since we already have implemented the function of adding a record, we can without any further problems add an option to edit it by using the same form: `UserForm`. Let's start by creating a custom view file *edit.phtml* with:

```
<div class="jumbotron">
    <h1><span class="zf-green">Edit User id: <?= $userId ?></span></h1>
    <?php
        $userForm->setAttribute('action', $this->url('users',
            [
            'action' => 'edit',
            'id' => $userId
        ]));
        $userForm->prepare();
        echo $this->form()->openTag($userForm);
        echo $this->formHidden($userForm->get('id'));
        echo $this->formRow($userForm->get('username'));
        echo $this->formSubmit($userForm->get('submit'));
        echo $this->form()->closeTag();
    ?>
</div>
```

It's obviously almost the same piece of code as in *add.phtml*, with the exception of changed action attribute, which is now `edit/[userId]`. Let's move quickly on the controller where much more happens.

```
public function editAction()
{
    $view = new ViewModel();
    $userId = (int) $this->params()->fromRoute('id');
    $view->setVariable('userId', $userId);
    if (0 == $userId) {
        return $this->redirect()->toRoute('users', ['action' => 'add']);
    }
    try {
        $userRow = $this->usersTable->getById($userId);
    } catch (\Exception $e) {
        return $this->redirect()->toRoute('users', ['action' => 'index']);
    }
    $userForm = new UserForm();
    $userForm->bind($userRow);
    $userForm->get('submit')->setAttribute('value', 'Save');
    $request = $this->getRequest();
    $view->setVariable('userForm', $userForm);
    if (!$request->isPost()) {
        return $view;
    }
    $userForm->setInputFilter($userRow->getInputFilter());
    $userForm->setData($request->getPost());
```

```
    if (!$userForm->isValid()) {
        return $view;
    }
    $this->usersTable->save($userRow);
    return $this->redirect()->toRoute('users', ['action' => 'index']);
}
```

We begin our edit logic by getting an identification number of the user from the URL address through `$this->params()->fromRoute('id')`. Then we should check it is not an empty value. If it's null, we redirect the user to the add page. If an `id` was passed in the URL address, then we need to try to find an user based on that value and use of the `getById()` inside a try section, which will call `catch()`, if it encounters an error (in our example user might not exist in the database). Then we create a form object and assign values of the fetched user model to the `userForm`, by which a form will be able to display data for modification. If form was submitted, we would perform a validation similar to `add()` method, and then store those updated details together with redirection to the index action.

5.5. Deleting a record

There is only one thing left – removal of records. Deleting records is a very delicate operation, so it will be much better if we present a confirmation prompt here, so that the user is aware that their decision is irreversible. We achieve that in our new view file called *delete.phtml*, we will display a modal message together with buttons: `Delete` and `Cancel`.

```
<div class="jumbotron">
    <h1><span class="zf-green">Delete User</span></h1>
    <p>
        Confirm deletion of user: "<?= $user->getUsername() ?>"
    </p>
    <form action="<?= $this->url('users', ['action' => 'delete', 'id' => $id]) ?>"
↪method="post">
    <div class="form-group">
        <input type="hidden" name="id" value="<?= (int) $user->getId() ?>" />
            <input type="submit" class="btn btn-danger" name="del" value="Delete" />
            <input type="submit" class="btn btn-success" name="del" value="Cancel" />
        </div>
```

```
    </form>
  </div>
```

We will enhance our controller `UsersController` with a new method, `deleteAction`, which will check if we are passing a correct user id, detect pressed confirmation button and execute a function `delete()` on `UsersTable`.

```
public function deleteAction()
{
    $userId = (int) $this->params()->fromRoute('id');
    if (empty($userId)) {
        return $this->redirect()->toRoute('users');
    }
    $request = $this->getRequest();
    if ($request->isPost()) {
        $del = $request->getPost('del', 'Cancel');
        if ($del == 'Delete') {
            $userId = (int) $request->getPost('id');
            $this->usersTable->delete($userId);
        }
        // redirect tot he users list
        return $this->redirect()->toRoute('users');
    }
    return [
        'id' => $userId,
        'user' => $this->usersTable->getById($userId),
    ];
}
```

Given the code aboce, we have to add a method to remove the data from our *UsersTable.php*; and the new method looks like:

```
public function delete($id)
{
    $this->tableGateway->delete(['id' => (int) $id]);
}
```

At the end our website should look similar to the screenshot below:

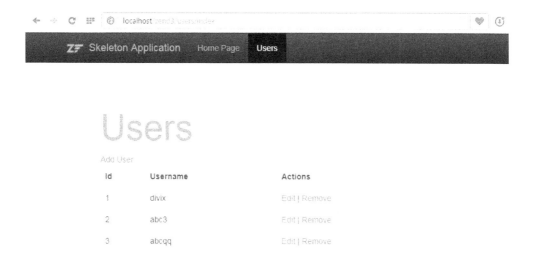

Image 5.1.

5.6. Adding a module through ZF2Rapid

Now that we know how to write our module from scratch, we will analyze the automatic process of creating example files for the new module via ZF2Rapid. You are probably wondering, why I am not using an official tool from Zend. *"ZFTool is not and it probably will not be compatible with new versions 2 & 3"*. This is the official statement I have received from one of the developers working on that project. On the other hand, ZFRapid is not fully compatible with ZF3, but some work around it has been started. Even though ZFFapid is not fully compatible with ZF3 we can reuse some of the available tools to create a file templates within seconds.

ZF2Rapid is a tool working in command line, allowing users to manage modules in Zend Framework 2 & 3. The primary functions of that library are: generating new projects, modules, controllers and single actions in the controllers. The additional functions of ZFF2Rapid are displaying loaded modules, a full diagnostics and creating the mapping classes.

67

The installation of this tool is done in a very easy and quick way by Composer, which we have already setup. We only need to open SHELL window, locate the main folder of our Zend application and run:

```
composer require zendframework/zf2rapid:dev-master
```

If we get a message about JSON error, we have to add another Zend JSON component to our application by typing:

```
composer require zendframework/zend-json
```

In a such way, we have an access to ZF2Rapid by running command:

```
vendor/bin/zf.php diag –v
```

The above line would return diagnostic information about our application. For more information about this tool you can visit: *https://github.com/zendframework/ZFTool*.

ZF2Rapid is however still in development phase, so it won't be discussed in this book.

5.7. What should be inside of a component?

There are two main principles of creating code logic in our application. Obviously, we will not mention about separating the presentation from business logic, but about splitting the logic so that we can write the most generic/modular modules. When writing a module, we should plan on using it in another project or in the same project two or three times. Thanks to that methodology we will be able to spread part of the logic and refactor methods and classes quicker, in order to make use of the same module in a slightly different configuration easier.

Fat controller, thin model – in this rule most of our operations we execute on the controller side, and the model or form stores only basic information about communication with tables in the database or cache.

Thin controller, fat model – in other words a reverse of the of the first rule, where most of business logic goes into models, forms and very often into additional helper classes, for instance with set interfaces.

In both cases it is worth noting the things that might be used or shared in other modules. We create these code sections in a folder with libraries, that is *vendor/*. Of course, you need to create your own unique namespace, which will determine a starting point of our libraries. For example if we would add our own implementation of debugging, then it could be called *DivixUtils/Debug.php*. It's mainly about libraries not overriding each other if they were in one folder and to share our ideas through the channels like GitHub with other developers.

When creating new classes and methods in a module, it's worth learning different types of code refactoring. The generation of a single interface together with drivers to the base class is one of the most often used examples. Thanks to that trick one class can have different triggers during the execution of single stages in code. An interesting detail is also a function parameterization, in which the primary achievement is to move defined variables into function parameters. By that we gain a bigger control of functioning of the method and we can use it in different places. More about refactoring can be read on the website: *https://sourcemaking.com/refactoring*.

Remember that all the elements, like images, fonts, JS or CSS files, are located in the folder *public/*, which is away from the main Application folder. Because of that, if our library or module has to use these related elements, we should create new folders in specific locations. For example, by using the previous `Debug` class, we can have an image linked with it in the path *public/img/debug/sample.jpg*. By doing so we are ensured that we won't override or interfere with any other resources.

## CHAPTER 6

MVC

The Model View Controller (MVC) is a common design pattern which describes where to put business logic, presentation layer and routing strategies. By splitting core aspects of the application, it provides a workflow and various dependencies between Model, View and Controller. Here is a sample diagram illustrating the concept:

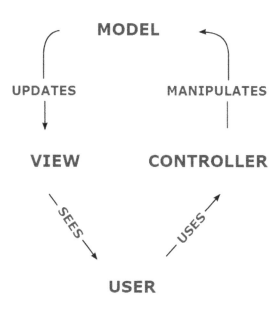

6.1. Model

A model layer is mainly for the modification of rows in database, sending requests, returning results and validation of parameters passed over. If you operate with a pattern operating on `AbstractTableGateway` (like we are going to do in this book), you will quickly notice that the base class allows you to only execute simple queries with one or two conditions.

```
$this->tableGateway->select(array('id' => $id))
```

What about more complex queries with many tables or specified sorting mechanism? Examples shown in chapter 8 "Databases" show how to write exactly those types of queries by using `Zend\DB\Sql`. How can we connect the usage of `Zend\DB\Sql` inside `TableGateway`? The answer is to call the method:

```
$this->tableGateway->getSql()->select()
```

or alternatively `update()` or `delete()`. How then do we integrate a run and return the results with a returned object through `->select()` and methods of `AbstractTableGateway` class? The solution are the methods ending with ...with(), so `selectWith()`, `updateWith()` and `deleteWith()`, those require `Sql` objects, like `select()`, `update()` and `delete()`. For example:

```
$select = $this->tableGateway->getSql()->select();
$select->where(array('avatar_id' => $id))
    ->order('date_added DESC');
$rowset = $this->tableGateway->selectWith($select);
$row = $rowset->current();
```

It is generally a good idea for every custom `save()` method to return a newly added or already existing identification number of the record. We can also set a property `id` in the `Rowset` object itself by `setId()`. It is a matter of taste.

This solution will have the same amount of haters who will deny it, saying that an object should not be changed without a controller's knowledge, as supporters who will start to like the ease of using this approach. Sometimes we would need `baseUrl` in our models, for instance for methods that return a file path to the images, like `getAvatarUrl()` or `getUploadedImages()`. How then can we get that path on the model layer? Zend Framework 3 is not offering us the possibility to grab a base path from the model. This is because the model part of an MVC application is very specific to the business logic of the application and it can requires different dependencies. However the base path is already available in the Service Manager. From that same place we are going to get and pass that extra information by using a constructor. By the way, we will move all models of type "identity", i.e. classes, with setters and getters into the subfolder *Rowset/* together along with the newly created abstract class `AbstractModel`.

Notice that we are talking about `baseUrl` which describes the main application folder on the server, not `basePath`. It returns a path on the server to the directory *public/*. Let's add that new value in configuration for `base_url`:

```
'view_manager' => [
    ...
    'base_url' => '/zend3/'
```

Let's check what has changed in the file *Module.php*:

```
'factories' => array(
    'UsersTableGateway' => function ($sm) {
        $dbAdapter = $sm->get('Zend\Db\Adapter\Adapter');
        $resultSetPrototype = new ResultSet();
        //get base url from config
        $config = $sm->get('Config');
        $baseUrl = $config['view_manager']['base_url'];

        //pass base url via cnstructor to the User class
        $resultSetPrototype->setArrayObjectPrototype(new User($baseUrl));
        return new TableGateway('users', $dbAdapter, null, $resultSetPrototype);
    },
```

We could also grab a path from the request itself, but the line below would not use the value set in configuration.

```
$baseUrl = $sm->get('Request')->getBasePath();
```

In order to finish our process of retrieving `$baseUrl` in model, we need to create a new class `AbstractModel` which contains an implementation of such a constructor. Thanks to that we will not have to repeat the same code in every other model to come.

```
namespace Application\Model\Rowset;
abstract class AbstractModel
{
    protected $baseUrl;
    public function __construct($baseUrl = null)
    {
        $this->baseUrl = $baseUrl;
    }
}
```

Check all the `import` declarations that should be now changed from use `Application\Model\User;` to `Application\Model\Rowset\User;`. From now on every model that requires an access to base url, will also need to extend the `AbstractModel` class, and then refer to `$this->baseUrl` at any time.

Let's finish this subsection with separating and creating a new abstract class `AbstractTable` to our table models, such as `UsersTable`. The primary task of the new class will be defining two methods: `saveRow()` and `deleteRow()`, and moving the class constructor. Let's then create `AbstractTable` inside of the same folder, *application/src/model*.

```
namespace Application\Model;
use Zend\Db\TableGateway\TableGateway;
use Application\Model\Rowset\AbstractModel;
class AbstractTable
{
    protected $tableGateway;
    public function __construct(TableGateway $tableGateway)
    {
        $this->tableGateway = $tableGateway;
    }
    public function saveRow(AbstractModel $userModel, $data = null)
    {
        $id = $userModel->getId();
        //if the parameter $data is not passed in, then update all of the object's properties
        if (empty($data)) {
```

```
            $data = $userModel->getArrayCopy();
        }
        if (empty($id)) {
            $this->tableGateway->insert($data);
            return $this->tableGateway->getLastInsertValue();
        }
        if (!$this->getById($id)) {
            throw new RuntimeException(get_class($userModel) .' with id: '.$id.'
not found');
        }
        $this->tableGateway->update($data, ['id' => $id]);
        return $id;
    }
    public function deleteRow($id)
    {
        $this->tableGateway->delete(['id' => (int) $id]);
```

Actually, we have moved the majority of logic from usersTable class, so that we can create new table classes more easily. A method saveRow() handles adding new records if the value of id is not set, otherwise it handles the update of existing record. Every time it returns an id value. An additional argument $data defines which data will be updated or entered. If we skip this parameter, the method will get all values of AbstractModel through getArrayCopy().

The final step is to replace the table class code. An example is UsersTable class which would look like:

```
namespace Application\Model;
use Application\Model\Rowset\User;
class UsersTable extends AbstractTable
{
    public function getById($id)
    {
        $id = (int) $id;
        $rowset = $this->tableGateway->select(array('id' => $id));
        $row = $rowset->current();
        if (!$row) {
            throw new \Exception('user not foound with id: '.$id);
        }
        return $row;
    }
    public function getBy(array $params = array())
```

```
    {
        $results = $this->tableGateway->select();
        return $results;
    }
    public function save(User $userModel)
    {
        $data = [
            'username' => $userModel->getUsername()
        ];
        return parent::saveRow($userModel, $data);
    }
    public function delete($id)
    {
        parent::deleteRow($id);
    }
}
```

Notice that our methods `save()` and `delete()` use methods from the base class `parent::saveRow()` and `parent::deleteRow()`. Thanks to that our class has been fully slimmed down and contains only specific lines, while the whole validation and conditions have been moved to the parent class.

Having the base class for table classes and rowsets, we can add new features to each class without actually modifying each of them individually. It will help us to hide not only related addresses like `baseUrl`, but also later the objects for internalizations, paginations or sessions.

6.2. View

A default Zend Framework 3 template looks like this:

```
<?= $this->doctype() ?>
<html lang="en">
    <head>
        <meta charset="utf-8">
        <?= $this->headTitle('ZF Skeleton Application')->setSeparator(' - ')->
```

```
↪setAutoEscape(false) ?>
        <?= $this->headMeta()
            ->appendHttpEquiv('X-UA-Compatible', 'IE=edge')
        ?>
        <!-- Style -->
        <?= $this->headLink(['rel' => 'shortcut icon', 'type' =>
↪'image/vnd.microsoft.icon', 'href' => $this->basePath() .
↪'/img/favicon.ico'])
            ->prependStylesheet($this->basePath
↪('css/bootstrap.min.css'))
        ?>
        <!-- Scripts -->
        <?= $this->headScript()
            ->prependFile($this->basePath('js/bootstrap.min.js'))
        ?>
    </head>
    <body>
        <div class="container">
            <?= $this->content; ?>
        </div>
        <?= $this->inlineScript() ?>
    </body>
</html>
```

Now, we are going to describe the biggest "magic" that happens here. First of all, we will start with `headMeta()` which generally generates just a `<meta>` HTML tag. We will learn how to make use of it properly. `Zend\View\Helper\HeadMeta`, which corresponds to the meta tag, does not define methods like `appendName()` or `offsetGetName()` in a normal way. This class is dynamic which means that all its public methods are appended "on the fly" in the magic methods like `__invoke()` or `__call()`. Available keys are:

```
protected $typeKeys = ['name', 'http-equiv', 'charset', 'property', 'itemprop'];
```

It means that each of them offers four variations of available methods. For instance, by using charset key we will be able to call `appendCharset()`, `offsetGetCharset()`, `prependCharset()` and `setCharset()`. We can also use `headMeta` helper in order to execute other features:

```
// turning off local cache
$this->headMeta()
    ->appendHttpEquiv('expires', 'Wed, 26 Feb 1997 08:21:57 GMT')
```

```
    ->appendHttpEquiv('pragma', 'no-cache')
    ->appendHttpEquiv('Cache-Control', 'no-cache');
// setting encoding and website language
$this->headMeta()
    ->appendHttpEquiv('Content-Type', 'text/html; charset=UTF-8')
    ->appendHttpEquiv('Content-Language', 'en-US');
// setting encoding on the HTML layer
$this->headMeta()->setCharset('UTF-8');
// setting redirect to another page after 5 seconds
$this->headMeta()
    ->appendHttpEquiv('Refresh', '5;URL=http://www.funkcje.net');
```

HeadLink and headScript, analogically to headMeta, generate tags
<link> and <script>. It's possible to add external files: CSS and JS based
on a specified order type. Along with that, we receive methods like:
append.., offsetSet.., prepend.. and set... For CSS styles we would
use appendStylesheet(), while for JavaScript scripts appendScript().
For clarity:

- append – adds a style declaration to the end of list;

- offsetSet – sets a new declaration to the specific place by pushing
  the others;

- prepend – adds a style declaration to the start of list;

- set – sets a specific list of styles

Each of these methods takes the same arguments, with the exception of
offsetSet method which takes an extra argument at the beginning -
$offset, that is the index number of the injected style.

```
//linkHead interface
appendStylesheet($href, $media, $conditionalStylesheet, $extras)
offsetSetStylesheet($index, $href, $media, $conditionalStylesheet, $extras)
prependStylesheet($href, $media, $conditionalStylesheet, $extras)
setStylesheet($href, $media, $conditionalStylesheet, $extras)

//styleHead interface
appendStyle($content, $attributes = array())
offsetSetStyle($index, $content, $attributes = array())
```

```
prependStyle($content, $attributes = array())
setStyle($content, $attributes = array())
```

The last of the "magic" methods in our default template file is `inlineScript()`. Its task is to add all scripts which need to be embedded together with the source code while being called within the `<body>` tags. It can cope with the plain JavaScript code or refer directly to another file. `inlineScript()` has the same methods signature as `headScript()`, so we can go ahead and use its possibilities.

```
<body>
    <?php
    echo $this->inlineScript()
        ->prependFile($this->basePath('js//style.js'))
        ->prependFile($this->basePath('js/vendor/jquery.js'));
    ?>
</body>

//will return:
<body>
    <script type="text/javascript" src="/js/vendor/jquery.js"></script>
    <script type="text/javascript" src="/js/style.js"></script>
</body>
```

To add a script of inline type we would use functions: `captureStart()` and `captureEnd()`.

```
<?php
$this->inlineScript()->captureStart();
echo "
    $(function(){
        alert('jquery loaded');
    });
";
$this->inlineScript()->captureEnd(); ?>
<?= $this->inlineScript() ?>

//will return:
<script type="text/javascript">
//<!--
$('select.dropdown').change(function(){
    location.href = $(this).val();
});
```

//-->
</script>

6.3. Controller

Each of the Zend MVC controllers, which extends the parent class `Zend\Mvc\Controller\AbstractActionController`, gives us the possibility of automatic integration with methods of type `addAction` not only to an URL address *controller/add*, but also to other methods of the base class `AbstractController`. We will briefly discuss all the available public methods in that last class:

- `onDispatch(MvcEvent $e)` – an event which processes a request in order to call the related action and method. It's an abstract method implemented on the `AbstractActionController` layer;

- `dispatch(Request $request, Response $response = null)` – executes a processed request through `onDispatch()`. By default it is executed automatically by Zend MVC;

- `getRequest()` – gets a request object sent to the server of type: `Zend\Http\HttpRequest`;

- `getResponse()` – get a response object sent back as an answer from the server of type : `Zend\Http\PhpEnvironment\Response`;

- `setEventManager(EventManagerInterface $events)` – sets an instance of Event Manager;

- `getEventManager()` – grabs a currently used instance of Event Manager;

- `getEvent()` – gets a merged event of type `MvcEvent`;

- `getPluginManager()` – returns an active instance of Plugin Manager.

From our point of view the most commonly used functions will be getting requests and responses together with receiving and modifying the Event Manager to modify available processes. Grabbing URL parameters and checking type of request are both available after calling `getRequest()`, which offers us useful functions like:

- `getQuery($name = null, $default = null)` – gets a parameter from super array `$_GET`, so the URL;

- `getPost($name = null, $default = null)` – returns a parameter from super array `$_POST`, so a submission passed via form;

- `getCookie()` – retrieves the whole `Cookies` header;

- `getFiles($name = null, $default = null)` – gets merged files;

- `getHeaders($name = null, $default = null)` – returns a specific request header;

- `isGet()` – returns `TRUE`, if request is of type: `GET`;

- `isPost()` – returns `TRUE`, if request is of type: `POST`;

- `isPut()` – returns `TRUE`, if request is of type: `PUT`;

- `isDelete()` – returns `TRUE`, if request is of type: `DELETE`;

- `isXMLHttpRequest()` – returns `TRUE`, if request is of type: `XML`;

- `isFlashRequest()` – returns `TRUE`, if request is send by `Flash` object;

Notice that methods responsible for retrieving data, like `getQuery()`, `getPost()`, `getFiles()` or `getHeaders()`, have two arguments. The first is the key name of the variable to find, while the second is the default value, returned when the expected variable does not exists or is equal to `NULL` value. On the other hand, object `Response` offers much less public methods. Here is the full list of them:

- `getVersion()` – gets a HTTP protocol version of response;

- `detectVersion()` – detect an active protocol version;

- `headersSent()` – returns an information if headers have been successfully sent;

- `contentSent()` – returns an information if content has been sent;

- `sendHeaders()` – sends HTTP headers;

- `sendContent()` – sends a content of response

- `send()` – begins the process of sending HTTP headers and contents

6.4. Router

Let's take a look at routing; in other words the rules that define where the users should be redirected to after hitting specific URL address in the browser. If you remember the first version of router in Zend Framework 1, you already know what these redirect rules look like in a Bootstrap file placed in method `_initFrontController()`:

```
protected function _initFrontController() {
    $this->frontController = Zend_Controller_Front::getInstance();
    $router = $frontController->getRouter();
    $router->addRoute('add_comics',
        new Zend_Controller_Router_Route_Static('/comics_list/add',
            array('controller' => 'comics', 'action' => 'add')
        )
    );
}
```

The rule allows to recognize an address of type: */comics_list/add* and executing `ComicsController` with its method named `addAction()`.

Zend Framework 3 has changed compared to its precursor, and it's a significant change. Most of all of our rules can be placed only in two ways: by using method `getRouteConfig()` inside the *Module.php* file, or in the configuration file itself *module.config.php*, by using a key `'router'` and `'routes'`, where we will add new stuff in. Taking into account above Zend 1 example, we will convert it to the new Zend format:

```
return [
    'router' => [
        'routes' => [
            'add_comics' => [
                'type' => Literal::class,
                'options' => [
                    'route' => '/comics_list/add',
                    'defaults' => [
                        'controller' => Controller\ComicsController::class,
                        'action' => 'add',
                    ],
                ],
            ],
        ]
    ],
    //don't forget about adding definition of new controller to the config
    'controllers' => [
        'factories' => [
            Controller\ComicsController::class => function($sm) {
                return new Controller\ComicsController();
            }
        ]
    ]
}
```

We should take a closer look mostly at the use of types and classes in string formats (`ClassName::class`) instead of creating new objects of type `Route_Router` etc. The rule identification however has not been changed and it is still required in every rule (`add_comics`), but in the new version it is also a key alias of these elements. So we need to ensure that each given alias is unique and unrepeatable, otherwise our router rules would be overridden by a last element. Parameter controller also has changed its format of receiving a controller; now we need to pass the class identification `::class` instead of just class name as a string. Thanks to that we are able to link the controller which exists in other module than Application. On top of that in Zend Framework 3 we must remember about initiating the newly linked controller via the key `'controllers'`.

Generally, in Zend Framework there are two mechanism to specify where the application needs to redirect a request: on the basis of a simple type (`Zend\Router\SimpleRouterStack`) and on the basis of a tree structure (`Zend\Router\Http\TreeRouterStack`).

SimpleRouterStack – is a straightforward mechanism of managing rules. There is a rule LIFO (Last In, First Out), so if we add two router rules, then that last added rule will be checked first, and if it does not match with the request, then the first rule will be executed, and those more broad, on the very end. It is especially important, because if the global rule was called before the more specific and custom one, then global rule would break the check of the other rules.

TreeRouterStack – as the name already says, it's a tree structure in which there is no nest limit. In other words, the tree of rules can be infinitely deep, depending on our requirements. Each tree of course needs its root key `'route'` and has to have optional plugins in `'route_plugins'` and flag `'may_terminate'` which describes the termination of continued rule mapping and obviously a key for another branch called `'child_routes'`.

```
return [
    'router' => [
        'routes' => [
            'comics' => [
                'type' => Literal::class,
                'options' => [
                    'route' => '/comics_list',
                    'defaults' => [
                        'controller' => Controller\ComicsController::class,
                        'action' => 'index',
                    ],
                ],
                'may_terminate' => true,
                'child_routes' => [
                'add' => [
                    'type' => 'literal',
```

```
            'options' => [
                'route' => '/add',
                'defaults' => [
                    'controller' => Controller\ComicsController::class,
                    'action' => 'add',
                ],
            ]
        ]
    ]
  ]
 ]
];
```

Note that we have defined a rule with name `'comics_list'` which has two internal rules. The first checks if the address begins with */comics_list*, then inside there is another check for the address */comics_list/add*, where we execute another controller's action. By using a flag `'may_terminate'` set to TRUE, we ensure that router stops searching in other rules, if the first one has mapped the request correctly. The next nested rules don't check previous matched conditions anymore, so we have not written */comics_list/add* but only a single word */add* in our rule `'add'`. The tree structure here starts to be useful and helpful, since we do not repeat the same mapping rules in the nested conditions.

Hostname Router

A component `Zend\Mvc\Router\Http\Hostname` allows mapping a request by the name of the host and subdomain. Below example will redirect the addresses like *user1.users.localhost* or *other_user.users.localhost* to the same Users controller and action name: `profileAction()`.

```
'profile_users' => [
    'type' => Hostname::class,
    'options' => [
        'route' => ':username.users.localhost',
        'constraints' => [
            'username' => '[a-zA-Z0-9_-]+',
        ],
        'defaults' => [
            'controller' => Controller\UsersController::class,
```

```
            'action' => 'profile',
            'custom_var' => 'something important'
        ],
    ]
],
```

Notice that we are using a colon before the content name, which functions as variable in URL address. In this example it is `:username` (we could also use `:username.:users`, then we could have two variables in the address); thanks to that each value will be matched to this rule with: *https://[anything].users.localhost*. Of course, we can easily change *localhost* to *domain.com* on the production server. Additionally, we are using a key `constraints`, which describes "restrictions" of our variables. We can use a regular expression here, like in the above code. The value of `:username`, will be mapped only when the value is contained with alphanumeric chars, numbers, underscores and dashes. The below address will be properly matched and will redirect to the profile action:

```
new_username.users.localhost
another_001-2.users.localhost
```

However, those addresses would NOT be matched:

```
completely_new_ąłż_user.users.localhost
weird_user<script>alert('xss');</script>.users.localhost
```

The first address is incorrect because of the usage of Polish characters, and the second is invalid due to the containment of unsupported special characters like: <, >, (,), or '.

Obviously in order to make our example work, we need an extra view file users/profile.phtml and extra action `profileAction()` in controller `UsersController`:

```
public function profileAction()
{
    $view = new ViewModel();
    $userName = $this->params()->fromRoute('username');
    $customVar = $this->params()->fromRoute('custom_var');
    $view->setVariable('userName', $userName);
    $view->setVariable('customVar', $customVar);
    return $view;
```

}

All the variables from router declaration are now available via the call of
`params()->fromRoute()`. For this example's needs, due to working at a
subdomain, we need to "hack" an instance of XMAPP. We just need to go
into the main folder of XAMPP */htdocs* and then edit file *index.php* like so:

```
//header('Location: '.$uri.'/xampp/'); //comment out this line
require_once('zend3/index.php'); //and add require_once
```

Of course, after testing above example, we should revert back the file
htdocs/index.php. An appropriate new site with user's profile data should be
presented (check image 6.1).

Literal Router

Literal Router maps the exact address that is passed in key route. This type of
routing is the simplest one and already has been covered in chapter 5.

Image 6.1.

Method Router

Method Router, so the class `Zend\Router\Http\Method`, is a method operating on the checks of the type of request. The possible types are `POST`, `GET`, `PUT`, and `DELETE`. The rule mentioned below will be only applied to the requests of types `PUT` and `DELETE`:

```
'edit_user' => [
    'type' => Method::class,
    'options' => [
        'verb' => 'put,delete',
        'defaults' => [
            'controller' => Controller\UsersController::class,
            'action' => 'edit'
        ],
    ]
],
```

Regex Router

Based on `Zend\Router\Http\Regex` class this is the mapping against a regular expressions and URL address. However, it's better to use methods that would return a related mapping key, than to relay on numeric values. In this instance we have neither a key route nor verb, instead, we use regex for the expression check and spec for mapping everything into one format:

```
'show_image' => [
    'type' => Regex::class,
    'options' => [
        'regex' => '/images/(?<id>[a-zA-Z0-9_-]+)(\.(?<format>(jpg|gif|png)))?',
        'defaults' => [
            'controller' => ImagesController::class,
            'action' => 'view',
        ],
        'spec' => '/images/%id%.%format%'
    ]
],
```

The above example has created a rule that can generate images on the fly by using an ID number and default format. For instance, address *images/12-image-name.jpg* means that controller `Images` will find an image with `ID 12` and will render an image in format JPG. Of course, a name of the image can be anything, it must, however, be composed of letters, numbers and dashes or underscores.

Scheme Router

`Zend\Router\Http\Scheme` is a routing type which refers to the type of the protocol in URL address. For example, we can check the protocol very easily whether the user is using `HTTPS` instead of `HTTP`. Thanks to the below example, every controller has an access to the variable `fromRouter('is_https')`, which is equal to `NULL` or `TRUE`.

```
'secure_page' => [
    'type' => Scheme::class,
    'options' => [
        'scheme' => 'http',
        'defaults' => [
            'is_https' => true
        ]
    ],
],
```

Segment Router

This type of routing has also been covered in chapter 5. To remind it, we will use a similar code.

```
'users_match' => [
    'type' => Segment::class,
    'options' => [
        'route' => '/users[/:action][/:id]',
        'constraints' => [
            'action' => '[a-zA-Z][a-zA-Z0-9_-]+',
            'id' => '[0-9]+'
        ],
        'defaults' => [
```

```
            'controller' => Controller\UsersController::class,
            'action' => 'index',
        ]
    ]
],
```

As you can see, we have added only a key 'constraints', which restricts the mapping of our address to just valid values, like *users/show/2*, and ignores things like *users/wrongAction/abc*. Of course, keys from the table constraints are assigned to the names from key route. By using an expression [/:action] we are letting Zend Router know that there might appear a backslash before the action name.

There are two different types of routers: Zend\Router\Http\Query and Wildcard. Both of them are equally marked as deprecated and it is not recommended to use them at all. First of them checked variables from a request and the other one marked mapping on every specified path. An example could be a combination of: Literal, and then object of the Wildcard type, so that all the characters were mapped after the specific symbol, like:

```
'child_routes' => array(
    'wildcard' => array(
        'type' => 'Wildcard',
    )
)
```

CHAPTER **7**.

Most important components

7.1. Event Manager

The Event Manager is a very characteristic tool, designed for specific solutions. If you are reading this book, you surely came across with one or more design patterns. They include such solutions as Strategy, Factory, Singleton or Observer; and the Event manager in Zend Framework 3 is exactly the last of these. Additionally, the Observer pattern is also used by Zend MVC, so you have already been using it in previous Zend version, without even noticing it.

In a nutshell, Event Manager takes the same solution logic like events in JavaScript or ActionScript. By this mechanism we can register or detach events based on specific functions through this mechanism. An event is actually just an information about current or incoming state. Each event can be listened by other registered listening objects. In this way, if we call for instance an event `add()`, then all the registered functions will be performed in a bubble format the way they have been attached for, or via the parameter `$priority`, which also controls the order of its custom settings.

The Event manager is built mainly from 4 main methods: `trigger()`, `triggerUntil()`, `attach()` and `detach()`. `Trigger()` is a method which executes a specific and already registered event. Thanks to that, listening objects receive information about the performed action. `TriggerUntil()`, same as `trigger()`, executes a given event but it has an additional argument in which we can inject logic describing how the event should react in a specific case; example:

```
$argv = array('var' => false);
$results = $this->getEventManager()->triggerUntil(function($var) {
    return ($var === true);
}, __FUNCTION__, $this, $argv);
```

Given trigger will be only executed once because our logic, passed in a parameter as a closure function, will return FALSE in the first iteration.

Closures are anonymous functions, added in PHP 5.3. They allow us to pass "callback" logic in function parameters into other class objects. An obvious thing for anonymous functions are their variables scope. By default closures only have access to the function parameters, if however we need to pass variables from the outside, we will have to use a key 'use', which will provide a given variable to the scope:

```
$custom->start(function($e) use ($debug) {
    $debug->log('info', 'start called');
});
```

The code above will give us object `$debug`, which can be freely used inside `start()` method in `$custom` object.

Additionally, `attach()`, as well as `detach()`, register events in a global array in the Event Manager and deletes them. Now that we have the solid basics, we can look at the example below, which is devoid of redundant logic. Our goal is: we have a `NewsTable` class which handles adding comments to each of the articles. Inside our core logic we will be triggering an event named `news.addcomment`, which later will be retrieved by another 2 classes: `Email` and `RSS`. They will be responsible for sending email messages and updating information in a RSS file. Let's begin from the class `NewsTable` – it will initiate the event with name `news.addcomment`.

```
namespace Application\Model;
```

```php
use Zend\Db\TableGateway\TableGateway;
use Zend\EventManager\EventManager;
use Zend\EventManager\EventManagerAwareInterface;
use Zend\EventManager\EventManagerInterface;

class NewsTable implements EventManagerAwareInterface
{
    public function __construct(TableGateway $tableGateway)
    {
        $this->tableGateway = $tableGateway;
    }
    public function addComment($comment, $userId)
    {
        $params = ['user_id' => $userId, 'comment' => $comment];
        $results = $this->getEventManager()->trigger('news.addcomment',
 $this, $params);
        //if event has been stopped by any of the class, then we would not add a record to
DB
        if (!$results->stopped()) {
            //add to DB
            echo 'SUCCESS';
            return true;
        }
        echo 'ERROR: Event has been stopped by the listener <br />';
        return false;
    }
    protected $events;
    public function setEventManager(EventManagerInterface $events)
    {
        $events->setIdentifiers([
            __CLASS__,
            get_class($this)
        ]);
        $this->events = $events;
    }
    public function getEventManager()
    {
        if (! $this->events) {
            $this->setEventManager(new EventManager());
        }
        return $this->events;
    }
}
```

The first thing we can spot, is an implementation of `EventManager`
↪`AwareInterface` interface that requires us to write one method:
`setEventManager()` (it sets an identification of our class as `NewsTable`).
Next, `getEventManager()` calls the previous method just once, in order not
to register any unnecessary class objects. In a method `addComment()` we
perform an initiation of the event with name `'news.addcomment'`, we also
pass an actual class object and parameters `$userId` and `$comment`. Next up,
we create simple libraries to handle `DivixUtils\Email` and
`DivixUtils\RSS`. In order to achieve that, we need to register our new
library DivixUtils in file *Module.php* first:

```
public function getAutoloaderConfig()
{
    return array(
        'Zend\Loader\StandardAutoloader' => array(
            'namespaces' => array(
                __NAMESPACE__ => __DIR__ . '/src/' . __NAMESPACE__,
                'DivixUtils' => __DIR__ . '/../../vendor/divixutils'
            )
        ),
    );
}
```

Afterwards we need to register our library in the Composer in *composer.json*
file:

```
"autoload": {
    "psr-4": {
        "Application\\": "module/Application/src/",
        "DivixUtils\\": "vendor/divixutils/src/DivixUtils"
    }
},
```

To make it work and update the Composer, we just need to reload its
references by running a command in `SHELL`:

```
composer update
```

We add all the new classes to the folder *vendor/divixutils/src/DivixUtils*,
accordingly to the PSR-4 specification. From now on we can create our two
classes inside of a new library:

```
namespace DivixUtils;
use Zend\EventManager\EventManagerInterface;
use Zend\EventManager\EventInterface;

class Email
{
    private $listeners = [];
    public function attachEvents(EventManagerInterface $eventManager)
    {
        $this->listeners[] = $eventManager->attach('news.addcomment',
↪[$this, 'send'], 2);
    }
    public function send(EventInterface $e)
    {
        $eventParams = $e->getParams();
        if (empty($eventParams['user_id']) || empty($eventParams['comment'])) {
            $e->stopPropagation(true);
            echo 'Email: user_id or comment is empty <br />';
        } else {
            echo 'Email: params: '.json_encode($eventParams).'<br />';
            echo 'Email: sending email <br />';
        }
    }
}
```

Notice that we have begun by attaching a listener by calling `attach()` which has the same identifier as `NewsTable`, and we pass a method name `'send'` which will be executed after the use of this event. The third argument of the method `attach()` is a priority number: the bigger the number is, the sooner our listener will be called. A method `send()` gets three parameters passed by the event and does a check of their correctness. If one of the fields is empty, the event is stopped by `stopPropagation(true)`, then it displays information about the error. Otherwise, it displays the variables in JSON format and informs about the successful execution of code.

```
namespace DivixUtils;
use Zend\EventManager\EventManagerInterface;
use Zend\EventManager\EventInterface;
class RSS
{
    private $listeners = [];
    public function attachEvents(EventManagerInterface $eventManager)
    {
```

```
        $this->listeners[] = $eventManager->attach('news.addcomment',
↪[$this, 'incrementUsersCount'], 1);
    }
    public function incrementUsersCount(EventInterface $e)
    {
        echo 'RSS: updating RSS<br />';
    }
}
```

Minimalistic RSS class is similar to Email, but it calls
incrementUsersCount() instead of send() and has a lower priority than
Email class with number 1.

At the very end, we just need to bring everything together in the new
controller called NewsController:

```
namespace Application\Controller;
use Zend\Mvc\Controller\AbstractActionController;
use Application\Model\NewsTable;

class NewsController extends AbstractActionController
{
    private $newsTable = null;
    public function __construct(NewsTable $newsTable)
    {
        $this->newsTable = $newsTable;
    }
    public function indexAction()
    {
    }
    public function addcommentAction()
    {
        $eventManager = $this->newsTable->getEventManager();
        $rssUtils = new \DivixUtils\RSS();
        $rssUtils->attachEvents($eventManager);
        $emailUtils = new \DivixUtils\Email();
        $emailUtils->attachEvents($eventManager);
        ob_start();
        //execution
        echo 'Scenario 1 <br />---<br />';
        $this->newsTable->addComment(", ");
        echo '<br /><br />Scenario 2 <br />---<br />';
        $this->newsTable->addComment('new comment', 2);
        $results = ob_get_contents();
```

```
        ob_end_clean();
        return ['results' => $results];
    }
}
```

An action with name `addcommentAction()` registers our classes from the library by `attachEvents()` and performs two scenarios: one faulty with missing parameters and one correct. in this example I have used `ob_start()` and `ob_get_contents()` in order not to display the results directly from the classes in the controller. Instead, we passed all the data to the view as a variable `$results`. The result of the above code will be:

```
Scenario 1
---
Email: user_id or comment is empty
ERROR: Event has been stopped by the listener
Scenario 2
---
Email: params: {"user_id":2,"comment":"new comment"}
Email: sending mail
RSS: updating RSS
SUCCESS
```

As you can see yourself, the `Email` class has blocked the execution of a code from `RSS` class by stopping an event. It has been called first, according to the higher priority number as expected. Received variables in scenario no. 2 are displayed properly, which confirms that everything went according to our expectations.

The Event Manager has been created to replace PHP hooks that are archaic and less effective. Additionally, developers have been passing anonymous functions, as parameters, more frequently into other methods, which causes the habits of Spaghetti Code anti-pattern. Thanks to the Event Manager we get an extra layer to register and detach any listeners, making our code more generic and easier to expand. The Event Manager fits perfectly when for example we create a custom library and we want to allow the execution from the outside, for instance inside of our private class methods.

Furthermore, by Event Manager we can group events properly, create our own Event classes and retrieve last returned results by the method `last()` when the event is stopped. Unfortunately, these more advanced implementations are beyond this book's scope.

7.2. Module Manager

A Module Manager is a component describing the file and folder structures inside of each module. The module in ZF3 world is a set of controllers, models, forms and other elements which define a set of features related to each other. For instance we could have a module for: administration panel, REST API or 3rd party integrations. In our examples we use just one module called Application. All modules need to be placed in the main folder *module/* and need to have the following architecture:

```
module_root/
    config/
        module.config.php
    public/
        images/
        css/
        js/
    src/
        Module.php
        autoload_classmap.php
        autoload_function.php
        autoload_register.php
        <module_namespace>/
            <our code>
    test/
        phpunit.xml
        <module_namespace>/
            <our code for tests>
    view/
        <module_namespace >/
            <folder-names-after-controllers >/
                <.phtml files>
```

Thanks to the optional files *autoload_*.php*, we can register additional embedded classes, functions (used for instance by `spl_autoload_register()`) or also callbacks. The main reason for using these files instead of other methods is launching the given module outside the Zend Framework environment without the Zend Module Manager component.

The Module Manager additionally describes the functionality of the *Module.php* file and defines which "magical" things we can link to our module engine.

The available events are:

- `loadModule()` and `loadModules()` – listen for events of loading a single or many extra modules;

- `loadModule.resolve()` and `loadModules.post()` – designed to check when a single or all modules are loaded;

- `mergeConflict()` – executes after a load sequence of all dependencies, so after `loadModules.post()`. Event `mergeConfig` is being captured by the class `Zend\ModuleManager\Listener\` ↪`ConfigListener` with priority of 1000 and is useful when we want to execute our code soon after all other listening objects. An example of use of the event `loadModules.post` can be code below:

```
use Zend\EventManager\EventInterface as Event;
use Zend\ModuleManager\ModuleManager;

class Module
{
    public function init(ModuleManager $moduleManager)
    {
        $events = $moduleManager->getEventManager();
        $events->attach('loadModules.post', array($this, 'loadComplete'));
    }
    public function loadComplete(Event $e)
    {
        // get our object and loaded modules
        $moduleManager = $e->getTarget();
        $loadedModules = $moduleManager->getLoadedModules();
        // retrieve CustomModule module name and its configuration
        $config = $moduleManager->getModule('CustomModule')->getConfig();
    }
}
```

By default *Module.php* has also built-in object listeners that require only a definition of given method in the class.

The available method listeners are:

- `getAutoloaderConfig()` – describes the extra configuration and passes it back to `Zend\Loader\AutoloaderFactory`;

- `getConfig()` – adds in an extra configuration to the main application configuration;

- `init()` – behaves the same as in Zend 1 and 2, so it is called as the first method soon after the module is loaded. Warning: this method is always executed with every request, hence you need to be careful with putting heavy things and logic or making database calls;

- `getModuleDependencies()` – executes a check of loaded modules correctness; if any of them is missing, it throws an exception: `MissingDependencyModuleException`;

- `onBootstrap()` – a method called by `Zend\MVC` during a bootstrap operation; so preparing a module to handle a request. The same way as in `init()`, it is executed every time, so let's keep only crucial and light scripts here;

- `getServerConfig()` – defines the factories or references to other classes like adapters implementations or object representing tables from databases. More about this method and usage examples will be found in the upcoming section 7.3. "Service Manager".

A simple usage of method `onBootstrap()` can be:

```
use Zend\EventManager\EventInterface as Event;
class Module
{
    public function onBootstrap(Event $e)
    {
        // get current application and service manager
        $app = $e->getApplication();
        $services = $app->getServiceManager();
    }
}
```

}

Additionally, when implementing the Module Manager, we need to take a closer look at a few crucial rules. First of all, it is recommended to contact neither a database directly – objects of `TableGateway` type are responsible for that – nor any save to file operation inside the module folder. If we are planning on creating files on the fly, we should expect a designed destination folder passed through configuration by the user which will be a location outside the main module folder (for example *public/*). If we are planning on sharing and publishing our module, we should add an id prefix, for instance `DivixNewsTools`, instead of `NewsTools`. All other linked services from that public module must also be prefixed. Thanks to that we will avoid the collision of names in other systems, for example the adapter: `MySqlAdapater` we might call `DivixNewsMySqlAdapter`.

7.3. Service Manager

In this subsection we will go back to the magical method `getServiceManagerConfig()` from previous section, which task is to set dependencies (services) to our main application module. A whole Service Manager component is really just an implementation of a Container Interoperability standard, in other words a jar of cooperation. Generally, this standard describes how the dependencies of Service Locators or Dependency Injections type are managed. The main reason behind applying the standard in this field is a better and faster integration of third-party libraries and projects with other projects and applications. The ZF3 Service Manager is fully PSR-11 compilant. PSR-11 standardize how frameworks and libraries make use of a container to obtain objects and parameters. A common standard means that we do not need any extra linking classes like Proxy Pattern or any other modification of the existing libraries, which should significantly improve the process of sharing and using other existing libraries created by other authors. According to the Container Interoperability, our serving dependencies "jar" must have at least two methods: `get()` to get a dependency based on the name and `has()` to check whether a given dependency has been already registered. The easiest use of Service Manager is creating custom container and assigning one dependency to it:

```
use Zend\Expressive\AppFactory;
use Zend\ServiceManager\ServiceManager;

$container = new ServiceManager();
$container->setFactory('AnExample', function ($container) {
    return function ($reqest, $response, $next) {
        $res->write('Example executed');
        return $res;
    };
});
$app = AppFactory::create($container);
$app->get('/', 'AnExample');
```

Above code uses just one PHP file for the purposes of explanation, so we are going to create the required application's classes such as `AppFactory` and the Service Manager container inside the same file. We will register our anonymous function as a key `'AnExample'`; apart from the function it might be also a class or method. We'll return another function inside our closure, which will print out "Example executed" as the result, thanks to the second parameter `$response`. Finally, we'll integrate the Service manager with an application by passing the object `$container` to the method `create()`. Now, when we simulate a call to home page with a proper key, a message from the anonymous function should appear.

The Service Manager was designed to improve and speed-up the process of grabbing and setting needed dependencies, so after multiple calls of the `get()` method with the same key we can get just the same instance of the class. For example, if we would want to obtain another object of the same class (for instance: we have a static class variables which we want to reset), then we should use the `build()` method instead of `get()`.

Some available keys for the Service Manager are:

- `services,`

- `factories,`

- `abstract_factories,`

- `aliases,`

- initializers,

- delegators,

- shared,

- lazy_services,

- shared_by_default.

Below is a brief overview of each key and its use.

Warning: the key `invokables` from ZF2 version has been removed and replaced with factories along with `InvokableFactory`.

7.3.1. Services

The easiest key called Services is used to register other services or other instances of the Service Manager objects. We can use it if, for example, our library already has its own Service Manager which we want to link inside our application and, at the same time, avoid problems with the keys being overridden.

```
use Zend\ServiceManager\Factory\InvokableFactory;
use Zend\ServiceManager\ServiceManager;
use Application\CustomServiceManager;

$serviceManager = new ServiceManager([
    'services' => [
        CustomServiceManager::class => new CustomServiceManager();
    ]
]);
```

7.3.2. Factories

Factories are probably the most commonly used keys in the Service Manager.

Thanks to them we are able to create almost any class which has its dependencies in the constructor or does not take any arguments. Of course, an utilization without extra parameters is much easier; enough will be the fact that we only need to use our class name with the package as a key name (for example using a shortcut ::class) and we would apply a class name and package InvokableFactory as a value. To create a class with dependencies, we would have to use anonymous functions.

```php
use Interop\Container\ContainerInterface;
use Zend\ServiceManager\Factory\InvokableFactory;
use Zend\ServiceManager\ServiceManager;
use Application\User;
use Application\UserSession;

$serviceManager = new ServiceManager([
    'factories' => [
        //User class creation without params but via InvokableFactory
        User::class => InvokableFactory::class,
        //class creation which require 1 parameter of: Application|User
        UserSession::class => function(ContainerInterface $sm, $name) {
            $userClass = $sm->get(User::class);
            return new UserSession($userClass);
        },
    ],
]);

//get new objects:
$serviceManager->get(User::class);
$serviceManager->get(UserSession::class);
```

As we have already mentioned above, the usage of ::class gives us the same results as writing: 'Application\User' in the script. However, if we use closures as values in our array, we will get an access to two variables: $sm and $name (optionally to the third one, $params, with extra options). The first parameter is always an object with interface ContainerInterface which we have mentioned (we know we can call methods like has() and get() on it). By variable $sm we get the User object we have written above. Next, we return a result class, passing at the same time a new get object $userClass.

7.3.3. Abstract Factories

It is a list of factory classes that are abstract and can only create objects based on their conditions. This key is most commonly used in classes which names we do not know, because they are generated on the fly. But they however have the same pattern of creating objects. Each of that abstract factory must have an interface of `Zend\ServiceManager\Factory\AbstractFactory` ↪`Interface` which requires from the other hand one method: `canCreate()`. Additionally, each abstract factory class must have its magical function `__invokable()` that describes the usage conditions of it more precisely. If, for example, we call on Service Manager object a command `get()` with not existing class name, the Service Manager executes methods of all the factories registered under key `abstract_factories` in a sequence `canCreate()`. If the first abstract factory returns `TRUE` for method `canCreate()`, then this class will be returned and a process of iteration will be stopped. It of course raises some problems with efficiency if we have many abstract factories. That is why we should use such factories only in special circumstances.

```
//sample class which we want to return
class User implements InputFilterAwareInterface
{
    ...
}

//sample abstract factory class
class MyAbstractFactory implements AbstractFactoryInterface
{
    public function canCreate(ContainerInterface $container, $requestedName)
    {
        return in_array('InputFilterAwareInterface',
↪class_implements($requestedName), true);
    }
    public function __invoke(ContainerInterface $container, $requestedName,
↪array $options = null)
    {
        return $requestedName();
    }
}

//manager registration
$serviceManager = new ServiceManager([
```

```
    'abstract_factories' => [
        MyAbstractFactory::class => new MyAbstractFactory()
    ]
]);


//call the object which doesn't exists
$serviceManager->get(InvalidClass::class);


//call the object which does exists
$serviceManager->get(User::class);
```

7.3.4. Aliases

Aliases, so the plain keys, are shortcuts to other services already available in the Service Manager. If for example we need to create a class User not only by passing `User::class` to `get()`, we can use any other key, for instance `'user_model'`, which also we place in the aliases key, remembering that we can link aliases between one another multiple times.

```
$serviceManager = new ServiceManager([
    'factories' => [
        User::class => InvokableFactory::class
    ],
    'aliases' => [
        'user_class' => User::class,
        'user_model' => 'user_class'
    ]
]);
$serviceManager->get('user_model');
```

7.3.5. Initializers

`Initializers` are yet another key that allows us to use an anonymous function or so-called callback or classes with interfaces: `Zend\Service ↪Manager\Initialier\InitializerInterface`. The main purpose of initializers is their initial run and execution of each registered service. They help out in passing the same dependencies into many classes or decorating them with other main objects, "wrappers". In a contrast to factories, initializers have only 2 arguments in method `__invokable(): $container` and `$instance` which captures an actually passed instance of the service.

```
$serviceManager = new ServiceManager([
    'factories' => [
        SessionToken::class => InvokableFactory::class
    ],
    'initializers' => [
        function(ContainerInterface $container, $instance) {
            if ($instance instanceof SessionInterface === false) {
                return;
            }
            $instance->setSessionToken($container->get(SessionToken::class));
        }
    ]
]);
```

In the given code, our initializer checks whether the returned object has an interface of `SessionInterface`. If it does, then it automatically adds an object `SessionToken` into same class instance. Similarly to `abstract_factories`, initializers can slow down an application due to the fact that they are called for every dependency.

7.3.6. Shared

Shared is really just an array with already registered keys from other keys which describes how the existing keys should be treated by `Boolean` value as `TRUE` (shared) or `FALSE` (unique). By default all the objects returned via `get()` method are locally cached, so their another call would not return a different object. However, shared gives us an ability to defines which services should be cached and which ones should not.

```
$serviceManager = new ServiceManager([
    'factories' => [
        User::class => InvokableFactory::class
    ],
    'shared' => [
        User::class => false
    ]
]);
```

```
//will return for us 2 different objects
$instance1 = $serviceManager->get(User::class);
$instance2 = $serviceManager->get(User::class);
```

7.3.7. Shared by Default

An Alternative to Shared, this option, instead of getting a whole array, gets only value TRUE/FALSE and defines whether or not all objects should be cached and returned.

7.3.8. Lazy Services

Delayed services are exactly what Lazy Services are. They are especially useful when we want to have a given object available in each class, but each class does not need to use that given object at all. If an object will not be used, then it won't be created. To understand this, we need to remember that the Service Manager creates each service at the very start. Classes inside lazy_services are created only when we refer to them via get() or build() method.

```
$serviceManager = new \Zend\ServiceManager\ServiceManager([
    'factories' => [
        User::class => InvokableFactory::class,
    ],
    'lazy_services' => [
        // we would use key: class_map, to define mapping of our class in key delegators
        'class_map' => [
            User::class => User::class,
        ],
    ],
    'delegators' => [
        User::class => [
            LazyServiceFactory::class,
        ],
    ],
]);
```

7.3.9. Delegators

Delegators are services that allow us to add a custom script into specific parts of code. It is practically the same rule as in the Event Manager. Everything is handled by `Zend\EventManager\EventManagerInterface` and methods `trigger()` (inside delegators) and `attach()` (outside of them) for adding your own piece of code.

```
//sample calss with extra method
class User
{
    ...
    public function getPoints()
    {
        return 'user have 10 points';
    }
}

//delegator/integration
use Zend\EventManager\EventManagerInterface;
class UserDelegator extends User
{
    protected $userClass;
    protected $eventManager;
    public function __construct(User $userClass, EventManagerInterface
↪$eventManager)
    {
        $this->userClass = $userClass;
        $this->eventManager = $eventManager;
    }
    public function getPoints()
    {
        $this->eventManager->trigger('getPointsEvent', $this);
        return $this->userClass->getPoints();
    }
}

//usage
$user = new User();
$eventManager = new Zend\EventManager\EventManager();
$eventManager->attach('getPointsEvent', function () { echo "Bonus! +1, "; });
```

```
$buzzer = new UserDelegator($user, $eventManager);
echo $buzzer->buzz();
//will return: Bonus! +1, user have 10 points
```

In order to use the Service Manager object, we would get the same result by calling:

```
//extra class, which is factory passed to delegators key
use Interop\Container\ContainerInterface;
use Zend\ServiceManager\Factory\DelegatorFactoryInterface;
class UserDelegatorFactory implements DelegatorFactoryInterface
{
    public function __invoke(ContainerInterface $container, $name, callable
↪$callback, array $options = null)
    {
        $userClass = call_user_func($callback);
        $eventManager = $serviceLocator->get('EventManager');
        $eventManager->attach('getPointsEvent', function ()
↪{ echo " Bonus! +1, "; });
        return new UserDelegator($userClass, $eventManager);
    }
}
```

Everything is linked with one script:

```
//usage of the new factory
$serviceManager = new Zend\ServiceManager\ServiceManager([
    'factories' => [
        User::class => InvokableClass::class,
    ],
    'delegators' => [
        User::class => [
            UserDelegatorFactory::class,
        ],
    ],
]);

//usage
$userDelegator = $serviceManager->get(User::class);
$userDelegator->getPoints();
//will return: Bonus! +1, user have 10 points
```

7.3.10. Plugin Managers

Plugin Managers are special objects designed to store scripts which are later used in many places at the same time. For instance, all validation services are defined in a plugin called `ValidatorPluginManager`. Plugin manager is also special because it extends the existing Service Manager - thanks to that it behaves exactly the same.

```
'factories' => [
    ValidatorPluginManager::class => function(ContainerInterface $container, $name) {
        return new ValidatorPluginManager($container, [
            'factories' => [
                StringLengthValidator::class => InvokableFactory::class,
            ],
        ]);
    },
],
```

To get that nested instance of `StringLengthValidator`, we need to call the method `get()` twice, first time from Service Manager and then the other one from the plugin itself:

```
$pluginManager = $serviceManager->get(ValidatorPluginManager::class);
$validator = $pluginManager->get(StringLengthValidator::class);
```

7.4. Hydrators

Hydrators are quite inconspicuous Zend components, without which of course we can work, but their size and purpose give an additional "taste" that should appeal to you. As you already know, each object can be also exported into an associative array format. The Hydrator is a component that reverts this operation. Hydrators are used to create objects from different PHP array formats. The main feature of each hydrator is a link between two separate layers, so that they are not cluttered up with unnecessary mappings, validations or filters in the classes, models etc. Someone once said that one example is worth more than 1000 words. That is why I am not going to write 1001 words in this section, instead, I will move straight away into a practical example.

Let take a look a situation where we have a linked object of the `User` class which is responsible for returned by us record from the table users, with a form to edit the user details. Our class User has a date of birth as a variable dateOfBirth. Obviously, we have a getter and setter, which looks like so:

```
public function getDateOfBirth()
{
    return $this->dateOfBirth;
}
public function setDateOfBirth(DateTime $date = null)
{
    $this-> dateOfBirth = $date;
    return $this;
}
```

Notice that method setDateOfBirth expects only a DateTime object or NULL. Exactly here the main problem raises – a linked form is passing a POST array with values of type string, so instead of DateTime object we would get, for instance "1988-01-02", which would cause an exception thrown by PHP core logic. In exactly this place we should use a hydrator that would format the date of birth accordingly, so that it fits to the interface of User class. All hydrators are created in a new single folder with name "Hydrator" in the folder *module/Application/src/*. Here is the first of them:

```
namespace Application\Hydrator;
use DateTIme;
use Zend\Stdlib\Hydrator\Strategy\DefaultStrategy;

class DateTimeStrategy extends DefaultStrategy
{
    /**
    * Converts a value of type string to the DateTime objects
    */
    public function hydrate($value)
    {
        if (is_string($value) && $value === '') {
            $value = null;
        } else if (is_string($value)) {
            $value = new DateTime($value);
        }
        return $value;
    }
```

}

We can use the `DateTimeStrategy` class by using a `Classmethods` that allows us to specify a base for methods get and set, by which it will be overridden by the hydrator. If we would pass a name `dateOfBirth` to the method `addStrategy`, the hydrator will be called for the reference of `getDateOfBirth()` and `setDateOfBirth()`. Note that our hydrator also checks an empty value of the form and passes an object null back to the `User` class, so that we can properly update a field in the column.

```
$user = new User();
$hydrators = new ClassMethods();
$dateTime = $hydrators->addStrategy('dateOfBirth', new DateTimeStrategy());
//assuming that $_POST have a variable dateOfBirth in a proper format
$hydrators->hydrate($_POST, $user);
```

Basically that is all. We just have to call `hydrate()` method from `ClassMethods`, which will call all the registered hydrators itself, and thanks to that our method `setDateOfBirth()` will be run with a parameter `DateTime` converted by the `DateTimeStrategy` class. Additionally, in the hydrator classes we can also define methods `extract()`, which as opposed to `hydrate()`, would export a value back to the initial state. In this situation, it would be a string with an initial date.

There are some other types of hydrators, such as:

- `Filters` – covers filtering of values returned by `extract()` or `hydrate()`;

- `Aggregate` – gives an ability to get Event Manager from the hydrator and later operating on those events;

- `IdentityNamingStrategy` – offers the creation of an object Entity from an associative array, where the array key equals to the class variable name;

- `MapNamingStrategy` – allows to define mapping from the array keys into other values required by class Entity;

- `UnderscoreNamingStrategy` – converts array naming into the camel case one when trying to hydrate, and back to the naming under case when `extract()` is called;

- `CompositeNamingStrategy` – gives an ability to set which naming strategy should be used for each of the keys separately during hydrating and extracting.

CHAPTER 8.

Databases

8.1. Adapters – MariaDB, MySQL, PostgreSQL etc.

Zend Framework 3 and its precursors support a lot of globally available database adapters. However, the new version also offers a support for a new database type called Maria DB. This new type of storing data has its own very untypical story. Maria DB is fully compatible with MySQL syntax. But since Oracale took over the Sun Microsystems corporation (along with its products such as Java or MySQL), the future of MySQL has changed. Formerly the Apache 2.0 license has been changed into multi licensing that offered free usage for noncommercial projects only.

Maria DB has also some improvements compared to MySQL: scalability and efficiency, so a key parameters of each database engine. The primary goal of Maria DB was to create a full open source product and share the engine on the GPL license. Let's however go back to the supported adapter types of DB. Zend Framework overall supports 7:

- IbmDb2 – a driver for `ext/ibm_db2`;

- Mysqli – a driver for `ext/mysqli`;

- `Oci8` – a driver for `ext/oci8`;

- `Pgsql` – a driver for `ext/pgsql`;

- `Sqlsrc` – a driver for `ext/sqlsrv` (Microsoft);

- `Pdo_Mysql` – a driver for MySQL and Maria DB with `PDO` extension;

- `Pdo_Sqlite` – a driver for SQLite with `PDO` extension;

- `Pdo_Pgsql` – a driver for PostgreSQL with `PDO` extension;

Now that we already know what Zend is compatible with, we can move on to find out what an object of the `Zend\Db\Adapter` needs to function normally. Presented below is a table with configuration keys, descriptions of each of them and options assigned to them.

Key name	Option	Description
driver	Required	One from the available adapter types, such as: `Mysqli`, `Sqlsrv`, `Pdo_Sqlite`, `Pdo_Mysql`, `Pdo`
database	Required	Name of the data base or file DB
username	Required	User name
password	Required	User password
hostname	Optional	IP address or host name to connect
port	Optional	Port number to connect
charset	Optional	Chars encoding type

The easiest way of creating a sample adapter is to pass an array with the keys above mentioned in one simple line:

```
$adapter = new \Zend\Db\Adapter\Adapter($config);
```

Additionally, a constructor of DB Adapter takes two optional arguments: `$platform`, so the database platform based on default adapter driver implementation, and `$queryResultSet` that represents our returned records in this adapter. In general, each adapter is constructed from three main objects:

- Connection – defines a way of connecting with database;

- Statement – describes how abstract methods of Zend Db are processed to the queries to the db;

- Result – outlines a format of returned records.

Thanks to them you will be able to for instance, modify connection to database or update default formats of returned results accordingly to your own classes and implementations. Zend Db uses default classes to adapters only when you will omit passing it into a constructor.

8.2. Simple queries

Once we will finally have an adapter object, we can use it to send some queries. And here is a big surprise. Methods like `fetchAll()`, `fetchOne` etc have been eliminated in favor of iterative PDO results. What does it mean for the developers of Zend Framework 1? It means that from now on we will be getting a result in an array format, without unnecessary extra methods. We will present below a code which will execute a query to a database, to get all results from table: `"users"`:

```
$sql = 'SELECT * FROM users';
$query = $adapter->query($sql);
$results = $query->execute();
foreach ($results as $row){
    print_r($row->toArray());
```

```
    }
```

The code looks very similar to standard PHP PDO queries, however it is missing a `fetch()` method, and while loop is now replaced with `foreach` statement.

If we don't need to return any results, for example with commands `UPDATE`, `ALTER`, or `DELETE`, we can short up our example code into just two lines:

```
$sql = 'ALTER TABLE ADD INDEX(`users_index`) ON (`id`)';
$adapter->query($sql, Adapter::QUERY_MODE_EXECUTE);
```

As it can be easily noticed, we don't need to call method `execute()` because we are passing a second parameter to the query() method. It informs then, that the query must be executed straight on (`QUERY_MODE_EXECUTE`).

And what if we need to pass parameters into queries? We are not just putting a variable into the SQL statement for sure! We can accomplish that in two ways. The first one is shorter and applies to the small queries, and the second one is longer but more readable. Both of them, however, protect us from attacks of "SQL injections". The first solution is to use question marks characters as placeholders in places where we want to input our variable.

```
$query = $adapter->query('SELECT * FROM users WHERE `id` = ?', [$userId]);
$query->execute();
```

As a second parameter we pass single level array with variables. However, a mechanism like that can easily confuse us; that is why the another way is more applicable to the more complex queries.

```
$adapter->query(
    'SELECT * FROM users WHERE `id` = :id AND username = :username'
);
$query->execute(['username' => $username, 'id' => $userId]);
```

Thanks to that approach, the order of the variables in second argument no longer has any importance. The keys with prefixed semicolons would be mapped to the keys in a passed array. Notice that we have moved a variables array into a method `execute()` instead of `query()`, and thanks to that we are able to build our table even after calling `query()`.

If you want to use abstract Zend methods such as in Table Gateway, but without application of this design pattern, Zend 3 gives you this possibility. Zend SQL Abstraction , because we are talking about it, offers all the features like `select()`, `from()`, `where()` and so on. We just need to create an object of `Zend\Db\Sql\Sql` and pass our database adapter into the constructor. Next, we call `prepareStatementForSqlObject()` method that is almost the same as a method `execute()` in the adapter itself. An example usage is described below:

```
$sql = new \Zend\Db\Sql\Sql($adapter);
$select = $sql->select();
$select->from('u' => 'users');
$select->where(['id' => 2]);
$statement = $sql->prepareStatementForSqlObject($select);
$results = $statement->execute();
```

We could also use a method `buildSqlString()` and pass `QUERY_MODE_EXECUTE` as a second argument of the `query()` method, but the first approach is more readable. Instead of the line `$select->from('users')`, we can pass another table name in SQL constructor: `($adapter, 'users')`.

In order to run simple `JOIN` of two tables, we just need to call a statement `join()` in the following way:

```
$select
    ->from(['u' => 'users'])
    ->join(
        ['up' => 'user_permissions'],
        'u.id = up.user_id',
        ['permission_name'],
        $select::JOIN_LEFT
    );
```

Above example would link the results from table `user_permission` with the records from users, on the condition that user's id would equals `user_id` in the table `user_permissions`. Additionally, a query will link a column with name `permission_name` to the records, if it finds a proper user or `NULL`, as we are using a linkage type of `LEFT JOIN`.

Surely you might be amazed by the structure of our code. Why are we not writing `$select->from()` and then `$select->join()`? Well, it's obviously a shortcut in writing, but you can ask a question: how is that possible? Almost all of the core methods like `join()`, `where()` or `from()` in object `Zend\Db\Sql\Select`, return an actual object via `return this;`. Thanks to that we are able to chain the methods together (chaining mechanism). It saves us time duplicating the same variables that store an object of the `Select`, `Insert`, `Update`, or `Delete`. We can find the same mechanism for instance in jQuery docs page:

```
$('.element').css('height', '200px').show();
```

As we can already expect, the object of a class `Select` offers other methods that additionally support `where()`. An example is statements GROUP BY or HAVING. The method `group()` eliminates duplicates in records, but `having()` gives us an option to filter returned records by condition WHERE.

```
$having = new \Zend\Db\Sql\Having();
$having->expression('LENGTH(password) = ?', 10);
$select
    ->from('users')
    ->where('id = 1')
    ->having('password')
    ->group('username');
```

By the way, we have presented an usage of method `expression()` from class `Having` that allows us to use keys like NOW(), CURDATE() or CURRENT_TIMESTAMP().

Sorting or limiting results is available under methods: `order()` and `limit()` / `offset()`. In example below, apart from sorting by user name and returning only two records, we will add extra conditions to the clause `where()`. We check if the username is not empty or if an id value is defined in our array.

```
$select
    ->from('users')
    ->where([
        new \Zend\Db\Sql\Predicate\IsNotNull('username'),
        'id' => [1, 2, 3]
    ])
    ->order('username ASC')
    ->limit(2)
```

```
->offset(0);
```

If we would want at any point to check if field is empty, that is `IS NULL`, we need to create an object `IsNull('column_name')` or, more easily, pass a condition: `'column_name' => null` into a `where()` method.

8.3. CRUD operations

CRUD queries, so the queries regarding Adding, Replacing, Updating and Deleting records, are easy to do by using `Zend\Db\Sql` object. If we want to add two new rows into a table, we should re-use the method `column()` to set column names into which we will be adding values in another method called `values()`. Let's have a look at the example:

```
$sql = new \Zend\Db\Sql\Sql($adapter);
$insert = $sql->insert();
$insert
    ->into('users')
    ->columns(['username', 'password'])
    ->values([
        'nowy1' => 'pass1',
        'nowy2' => 'pass2',
    ]);
```

Optionally, we can append the second argument with method `values()`, like `$insert::VALUES_MERGE`, to merge all the records with the same query. By default this option is set on `VALUES_SET`, so without merges.

Records updating takes place analogically to adding, except that instead `column()` we would call `set()`, `values()` is replaced with method `where()`, while `into()` we change into `table()`.

```
$update = $sql->update();
$update
    ->table('users')
    ->set([
        'username' => 'nowa_nazwa',
        'password' => 'nowe_haslo',
```

```
])
    ->where(['username' => 'new 1']);
```

Take a close look, that "`set`" takes an array in format: `column_name = > value`, the same as a method defining query conditions `where()`. But "`where`" must be more functional to execute more sophisticated comparisons like "`like, between, more than/less than`", etc. For instance, we can change above example into `LIKE` usage in the following way:

```
$update
    ->table('users')
    ->set([
        'username' => 'new_name',
        'password' => 'new_pass',
    ]);
$where = $update->where();
$where->like['username' => 'new%']);
```

Thanks to that, we will be able to add much more conditions by using an object `$where`. A list of all available methods of the object `Zend\Db\Sql\Where` is presented below:

- `nest()`

- `setUnnest(predicate)`

- `unnest()`

- `equalTo(left, right, leftType, rightType)`

- `notEqualTo(left, right, leftType, rightType)`

- `lessThan(left, right, leftType, rightType)`

- `greaterThan(left, right, leftType, rightType)`

- `lessThanOrEqual(left, right, leftType, rightType)`

- `greaterThanOrEqual(left, right, leftType, rightType)`

- `like(column, value)`

- `notLike(column, value)`

- `literal(literal)`

- `expression(expression, params)`

- `isNull(column)`

- `isNotNull(column)`

- `in(column, values)`

- `notIn(column, values)`

- `between(column, min, max)`

- `notBetween(column, min, max)`

- `predicate(predicate)`

A "magical" class `Predicate` in `setUnnset()` and `predicate()` is a base class for `Zend\Db\Sql\Where` and `Having`. The class `Predicate` offers the same methods as displayed list of class `Where`.

At the end, we have left the easiest function of deleting records. It uses already known methods as `from()` and `where()`. To delete a user with name `new2`, we just need this script:

```
$delete = $sql->delete();
$delete
    ->from('users')
    ->where(['username' => 'new2']);
```

8.4. Table Gateway

A component Table Gateway is a design pattern of database tables represented in an object-oriented format. What does that mean? In a nutshell, this pattern requires from a programmer to create one new class for each table with interface of `Zend\Db\TableGateway\TableGateway` ↪`Interface`, (or, alternatively and more easily, to extend an abstract class `AbstractTableGateway` from the same package name as the interface). A primary rule both implementations is having the five methods: `getTable()`, `select()`, `insert()`, `update()` and `delete()`. They define the basic tasks of each `TableGateway` class and make our life easier when later communicating with a model to create a business logic. An important thing in the Table Gateway pattern is a separation, so-called an encapsulation of a logic linked with getting or modifying the data of one table in just one class in the whole project. To illustrate above description, we will present a new class `AvatarsGateway`:

```
class AvatarsGateway extends \Zend\Db\TableGateway\TableGateway
{
    public function __construct($adapter)
    {
        parent::__construct('avatars', $adapter);
    }
}
```

And there is a way of using that class to get some results via method `select()` that takes the same parameters as `where()` in the previous section.

```
$gatewayTable = new TableGateway('project', $adapter);
$rowset = $gatewayTable->select(['username' => 'new']);

foreach ($rowset as $row) {
    echo $row['name'].PHP_EOL;
}
//or to get first element in array:
$row = $rowset->current();
echo $row['username'].PHP_EOL;
```

Take a look at the execution of constructor of abstract class, into which we first passed a table name, and later DB adapter. Those two first parameters are the only ones required to create correct object. However, the constructor of class `TableGateway`, which extends `AbstarctTableGateway`, has three other arguments. The whole method signature looks like below:

```
public function __construct(
    string|TableIdentifier $table,
    AdapterInterface $adapter,
    Feature\AbstractFeature|Feature\FeatureSet|Feature\AbstractFeature[]
↪$features = null,
    ResultSetInterface $resultSetPrototype = null,
    Sql\Sql $sql = null
);
```

The third parameter, `$features`, describes the set of "extra improvements" that add new features to our `TableGateway` class. We can use an array of these features or just pass a single one that can be any of these types:

- `EventFeature` – gives an ability to create Event Manager that listens for different cycles/stages during the request of a database;

- `GobalAdapterFeature` - offers defining of a global adapter for all classes of `AbstarctTableGateway` type; a useful option if we have only one adapter and one database in a project;

- `MasterSlaveFeature` – requires two adapters, where master is responsible for operations of type: `insert()`, `update()` or `delete()`, and a second adapter is responsible for execution of `select()` queries only;

- `MetadataFeature` – extends the functionality by adding extra information about the columns from the `Metadata` object into returned records;

- `RowGatewayFeature` – adds an ability to extend `select()` method that stars returning objects extended with functionality of `RowGateway`, allowing the later modification back to the database. You can find more about `RowGateway` in the next section.

A fourth constructor parameter is `$resultSetPrototype`. It deals with a type of objects returned by the method `select()`.The models with getters and setters and `toArray()` are the most common. The fifth and last argument is `$sql`, which is of a `Zned\Db\Sql\Sql` type and, as you might guess, it replaces a default `Sql` object attached to the given adapter in a second parameter.

You may wonder why we have used a `TableGateway` class instead of `AbstarctTableGateway`. There are two simple answers. First, the abstract class does not have a defined constructor, which makes it harder to use at first. The second argument is an additional validation of passed parameters in `TableGateway` that do not entirely exist in `AbstractTableGateway`, which is the nature of this class.

8.5. Row Gateway

A design pattern Row Gateway is sort of an extension to the previous pattern Table Gateway, at least when it comes to its implementation in Zend Framework 3. In comparison to Table Gateway, Row Gateway is a pattern replicating not a table, but a record from the database table. Apart from `insert()`, `update()` etc., there are two already implemented methods: `save()` and `delctc()` in our class. Thanks to this approach we will be able to modify our returned cords from the database and call the method `save()` that determines which fields have been changed and which ones need an update in the table. However, the method `delete()` will remove a result based on the primary key in the table. The primary key is passed to the constructor of `RowGatewayTable`.

```
use Zend\Db\TableGateway\TableGateway;
use Zend\Db\TableGateway\Feature\RowGatewayFeature;

$table = new TableGateway('avatars', $adapter, new RowGatewayFeature('id'));
$results = $table->select(['id' => 1]);
$avatarRow = $results->current();
$avatarRow->src = 'new_src.jpg';

//here we save data to database with changed column 'src'
```

```
$avatarRow->save();
```

As you already know, the last option of the variable $features in previous section is RowGtewayFeature(column) executed in line that initializes the TableGateway class. Next, we do a query in order to get a single record from the table avatars and we are changing the value of src. Using the same object returned by select() and current(), we perform an update through the save() method.

A very popular technique among the Zend Framework 1 programmers was using so-called Active Record pattern, which assumed that all the functionalities regarding saving or deleting the data needed to be concluded in class TableGateway. The whole business logic concerning modifications of a given table could be placed only in a given class. It meant nothing else than overriding methods save(), delete() or adding extra methods to help manipulating the data. As an example, if we add a record to the database and we want to apply by the way another record modification at the same time, then we need to reuse a design pattern Active Records , which gives us a possibility to override save() and delete().

```
use Zend\Db\TableGateway\Feature\RowGatewayFeature;
use Zend\Db\TableGateway\TableGateway;
use Zend\Db\RowGateway\RowGatewayInterface;

class Avatar implements RowGatewayInterface
{
    protected $adapter;
    public function __construct($adapter)
    {
        $this->adapter = $adapter;
    }
    //override method save and delete
    public function save()
    {
        //custom implementation
        parent::save();
    }
    public function delete()
    {
        //custom implementation
        parent::delete();
    }
}
```

```
public function reset()
{
    //here we can for instance delete few class variables
    unset($this->date);
    unset($this->src);
}
}
```

Instead of the column name, we are passing this new class to the constructor
of `RowGatewayFeature`, remembering about passing an adapter of a new
class as well.

```
$table = new TableGateway('artist', $adapter,
↪new RowGatewayFeature(new Avatar($adapter)));
```

CHAPTER 9.

View templates

9.1. Default views

The same as in previous Zend Framework versions, default views are written in Zend View, in other words the files with *.phtml* extension. They are based on regular HTML files with short tags `<?= ?>`, or with standard ones `<?php ?>`. Of course, every view has an access to the passed variables from the controller's level. Just return a single action like `indexAction()`, an object of `ViewModel()` or a regular associative array. Each given array will be converted into an instance of the mentioned object anyway. Calling the `setVariable()` method:

```
$view = new ViewModel();
$view->setVariable('test', 'values');
$view->setVariable('letters', ['a', 'b', 'c', 'd']);
```

It means that in view file we will be able to use a variable `$test` in order to display a logical condition. We can pass any other type of the variable – it could be `string`, `integer`, `object` or `array`. In order to display the sample variables, we will present a demo view in *.phtml* file:

```
<?php if ($test === 'values'): ?>
    <b><?= $test ?>:<br /></b>
    <p>
```

```php
    <?php foreach ($letters as $letter) : ?>
        <?= $letter?> <br />
    <?php endforeach; ?>
  </p>
<?php endif (); ?>
```

//will return
values:
a
b
c
d

It's worth to mention that we are using an alternative syntax of control structures in the view files. It is a usage of type like `if()` : with the colon at the end and the ending such as `endif`, without the need of adding curly brackets. It is a recommendation syntax to use inside each view where quite often we have a lot of nested conditions that could potentially break the readability of the file. Thanks to using `endif` or `endforeach` we can analyze the code and separate conditions easier than using the curly brackets. An alternative syntax is available for the structural blocks such as: if, while for, `foreach` and switch.

Often, however, you might want to create additional view files, which can be used in a couple of other actions. These files usually consist of parts of the sites that repeat two or more times on a single site; elements such as: logged in user menu or search bar. The easiest way of embedding these views is executing a method `<?= $this->render('file.phtml'); ?>`, but it is best to keep these dependencies in the controller by using `ViewModel` and the method `addChild()`:

```php
class AvatarsController extends AbstractActionController
{
    public function indexAction()
    {
        $view = new ViewModel();
        $searchView = new ViewModel();
        $searchView->setTemplate('_shared/search');
        $view->addChild($searchView, 'searchView');
        return $view;
    }
}
```

With such control of values our view file becomes much smaller and more readable:

```
<div class="row content">
    <?= $this->searchView ?>
</div>
```

Due to the fact, that we are passing a view by using `addChild`, not `setVariable()`, we have to refer to the `ViewModel` object by `$this->`, and then to the value of `searchView` defined in the second argument of the `addChild()` method in the controller. A method `setTempalte()` overrides a default path to the *.phtml* view file, thanks to which we can generate such paths in the controller itself.

It is easy to realize that defining links to other views, which require a lot of variables in the controller, is not that affordable and it "clogs" the logic of controller. That's why in my opinion in the case of passing a huge amount of the variables or nested views it is much better to use good old calls of `partial()`. This method works in a similar way to `$this->render()`, but it gives us a possibility to pass the view parameters to the embedded views.

```
<?= $this->partial('application/_shared/search.phtml', array(
    'letters' => $letters,
    'var2' => 'value2'
))?>
```

In the following sections of this book we will be using an alternative syntax and methods of `partial()`. Another method worth to mention is `setTerminal()` that takes a parameter of `Boolean` type and determines whether `ZendMvc` needs to stop rendering the layout and only return the content of a single view.

```
public function imagesAction()
{
    $view = new ViewModel([
        'message' => 'Your Images',
    ]);
    // stop rendering a whole layout, instead display just the contents of images.phtml
    $view->setTerminal(true);
    return $view;
}
```

At the end, a nice function of the basic views is the protection from an XSS (Cross Site Scripting), or from other attempts of trying to generate other than expected data from views. Zend View has a few of these methods to protect and escape the view variables:

- escapreHtml – used to convert HTML tags into entities;

- escapeHtmlAttr – converts quotes and other special characters that could unexpectedly close HTML tag;

- escapeJs – protects all cases of passing JavaScript code;

- escapeCss – protects all cases of passing CSS code;

- escapeUrl – converts URL address in the same way as urlencode().

For example:

```
echo $this->escapeUrl('http://aaa.com');
//return: http|3A |2F |2F aaa|2E pl

<?= $this->escapeCss('.container { width: 100%; }') ?>
//return: |2E container|20 |7B |20 width|3A |20 100|25 |3B |20 |7D
//never trust variables contents if they are comming from inputs

<script type="text/javascript">
var variable = "<?= $this->escapeJs('"; alert("XSS");') ?>";
</script>
//return:
<script type="text/javascript">
var variable = "\x22\x3B\x20alert\x28\x22XSS\x22\x29\x3B";
</script>
```

9.2. View template engines – Smarty, Twig

Template Engines are an additional layer sitting between a view and resulted code for the web browser. View engines from a definition, sets their own syntax and the usage of the variables from controllers. The main goal of a such engine is a maximum separation of PHP script and template files. Thanks to that operation, a code in the view templates is cleaner and easier to understand and modify for a person who does not develop a PHP code on the daily basis. People like front end developers, working on HTML and JavaScript mainly, do not want to browse and read PHP codes in files they regularly update almost every day, if a client is changing its requirements all the time. When a PHP code is mixed with a presentation, it's much easier for new bugs and unstable integration to come up, which results in a harder to ensure stability of a given application. In this book we are going to present two the most popular template engines: smarty (cause it's mostly used in Zend Framework 1 applications) and Twig (an innovative and modern platform).

9.2.1. Smarty

Smarty, as the precursor of Template Engines, has started in 2002 and has developed to the version 3.1.30, released in August 2016. It can be easily used via creating a class object, setup of access paths, adding required variables and executing the whole thing:

```
$smarty = new Smarty();
$smarty->template_dir = './templates/';
$smarty->compile_dir = './templates/compile/';
$smarty->assign('title', 'some title');
$smarty->assign('body', 'some contents');
$smarty->display('index.tpl');
```

However, all the template files should be ending with extension *.tpl* (tpl is a short cut of a word template) and look like a linkage of a simple HTML, JS and CSS with blocks of type {block}. If we require the use of passed variables from a controller, for example of index.tpl, then it might look as below:

```html
<html lang="en">
    <head>
        <title>{$title|escape}</title>
    </head>
    <body>
        {$body}
    </body>
</html>
```

By adding a pipe character | after the variable name, we are able to call any built-in PHP function. `{$title|escape}` is the same as `escape(title)` in plain PHP. Smarty obviously supports layouts as well and can integrate with any Zend Framework version. After integrating with the latest version we will be using a project ZF3 Smarty Module from the website: *https://github.com/skillfish/zf3-smarty-module.* In order to start the installation, we have to first import a new project to the existing application. To do that we need to of course use a command line and Composer:

```
composer require skillfish/zf3-smarty-module
```

If we do not get any errors with dependencies, we can add a new record called `'Smarty'` into *config/modules.config.php.* Another step is to modify the application configuration in *application/config/module.config.php.* We must first change our existing declaration of template_map, in order to make it refer to the files with *.tpl,* instead of *.phtml.* Next, we need to tell Zend View that we are going to use another view rendering method by defining a strategy.

```php
'template_map' => [
    'layout/layout' => __DIR__.'/../view/layout/layout.tpl',
    'application/index/index' => __DIR__.'/../view/application/index/index.tpl',
    'error/404' => __DIR__.'/../view/error/404.tpl',
    'error/index' => __DIR__.'/../view/error/index.tpl',
],
'strategies' => [
    'Smarty\View\Strategy'
],
```

The last task is to add a new module Smarty into the list of active modules in file *modules.config.php*:

```php
'Smarty',
```

Now we can modify our sample method `indexAction()`, in which we would set a termination of rendering of Zend's layout and, pass a variable `baseUrl`, in order to properly display all the assets on site, such as JS/CSS.

```
public function indexAction()
{
    $view = new ViewModel();
    $model = $this->usersTable;
    $row = $model->getById(1);
    $view->setVariable('id', $row->getId());
    $view->setVariable('username', $row->getUsername());
    $view->setVariable('password', $row->getPassword());

    //we are terminating further rendering of main template, instead of that we would call a template
    // from the file index.tpl
    $view->setTerminal(true);
    //we are passing a base URL, as Smarty does not have an access to the  basePath() method
    $view->baseUrl = $this->getRequest()->getBaseUrl().'/public';
    return $view;
}
```

Of course we could define `$view->baseUrl` in abstract controller, then all other controllers would have a direct access, but to keep a simplicity in our example we should leave it there in the controller's method.

Now we just need to create new tpl files we have referenced in the configuration. To start with, a file *application/view/application/index/↪index.tpl*:

```
{extends 'layout/layout.tpl'}
{block 'content'}
    <div class="jumbotron">
        <h1><span class="zf-green">Zend Framework 3</span></h1>
        <p>
            Found user:<br /><br />
            Id: {$id}<br />
            Name: {$username}<br />
            Password: {$password}
        </p>
    </div>
{/block}
```

135

Take a look at the first line of the Smarty file: {extends 'layout/layout.tpl'}. It informs template engine that the actual file is using layout.tpl file to generate the whole. Another important issue is adding block as {block 'content'}, which later defines for us a variable with name {$content} in a file *layout.tpl*. Analogically, we create error files too, like *error.tpl* and *404.tpl* (as we want), remembering about extending a template: *layout.tpl*. A crucial issue is, however, the single template file, which sets our whole HTML structure:

```
<html lang="en">
    <head>
        <meta charset="utf-8">
        <title>ZF Skeleton Application</title>
        <link href="{$baseUrl}/img/favicon.ico" rel="shortcut icon"
↪type="image/vnd.microsoft.icon" />
        <link href="{$baseUrl}/css/bootstrap-theme.min.css" rel="stylesheet"
↪type="text/css" />
        <link href="{$baseUrl}/css/style.css" rel="stylesheet" type="text/css" />
        <link href="{$baseUrl}/css/bootstrap.min.css" rel="stylesheet"
↪type="text/css" />
        <!-- Scripts -->
        <script type="text/javascript" src="{$baseUrl}/js/
↪bootstrap.min.js"></script>
        <script type="text/javascript" src="{$baseUrl}/js/jquery-2.2.4.min.js">
↪</script>
    </head>
    <body>
        <nav class="navbar navbar-inverse navbar-fixed-top" role="navigation">
            <div class="container">
                ...
                <div class="collapse navbar-collapse">
                <ul class="nav navbar-nav">
                    <li class="active"><a href="{$baseUrl}
↪">Home Page</a></li>
                    <li class=""><a href="{$baseUrl}/users/index">
↪Users</a></li>
                    <li class=""><a href="{$baseUrl}/news/index">
↪Articles</a></li>
                </ul>
            </div>
        </nav>
        <div class="container">
            {block 'content'}{/block}
```

```
        <hr>
      </div>
    </body>
  </html>
```

Above example should give the same result as in chapter 5, that is the display of an information about user with id: `1`.

Smarty offers also a more complex usages like `{foreach}`, `{while}`, `{if}`, `{else}`, `{include}`, and ending at advanced plugins and own caching. All the information can be found on the official Smarty documentation: *http://www.smarty.net/docs/en/*.

9.2.2. Twig

Twig, on the other hand, is a fresh approach to the template engines subject. Initially not very popular, but after included into Symfony package and taken over by SensioLabs, has become almost as popular as the previously covered Smarty. Twig has other syntax structure than Smarty. It operates on double curly brackets to display variables, for example: `{{ variable }}`, and on syntax similar to EJS files, when defining blocks, loops or if conditions: `{% if online == false %}`. There are different end tags too. They do not relate, like in Smarty, to the XHTML, like endings like `{/if}` or `{/for}`, but correlate to the word: end: `{% endif %}`, `{%endfor %}`. The solution is similar like in PHP alternative syntax for control structure: `<?php endif; ?>` etc.

Unfortunately, an actual Twig integration with Zend in version 3 doesn't exist. There are, however, implementations for ZF2, which require a few alterations in order to make them work for the latest version too. In this book we will use a forked branch: *https://github.com/ZF-Commons/ZfcTwig*; our version, however, has an address: *https://github.com/divix1988/ZfcTwig*. Let's begin the installation by modifying contents of *composer.json*. Due to the fact that we will be including the patched version of the library and not just original lib, we first need to add a key into require:

```
"zf-commons/zfc-twig": "dev-dev-bugfix"
```

Notice that we are refering to a non-existing branch name: dev-dev-bugfix. We do that because by default composer will not load our forked branch, since it's not a valid distributed channel. A channel with name `dev-bugfix` is however in repository `divix1988/zfctwig` - that's why we have to refer to that name by adding a new key called repositories into composer. It looks like the following:

```
"repositories": [
    {
        "type": "vcs",
        "url": "https://github.com/divix1988/zfctwig"
    }
],
```

Now we can finally call a command composer update to get our new library and Twig integration. We should see a success message about the update:

```
# composer update
Loading composer repositories with package information
Updating dependencies (including require-dev)
- Installing zf-commons/zfc-twig (dev-dev-bugfix 5a11e23)
Cloning 5a11e23433034bbb10418bdeda8f447b4f57069e
Downloading 100%
Now trying to download from dist
- Installing zf-commons/zfc-twig (dev-dev-bugfix 5a11e23)
Downloading: 100%
```

If we already have downloaded the libraries, we can have a look at their configuration. The whole process is really very alike to the Smarty template engine integration. We begin with defining paths to our templates:

```
'template_map' => [
    'layout/layout' => __DIR__.'/../view/layout/layout.twig',
    'application/index/index' => __DIR__.'/../view/application/index/index.twig',
    'error/404' => __DIR__.'/../view/error/404.twig',
    'error/index' => __DIR__.'/../view/error/index.twig',
],
```

Later we register a new module in file *modules.config.php*, ZfcTwig, and we add new files with *.twig* extensions. By the way we delete the previous Smarty module, which collides with Twig. As an example our file *error/index.twig*, which displays various errors, will look like this:

```
<h1>Error</h1>
<h2>{{ message }}</h2>
{{ display_exceptions }}
{{ exception }}
<hr/>
<h2>Additional information:</h2>
<dl>
    <dt>File:</dt>
    <dd>
        <pre class="prettyprint linenums">{{ exception.getFile() }}:{{
↪exception.getLine() }}</pre>
    </dd>
    <dt>Message:</dt>
    <dd>
        <pre class="prettyprint linenums">{{ exception.getMessage() }}</pre>
    </dd>
    <dt>Stack trace:</dt>
    <dd>
        <pre class="prettyprint linenums">{{ exception.getTraceAsString()
↪}}</pre>
    </dd>
</dl>
```

Our *index/index.twig* file differs from Smarty just by other syntax usage, commands however remain the same.

```
{% extends 'layout/layout.twig' %}
{% block content %}
<div class="jumbotron">
    <h1><span class="zf-green">Zend Framework 3</span></h1>
    <p>
        Found user:<br /><br />
        Id: {{id}}<br />
        Name: {{username}}<br />
        Password: {{password}}
    </p>
</div>
{% endblock %}
```

Block `extends` renders for us a layout contents in: *layout.twig*, and a block with name content declares a variable we pass to the layout file. The main difference is an `IndexController` file, in which we no longer need the declaration of: `$view->setTerminal(true);`. Twig automatically configures this for us and simplifies the whole process of embedding and declaring views strategies. We will not display a whole file of *layout.twig*, as it does not differentiate much from the Smarty one. But it's worth to mention a single fragment of it:

```
<div class="container">
    {% block content %}{{ content|raw }}{% endblock content %}
    <hr>
```

The block content of course defines a place, in which our *index/index.twig* contents need to be displayed. A call `content|raw` means that the content of content var will not be changed or escaped to a safe form, as our code from *index.twig* contains special characters and HTML code. As opposed to the function raw there is a function `escape()`, which works analogically to the Smarty function called: `$this->escapeHtml()`.

9.3. Layouts and helpers

Layouts, so-called structural definitions of views, we can change on the fly in our controllers in a very easy way. By running a command `$this->layout()` we can get an actually used layout, and then we can execute the same method as for the view object to change phtml file by `setTemplate()`.

```
public function Action()
{
    //get an active layout and change it to the other, fe. with alterantive skin
    $layout = $this->layout();
    $layout->setTemplate('layouts/green_theme');
    //attach to the green_theme.phtml file a content variable
    $view = new ViewModel(['content' => $content]);
    return $view;
}
```

What if a couple of our controllers return JSON objects and another XML? We won't be duplicating a `layout()` definition over and over and create an empty layout objects to fulfill that, right? Luckily, Zend (apart from the controller of type RestfulController) gives us an option to set view generation modes. For this purpose we should use so-called strategies, so custom interference of implementations, via the Event Manager. Zend View actually holds its whole implementation in the executed by it three main events: renderer, dispatch and response.

```php
namespace SecondApplication;

class Module
{
    public function onBootstrap($e)
    {
        //register setLayout() method with render event
        $app = $e->getApplication();
        $app->getEventManager()->attach('render', [$this, 'setLayout'], 100);
    }
    public function setLayout($e)
    {
        $matches = $e->getRouteMatch();
        $controller = strtolower($matches->getParam('controller'));

        if (strpos('api', $controller) !== false) {
            // controller of type JSON
            $strategy = 'ViewJsonStrategy';
        } else if (strpos('feed', $controller) !== false) {
            // controller of type XML
            $strategy = 'ViewFeedStrategy';
        } else {
            //do not modify a default strategies for other controllers
            return;
        }

        // get Service Manger object together with its relative view strategy object
        $app = $e->getTarget();
        $locator = $app->getServiceManager();
        $view = $locator->get('Zend\View\View');
        $viewStrategy = $locator->get($strategy);
        // set new strategy for Zend View
        $view->getEventManager()->attach($viewStrategy, 100);
    }
}
```

Now for each controller of type `ApiAvatarsController` or `AvatarsApiController`, we will be executing a view of type `ViewJsonStrategy`. As an example: for controller with xml in name (`XmlResultsController`) we execute a view `ViewFeedStrategu` that will handle the retuning of XML contents in a proper manner.

We will move on into methods that support views, so-called mechanisms like generating paginations, URL addresses or HTML blocks. Zend MVC follows the Model View Controller design patter, so you should already know that the view should not call methods from controller directly. In that way, how should we should then execute a generating of ready-made elements? An answer is Plugin manager, which contains plugins responsible for various kinds of support of our views. Each registered plugin has at least two methods: `getView()` and `setView()` that take a class instance of `Zend\View\Renderer\RendererInterface`. A list of built-in plugins is presented below; in this chapter we will cover just a few most crucial ones. Most of these plugins will be outlined in next chapters of this book.

- `BasePath` – a tool for generating root http path to the project; in previous Zend version known as `baseUrl`;

- `Cycle` – allows a character array declaration and displaying it in the order in a loop by using foreach, while or for;

- `Doctype` – displays a HTML tag declaring document type;

- `FlashMessenger` – a powerful tool to display information and errors in such elements as form elements;

- `Form` – a set of tools to generate single form elements like: `openTag()`, `formElement()` or `formElementErrors()`;

- `Gravatar` – a helper to generate images `<img>` hosted on the Gravatar service;

- `HeadLink` – creates a HTML tag for embedding CSS files, `<link>`;

- `HeadMeta` – creates a HTML tag for defining meta data, `<meta>`;

- `HeadScript` – creates a HTML `<head>`;

- `HeadStyle` – creates a HTML tag for embedding CSS styles, `<style>`;

- `HtmlList` – generates a list of HTML elements, via `<ul>`, `<ol>` or

`<li>` for the given PHP array;

- HTML Object Plugins – creates a HTML tag for embedding interfactive elements, like Flash or JAVA, `<object>`;

- `I18n` – a tool used more or less to display a translated word into correct language linked with the translation key;

- `Identity` – allows the quick access to the actual logged in user's object;

- `InlineScript` – creates a HTML tag for embedding files and plain code of JavaScript, `<script>`;

- `JSON` – a tool for setting a page header with a type of application/json;

- `Navigation` – a set of tools for generating menu, site maps, navigations and pathway;

- `Pagination` – made for generating paginations with page numbers for the search results;

- `Partial` – attaches other view file into actual view and enables passing extra arguments into that view;

- `Placeholder` – made mainly for handling data between the views;

- `Url` – a tool to help generate URL links with own their variables.

9.3.1. FlashMessenger

As we have already mentioned, it is a tool for displaying based on a session messages for the user. From the controller layer, without much problems we can get an instance of such plugin and add an example message:

```
$this->flashMessenger()->addMessage('A message from controller.');
```

Thanks to that, in combined view file we can display such message by:

```
echo $this->flashMessenger()->render();
```

A default format of such displayed text will be default. If we want to change the style of a given message, we can pass a name of expected format in a first method parameter `render()`. Available modes are: success, warning, error and info.

```
echo $this->flashMessenger()->render('error');
```

An above example will return the same message as the previous line, but in error format (in red).

It is possible to further decorate and interchange a HTML code structure, which sits around our message – for this purpose we would use a second argument. This parameter takes an array format and sets class names which need to be attached to the main element.

```
echo $this->flashMessenger()->render('success', ['alert', 'alert-success']);
```

Given line will display a message in a standard form of `<ul>` and `<li>` tags:

```
<ul class="alert alert-success">
    <li>A message from controller.</li>
</ul>
```

Apart from the `addMessage()` method from the controller's level, we can also execute methods like `hasMessage()`, `getMessages()`, or `clearMessages()`, in order to control messages and check contents of these messages in other action methods.

9.3.2. Identity

Identity plugin takes care of keeping information about logged in user and verification if such user has logged in to the system correctly. A call `$this->identity()` returns for us an object of type `Zend\Authnetication\`↪`Adapter\AbstractAdapter`, in which we have an access to the presented methods:

- `getUsername()` – gets account's name,

- `getPassword()` – returns encrypted account's password,

- `getRealm()` – determines a type of that account.

In order to verify if user is logged in, we just need to see if a returned object from `identity()` is not empty or does not equal `FALSE`, like in the example:

```php
public function userAction()
{
    if ($user = $this->identity()) {
        //logged in
    } else {
        //unauthorised
    }
}
```

9.3.3. Placeholder

Placeholder is a tool not that commonly used and it's very underestimated by developers. In a nutshell, with its help we are able to move and display previously defined data between the views. Same as in the cases with Smarty or Twig, Zend View by default uses `captureStart()` method instead of definitions `{block name}` to begin registering a view and `captureEnd()` to end capturing.

```php
//define a block with name infoBox
<?php $this->placeholder('infoBox')->captureStart();
<div class="box">
    <h2><?= $info ?></h2>
</div>
<?php $this->placeholder('infoBox')->captureEnd() ?>
//display contents from key infoBox
<?= $this->placeholder('infoBox') ?>
```

Apart from registering code blocks in one line, we can use Placeholder plugin as a simple `"container"` to store a similar information into one place. Additionally, when to such `Placeholder` we add an array, we can define, in which presentation format data need to be presented. An example of a simple use of all available helper methods can be something similar to this:

```
//set infoBox value
<?php $this->placeholder('infoBox')->exchangeArray(array('a', 'b', 'c')) ?>
<?php
$this->placeholder('infoBox')
    ->setPrefix("<div>\n <span>") //set prefix of whole array
    ->setSeparator("</span><span>\n") //define sepearators between records
    ->setIndent(4) //set an amount of space characters
    ->setPostfix("</span></div>\n"); //set postfix of whole array
?>

//display an array
<?= $this->placeholder('infoBox') ?>

//will return:
<div>
<span>a</span>
<span>b</span>
<span>c</span>
</div>
```

CHAPTER 10.

Forms

The forms in Zend Framework have always been a layer between views and models. Sometimes they also contain their own validation rules or data filters, thus they might be self-sufficient. Hydrators easily intercept and format the data from forms and return it to the model object. Each form is always built from elements with a single name or an array of arguments. Forms can also group these elements by using filedsets that, on the other hand, might contain other nested fieldsets.

Forms can be created in two ways: by extending a base class of Zend\Form\Form, or by using factories. The first and simpler example of such form has already been created in chapter 5; that is why we will display just a way to create it with factory.

```
use Zend\Form\Element;
use Zend\Form\Factory;
use Zend\Hydrator\ArraySerializable;
$factory = new Factory();
$form = $factory->createForm([
    'hydrator' => ArraySerializable::class,
    //define two fieldsets: user_basic and user_info
    'fieldsets' => [
        [
            'spec' => [
                'name' => 'user_basic',
```

```
'elements' => [
    [
        'spec' => [
            'name' => 'username',
            'options' => [
                'label' => 'User name',
            ],
            'type' => 'Text'
        ],
    ],
    [
        'spec' => [
            'type' => Element\Email::class,
            'name' => 'email',
            'options' => [
                'label' => 'Email address',
            ],
        ],
    ],
],
],
[
    'spec' => [
        'name' => 'user_info',
        'elements' => [
            [
                'spec' => [
                    'name' => 'gender',
                    'options' => [
                        'label' => 'Gender',
                        'value_options' => [
                            'male' => 'Male',
                            'female' => 'Female',
                        ],
                    ],
                    'type' => 'Radio',
                ],
            ]
        ],
    ],
],
]
//validators and formatters definitions
```

```
    'input_filter' => [
        /* ... */
    ],
]);
```

The given example will generate a form with two groups: user_basic and user_info, where we will have text fields as: username or email, and two buttons of type Radio Buttons to choose the user gender. Designing forms by factories is however less popular and not that useful; the main advantage of such approach is defining a whole form structure, for instance in the configuration file separately. With that, generating feels more dynamic and dependent on the outside data. However, in this book and generally in Zend MVC environment it is recommended to extend the object by creating a new class instead of using factories for all forms.

10.1. Generating

Before even generating a sample form we should first modify the same UserForm, which from now on will additionally contain the following elements: email, gender, dropdown list with education and preference regarding the newsletter.

```
$this->add([
    'name' => 'email',
    'type' => Element\Email::class,
    'options' => [
        'label' => 'Email Address'
    ],
    'attributes' => array(
        'required' => 'required'
    )
]);
$this->add([
    'type' => UserInfoFieldset::class,
    'name' => 'user_info',
]);
```

The first element is of course of type email that gets an attribute `'required'` – this will require providing a value by the client. Remember to add a line importing the `Form Element`:

```
use Zend\Form\Element;
```

Otherwise we would get an information about the error with searching for `Application\Form\Element\Email` class. Next task is to add a `fieldset` with name `UserInfoFieldset`, which we will create in a moment in the other file. The remaining elements will be placed in that new class, which gives us an option to reuse these form elements group in other forms. We can agree that `UserForm` will be a form just for registering users, and then `UserInfoFieldset` will be used in another form for editing user information, like `UserEditForm`. Let's then create a new class `UserInfoFieldset` in the same folder as `UserForm`, just with gender selection, in order not to overcomplicate our `fieldsets` introduction:

```php
namespace Application\Form;
use Application\Entity\Product;
use Zend\Form\Fieldset;
use Zend\InputFilter\InputFilterProviderInterface;
use Zend\Form\Element;
class UserInfoFieldset extends Fieldset implements InputFilterProviderInterface
{
    public function __construct()
    {
        parent::__construct('user_info');
        $this->add(array(
            'name' => 'gender',
            'type' => Element\Radio::class,
            'options' => array(
                'label' => 'Gender',
                'value_options' => [
                        'male' => 'Male',
                        'female' => 'Female',
                ]
            ),
            'attributes' => array(
                'required' => 'required'
            ),
        ));
    }
```

```
    public function getInputFilterSpecification()
    {
        return array(
            'gender' => array(
                'required' => true,
            )
        );
    }
}
```

First thing we can observe is an extension of Zend\Form\Fieldset and implementation of interface for InputFilters, which requires a definition of getInputFilterSpecification(). This method sets mostly the validation rules and type of formatting. In a constructor we add the elements in the same way we did in the regular form object. Then we add an element of type Zend\Form\Element\Radio and name gender with two available options: *Male, Female* and we mark it as required.

Now we will move into a view file to display our additional information of the form.

```
echo $this->form()->openTag($userForm);
echo $this->formHidden($userForm->get('id'));
echo $this->formRow($userForm->get('username'));
echo $this->formRow($userForm->get('email'));
echo $this->formRow($userForm->get('user_info')->get('gender'));
echo $this->formSubmit($userForm->get('submit'));
echo $this->form()->closeTag();
```

For the rest of the elements we use the same type of display like for the email and gender element, except that we first must get a fieldset by name (in above example it is user_info), and then its embedded element. By using a small CSS code, we will be able show our updated form in a nice way:

```
<style type="text/css">
    form label {
        display: block;
    }
    form label span {
        width: 130px;
        display: inline-block;
        margin: 5px 0;
```

```
    }
</style>
```

And here it is - our first form with the grouped elements used.

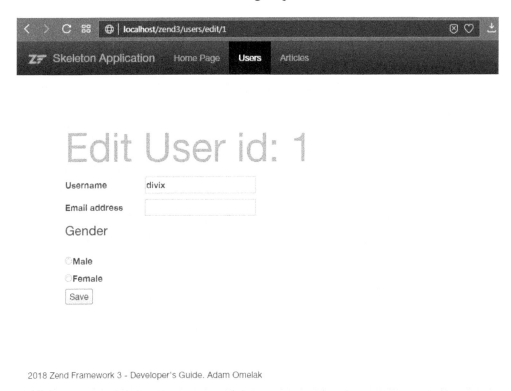

Image 10.1.

If our simple example does not work as expected, we can add missing fields: dropdown list and checkboxes to the `UserInfoFieldset` class.

```
$this->add(array(
    'name' => 'education',
    'type' => Element\Select::class,
    'options' => array(
        'label' => 'Education',
        'value_options' => [
            'primary' => 'Primary',
            'college' => 'Secondary',
            'highschool' => 'High school',
```

```
            'graduate' => 'Graduate'
        ]
    ),
    'attributes' => array(
        'required' => 'required'
    ),
));

$this->add(array(
    'name' => 'hobby',
    'type' => Element\MultiCheckbox::class,
    'options' => array(
        'label' => 'Interests',
        'value_options' => [
            'books' => 'Books',
            'sport' => 'Sport',
            'movies' => 'Movies',
            'music' => 'Music'
        ]
    ),
    'attributes' => array(
        'required' => 'required'
    ),
));
```

You can notice that both of the new elements look very alike to the `'gender'` element, where we use `'required'` attribute and `'value_options'` to embed the values. It is worth to mention that we don't use class `Element\Checkbox`, but `MultiCheckbox` for the element of type checkbox. It is a second class that will group our values into one array and will pass these as one form parameter.

Zend Form also defines a lot of other elements that offer different functions. We will describe and apply most of them in our sections to come in this chapter. Here is a list of some of these elements:

- `Button` – used to display form buttons;

- `Captcha` – generates a filed verification for anti-bots `CAPTCHA`;

- `Collection` – repeats given element many times depending on the needs;

- `Color` – prepares an element of type color, according to HTML5;

- `CSRF` – avoids CSRF like hacker attacks; secures our form from execution by other sites;

- `Date` – prepares an element of type date, according to HTML5;

- `DateTime` – generates an element of type `DateTime`, according to HTML5;

- `DateTime-Local` – generates an element of type local `DateTime`, according to HTML5;

- `Email` – displays an element of type email, according to HTML5;

- `File` – creates a form element that accepts files;

- `Month` – prepares an element of type month, according to HTML5;

- `MonthSelect` – defines a link element to Month to create a pair of month – year;

- `Number` – generates an element of type number according to HTML5;

- `Password` – creates an input field to enter passwords securely;

- `Range` – creates an element, which will define a minimal and maximal value together with interval;

- `Search` – prepares an element of type search according to HTML5;

- `Tel` – generates an element of type telephone according to HTML5;

- `Textarea` – adds a big element of text field;

- `Time` – creates an element of type time according to HTML5;

- `Url` – prepares an element to enter URL addresses according to HTML5;

- `Week` – used to insert a filed taking values of week day according to HTML5;

10.2. Validation

Let's go back to our form and add validators into our new fields: `gender`, `education` and `hobby` in `UserInfoFieldset` and in method: `getInputFilterSpecification()`.

```
public function getInputFilterSpecification()
{
    return array(
        'gender' => array(
            'required' => true,
            'validators' => [
                [
                    'name' => Validator\Regex::class,
                    'options' => [
                        'pattern' => "/^[a-z]+$/"
                    ]
                ]
            ]
        ),

        'education' => array(
            'required' => true,
            'validators' => [
                [
                    'name' => Validator\Regex::class,
                    'options' => [
                        'pattern' => "/^[a-z]+$/"
                    ]
                ]
            ]
        ),

        'hobby' => array(
            'required' => true
        )
    );
}
```

As you have already spotted, we have a lot of repetitions here, we use a single validator in three different elements. A newly added validator `Regex` checks if the passed value is in a form of regular letters from a do z. As this is quite popular format of checking valid data, we will take a look at creating a custom validator in order to avoid the code duplication. We will call the newly file *Alpha* and insert it into the newly created folder: *Application/Form/Validator*.

```php
<?php
namespace Application\Form\Validator;
use Zend\Validator\AbstractValidator;
use Zend\Validator\Regex;

class Alpha extends AbstractValidator
{
    const STRING_EMPTY = 'alphaStringEmpty';
    const INVALID = 'alphaInvalid';
    /**
     * Static instance of Regex class, avoids creating multiple instances of the same class
     *
     * @var Zend|Validator|Regex
     */
    protected static $regexValidator;
    /**
     * Messages about errors
     *
     * @var array
     */
    protected $messageTemplates = [
        self::STRING_EMPTY => "Element is empty",
        self::INVALID => "Invalid format, required alphanumeric characters ",
    ];
    /**
     * Returns true, if value of $value contains with just characters from a-z
     *
     * @param string $value
     * @return bool
     */
    public function isValid($value)
    {
        if (!is_string($value)) {
```

```
            $this->error(self::INVALID);
            return false;
        }
        $this->setValue((string) $value);

        if (empty($this->getValue())) {
            $this->error(self::STRING_EMPTY);
            return false;
        }
        if (static::$regexValidator == null) {
            static::$regexValidator = new Regex(['pattern' => "/^[a-z]+$/"]);
        }
        if (!static::$regexValidator->isValid($this->getValue())) {
            $this->error(self::INVALID);
            return false;
        }
        return true;
    }
}
```

To create our new class we will use an abstract class of `Zend\Validator\AbstractValidator`. A static instance of `$regexValidator` is only a cosmetic efficiency – no matter how many times we have used the new `Alpha` validator, there will be only one `Regex` class instance created. Values of `const`, like `STRING_EMPTY`, are keys to the class array `$messageTemplates`, which is required while creating custom messages. We also have to override `isValid()` method, which checks if entered value is correct or not. Important things in creating and data checking inside `isValid()` is first of all setting an initial potential value by `$this->setValue($value)`, and then using it by a getter: `$this->getValue()`. We achieve exactly this in the last if condition by using `Validator\Regex` object. Now we just need to update and refactor a bit our code in `UserInfoFieldset`.

```
public function getInputFilterSpecification()
{
    return array(
        'gender' => array(
            'required' => true,
            'validators' => [$this->getAlphaValidator()]
        ),
        'education' => array(
```

```
              'required' => true,
              'validators' => [$this->getAlphaValidator()]
          ),
          'hobby' => array(
              'required' => true
          )
      );
  }

  private function getAlphaValidator()
  {
      return [
          'name' => CustomValidator\Alpha::class
      ];
  }
```

Of course, we have to remember about adding a new use declaration into our path with custom validators at the beginning of the file:

```
use Application\Form\Validator as CustomValidator;
```

As the alias Validator is already occupied by the previous declaration of Zend\Validator, we need to use other names, thus in this file we use name CustomValidator.

We have significantly reduced our code concerning validation rules and have moved a duplicated code into a new private method getAlphaValidator(). Now our fieldset looks much neater and clearer, and we will be able to use it in other forms within an application. Notice that elements hobby, so-called checkboxes, do not have any validators because the value of this field is an array and not plain string. Secondly, by default Zend offers a validator InArray for each element of type MultiCheckbox. and Checkbox. Available values are keys passed in option: value_options. For that reason we just add a flag, meaning that its required, and the rest will be handled by Zend Framework.

We can also choose which fields need to be marked as valid, ignoring their validators, so that the method isValid() would return TRUE, checking only two or three elements. For such organization we use a method set:

```
$form->setValidationGroup('username', 'email', 'user_info' => ['gender']);
$form->setData($data);
```

```
if ($form->isValid()) {
    $data = $form->getData();
}
```

Above call `isValid()` would return `TRUE`, only then, when correctly filled elements will be: `username`, `email` and `gender` from element group `info_user`. To reset the validation option back to the default behavior, that is checking all the fields, we need to pass the value of the constant `FormInterface::VALIDATE_ALL` to the method `setValidationGroup()`.

Additionally, Zend Framework 3 offers other types of the validators to the various popular things:

- `Barcode` – checks if given value could be saved in form of barcode;

- `Between` – checks if given value fits between specified numerical range;

- `Callback` – gives an option to pass an anonymous function or just a function name to execute;

- `CrediCard` – checks given credit card number;

- `Date` – sets if value is in date format;

- `Db\RecordExists` – checks if given record exists in database;

- `Digits` – ensures that the string only consists of numbers;

- `EmailAddress` – checks if given value is a valid email;

- `GreaterThan` – defines if a value is greater than from a specified value;

- `Hex` – verifies if value is of a type: hexadecimal;

- `Hostname` – checks a correctness of the host name;

- `Iban` – performs a check of bank ID format of type IBAN;

- `Identical` – ensures that given value is exactly the same as specified string;

- `Ip` – verifies if a value is a correct IP number;

- `Isbn` – performs a check of a book ID format of type ISBN;

- `InstanceOf` – ensures that given value is an instance of the specified class;

- `LessThan` - defines if a value is less than a specified value;

- `NotEmpty` – checks if an element is not empty or null;

- `PostCode` – verifies a post code format;

- `Regex` – performs a check of the value by using regular expressions;

- `Sitemap` – contains a set of methods to check the correctness of values inside a site map, for instance `Sitemap\LastMode()` or `Sitemap\Priority();`

- `Step` – checks if a resulted value can be used as incremenet/decrement to the numerical values;

- `StringLength` – sets a minimal and maximal range of characters length;

- `Timezone` – verifies if a given value is of a format Timezone;

- `Uri` – checks if given value is a correct Uri address;

- `Uuid` – ensures that the element is of type UUID.

10.3. Filters

Filters are nothing else than validators, but instead of throwing errors they format passed in values according to the defined template. The amount of filters in Zend Framework 3 exceeds 35. In this section we will use a few of them and will introduce with the most popular filter in the dev environment.

Most of all, each of the filters has a method `filter()`, which takes a parameter as an input value. A formatted text is returned by the same method:

```
$strtolower = new Zend\Filter\StringToLower();
echo $strtolower->filter('Zend Framework 3');
//return zend framework 3
```

There is a possibility also to call filters via the magical method `__invoke` in the following way:

```
$strtolower = new Zend\Filter\StringToLower();
echo $strtolower('Zend Framework 3');
//returns: zend framework 3
```

Both approaches would return exactly identical results, however they require creating a class instance of `StringToLower()`. An alternative would be to use a static point, where different filters would be kept as static instances. Thankfully, Zend's authors has foreseen this situation and they offer us a class `StaticFilter`. A class is in package `Zend\Filter` and has three static methods: `setPluginManager`, `getPluginManager()` and `execute()`. That last one could be used as a bridge to execute `filter()` methods of single filter classes.

```
echo StaticFilter::execute(
    'Zend Framework 3',
    'StringToLower',
    ['key' => parameter]
);
```

First argument is obviously an input value, second is a filter name and third an optional: a list of parameters passed directly into filter. First two `StaticFilter` class methods are used for adding new and custom filters to the static class and for retrieving them.

```
$pluginManager = StaticFilter::getPluginManager()->setInvokableClass(
    'newFilterName',
    'Package\Subpackage\NewFilterName'
);
```

It is often to execute filters in the specific order, for instance when we change HTML tags into entities and then we want to delete all the characters like <>. In these cases we can use `FilterChain`, thanks to which we can add a couple of filters into one combined chain. By using this technique we can define more advanced filtering rules of specified variable types.

```
$filterChain = new Zend\Filter\FilterChain();
$filterChain
    ->attach(new Zend\I18n\Filter\Alpha(), 1000)
    ->attach(new Zend\Filter\StringToLower(), 1001);
echo $filterChain->filter('Zend Framework 3');
```

//return: zend framework

A method `attach()` adds another filters to the list, while a call `filter()` from `FilterChan` executes an iteration of the added validation filters and executes their logic contained in `filter()` methods.

A second argument of `attach()` method is a priority number. By default all the filters get a priority of 1000, and these with larger priority number are executed first. In above example `StringToLower` filter will be executed first, and then `Alpha`. The same as in case `StaticFilter` class, to add your own filter into chaining class `FilterChaing`, you need to use Plugin Manager and `setInvokableClass()`.

```
$filterChain = new Zend\Filter\FilterChain();
$filterChain
    ->getPluginManager()
    ->setInvokableClass('newFilterName', 'Package\Subpackage\NewFilterName');
```

Here are just a few most used filters in the everyday work:

- `Alnum` – converts the value into an alphanumeric string;

- `Alpha` – changes given value into a string of A-Z;

- `BaseName` – retrieves just a name of the file from the specified path;

- `Blacklist` – defines a forbidden string array and returns `NULL` if such value is passed in;

- `Boolean` – converts the value into a `Boolean` type;

- `Callback` – allows to apply a filtering method by passing an anonymous function;

- `Compress/decompress` – allows compressing and decompressing of strings, files and folders according to the selected method;

- `Digits` – converts the value into numbers only;

- `Dir` – returns a last folder in given file path;

- `Encrypt/Decrypt` – encrypts or decrypts an initial value, key, mode and vector according to the specified algorithm;

- `HtmlEntities` – converts HTML tags into entities;

- `ToInt` – allows converts strings into integers;

- `ToNull` – converts the value into a `NULL` format;

- `NumberFormat` – converts numbers into their local forms;

- `PregReplace` – searches a string according to the set regex;

- `RealPath` – converts paths into absolute paths;

- `StringToLower` – changes all uppercase letters into the small ones;

- `StringToUpper` – changes all lowercase letters into the big ones;

- `StringTrim` – deletes unnecessary white space characters from the beginning and the end of a string;

- `StripNewlines` – removes all representations of new lines chars;

- `StripTags` – removes all tags from a string;

- ▪ `UriNormalize` – sets a prefix to the `Uri` identifications if it's not set;

- ▪ `Whitelist` – defines an array of accepted strings and returns `NULL` if at least one white value is not passed in.

10.4. Decorators

You already know how to render different types of form elements by using a `fromRow()` method. What if you want to change a form's structure?

```
$formLabel = $this->plugin('formLabel');
<div class="form_element">
    <?php
    $userName = $form->get('username');
    echo $formLabel->openTag() . $userName->getOption('label');
    echo $this->formInput($userName);
    echo $this->formElementErrors($userName);
    echo $formLabel->closeTag();
    ?>
</div>

//return:
<div class="form_element">
    <label>
        Name
        <input type="text" name="username" />
        <ul><li>Value is required and can't be empty</li></ul>
    </label>
</div>
```

A call to `formInput()` instead of `fromRow()` gives us much more flexibility in positioning labels or attaching extra HTML elements. By a call `formElementError()` we can determine a place, in which errors linked to the given element will be displayed. If however, you want to define one rendering format of each element, you can use view helpers that we define in the configuration by:

```
return [
```

```
    'view_helpers' => [
        'factories' => [
            View\Helper\Form::class => Application\View\Helper\FormFactory::class
        ],
    ],
];
```

Have a look that we use default view keys, so we can override these keys with our own implementations. A further implementation in form class will be brought to override `render($element)` method, where we will be able to set a generated HTML code. Our example helper view class `FormFactory` can look like:

```
namespace Application\View\Helper;
use Zend\View\Helper\AbstractHelper;
use Interop\Container\ContainerInterface;
class FormFactory extends AbstractHelper
{
    public function __invoke(ContainerInterface $container)
    {
        return new Form();
    }
}
```

More information about view helpers will be in chapter 20, where we will start generating our own form's codes based on the Bootstrap CSS layout and styling. At the end, let's mention that **the form decorators have been completely removed in Zend Framework 3** and it is a recommended to use view helpers instead.

10.5. Finishing the user form

Let's go back to filling code, which will be updating all the data from the edit user form to the database. We will begin with modification to our actual DB table users and adding a new table `user_hobbies`:

```
ALTER TABLE `users` ADD `email` VARCHAR(100) NOT NULL , ADD `gender`
↪VARCHAR(10) NOT NULL , ADD `education` VARCHAR(50) NOT NULL ;

CREATE TABLE IF NOT EXISTS `user_hobbies` (
    `id` int(10) unsigned NOT NULL,
    `user_id` int(11) NOT NULL,
    `hobby` varchar(50) NOT NULL
)
```

Now let's add three missing elements into `Rowset\User` class for email address, gender and education, at the same time skipping elements we already have in this class, to save space on paper of this book:

```
public $email;
public $gender;
public $education;
...
public function exchangeArray($row)
{
    $this->id = (!empty($row['id'])) ? $row['id'] : null;
    $this->username = (!empty($row['uscrname'])) ? $row['username'] : null;
    $this->password = (!empty($row['password'])) ? $row['password'] : null;
    $this->email = (!empty($row['email'])) ? $row['email'] : null;
    $this->gender = (!empty($row['gender'])) ? $row['gender'] : null;
    $this->education = (!empty($row['education'])) ? $row['education'] : null;
}
...
public function getEmail() {
    return $this->email;
}
public function getGender() {
    return $this->gender;
}
public function getEducation() {
    return $this->education;
}
...
```

```php
public function getArrayCopy()
{
    return [
        'id' => $this->getId(),
        'username' => $this->getUsername(),
        'email' => $this->getEmail(),
        'gender' => $this->getGender(),
        'education' => $this->getEducation()
    ];
}
```

Next, let's add two classes: `Application\Model\Rowset\UserHobby` with fields `userId` and `hobby` and class `Application\Model\UserHobbiesTable`, which will interact with DB table `user_hobbies`.

```php
namespace Application\Model;

class UserHobbiesTable extends AbstractTable
{
    public function getPlainHobbies($userId)
    {
        $output = [];
        $userHobbies = $this->getByUserId($userId);
        foreach ($userHobbies as $hobbyRow) {
            $output[] = $hobbyRow->getHobby();
        }
        return $output;
    }
    public function getByUserId($userId)
    {
        $rowset = $this->tableGateway->select(array('user_id' => (int) $userId));
        return $rowset;
    }
    public function getBy(array $params = array())
    {
        $results = $this->tableGateway->select($params);
        return $results;
    }
    public function save($userId, array $hobbies)
    {
        //remove old links to hobby
        $this->deleteByUserId($userId);
        foreach ($hobbies as $hobby) {
            $data = [
```

```
            'user_id' => $userId,
            'hobby' => $hobby
        ];
        $this->tableGateway->insert($data);
    }
    return true;
}
public function deleteByUserId($userId)
{
    $this->tableGateway->delete(['user_id' => (int) $userId]);
}
}
```

Apart from already explained methods as getBy(), save() or deleteByUserId(), we also have getByUserId() that is just an alias to the getBy() method with already defined parameters and getPlainHobbies(). This method returns a simple one-dimensional array of hobby identification keys in order to pass such result to the element MultiCheckbox to display actual linked hobbies.

Another step will be to register our UserHobbiesTable class by adding a record to *Module.php*, inside factories key:

```
'UserHobbiesTableGateway' => function ($sm) {
    $dbAdapter = $sm->get('Zend\Db\Adapter\Adapter');
    $resultSetPrototype = new ResultSet();
    $resultSetPrototype->setArrayObjectPrototype(new Rowset\UserHobby());
    return new TableGateway('user_hobbies', $dbAdapter, null, $resultSetPrototype);
},

'Application\Model\UserHobbiesTable' => function($sm) {
    $tableGateway = $sm->get('UserHobbiesTableGateway');
    $table = new UserHobbiesTable($tableGateway);
    return $table;
},
```

They look, obviously, very similar to the UsersTableGateway keys and Application\ModelUserTable, but our object Rowset\UserHobbies does not need an access to the $baseUrl variable. Next, we will modify a definition of creating a controller UsersController in file *module.config.php*, because we are adding another parameter UserHobbiesTable to it:

```
Controller\UsersController::class => function($sm) {
    $usersTable = $sm->get('Application\Model\UsersTable');
    $userHobbiesTable = $sm->get('Application\Model\UserHobbiesTable');
    return new Controller\UsersController($usersTable, $userHobbiesTable);
},
```

Only at the very end, we edit a controller's constructor (remember to add the missing use definitions):

```
use Zend\Mvc\Controller\AbstractActionController;
use Zend\View\Model\ViewModel;
use Application\Model\UsersTable;
use Application\Model\UserHobbiesTable;
use Application\Model\Rowset\User;
use Application\Form\UserForm;
class UsersController extends AbstractActionController
{
    private $usersTable = null;
    private $userHobbiesTable = null;
    public function __construct(UsersTable $usersTable, UserHobbiesTable
↪$userHobbiesTable)
    {
        $this->usersTable = $usersTable;
        $this->userHobbiesTable = $userHobbiesTable;
    }
```

Finally, we will also drastically modify the method `editAction()`, which from now on will be getting an actual data about the user and store all the entered changes.

```
public function editAction()
{
    $view = new ViewModel();
    $userId = (int) $this->params()->fromRoute('id');
    $view->setVariable('userId', $userId);
    if ($userId == 0) {
        return $this->redirect()->toRoute('users', ['action' => 'add']);
    }
    // get user data; if it doesn't exists, then redirect back to the index
    try {
        $userRow = $this->usersTable->getById($userId);
    } catch (\Exception $e) {
        return $this->redirect()->toRoute('users', ['action' => 'index']);
    }
```

```
$userForm = new UserForm();
$userForm->bind($userRow);
$userForm->populateValues(
    [
        'user_info' => [
            'gender' => $userRow->getGender(),
            'education' => $userRow->getEducation(),
            'hobby' => $this->userHobbiesTable->getPlainHobbies($userId)
        ]
    ]
);
$userForm->get('submit')->setAttribute('value', 'Save');
$request = $this->getRequest();
$view->setVariable('userForm', $userForm);

if (!$request->isPost()) {
    return $view;
}
$userForm->setInputFilter($userRow->getInputFilter());
$userForm->setData($request->getPost());

if (!$userForm->isValid()) {
    return $view;
}
$extraUserdata = [
    'gender' => $userForm->get('user_info')->get('gender')->getValue(),
    'education' => $userForm->get('user_info')->get('education')->getValue()
];
$hobbies = $userForm->get('user_info')->get('hobby')->getValue();
$this->usersTable->save($userRow, $extraUserdata);
$this->userHobbiesTable->save($userRow->getId(), $hobbies);
// data saved, redirect to the users list page
return $this->redirect()->toRoute('users', ['action' => 'index']);
}
```

The most crucial are bind method calls: `bind($userRow)` and `populateValues()` from the form object `$userForm`. The first method, as we have already mentioned, applies values linked with the class object `Rowset\User`, however the second one works in a similar way but accepts a multi-dimensional arrays. Thanks to that we are able to pass `fieldset` values by transmissing another array by the key name of a such grouped element. We also use a method `getPlainHobbies($userId)`, which returns an accepted format of the form's element. Afterwards, we prepare data to save after checking if the form is correctly filled and we execute two methods: `save()` — one from `usersTable` and another one from `usersHobbiesTable`.

```
$extraUserdata = [
    'gender' => $userForm->get('user_info')->get('gender')->getValue(),
    'education' => $userForm->get('user_info')->get('education')->getValue()
];
$hobbies = $userForm->get('user_info')->get('hobby')->getValue();
$this->usersTable->save($userRow, $extraUserdata);
$this->userHobbiesTable->save($userRow->getId(), $hobbies);
```

Pay attention that fields `gender` and `education` must be passed separately as `$extraUserdata` because they are inserted from the `UserInfoFieldset` layer in the form itself; that's why they won't be mapped by default by `Rowset\User` object. As you can see, we have to override a bit our `save()` method in order to pass an additional parameter in `UsersTable` class:

```
public function save(User $userModel, $extraData = [])
{
    $data = [
        'username' => $userModel->getUsername(),
        'email' => $userModel->getEmail()
    ];
    if (!empty($extraData)) {
        $data = array_merge($data, $extraData);
    }
    return parent::saveRow($userModel, $data);
}
```

We link extra data with the preformatted arrays username and email, and pass them back to the update mechanism via `parent::saveRow()`. The second method, `save()` in `userHobbiesTable`, accepts only an identification user number and array of linked hobbies, so there is nothing too complex.

In order to check our new form we must also modify related two view files; first *users/edit.phtml*:

```php
echo $this->form()->openTag($userForm);
echo $this->formHidden($userForm->get('id'));
echo $this->formRow($userForm->get('username'));
echo $this->formRow($userForm->get('email'));
echo $this->formRow($userForm->get('user_info')->get('gender'));
echo $this->formRow($userForm->get('user_info')->get('education'));
echo $this->formRow($userForm->get('user_info')->get('hobby'));
echo $this->formSubmit($userForm->get('submit'));
echo $this->form()->closeTag();
```

Then we use *users/index.phtml* and `indexAction()` from `UsersController`, to display our new data:

```php
<?php foreach ($userRows as $user): ?>
    <tr>
        <td><?= $user->getId() ?></td>
        <td><?= $user->getUsername() ?></td>
        <td><?= $user->getEmail() ?></td>
        <td><?= $user->getGender() ?></td>
        <td><?= $user->getEducation() ?></td>
        <td><?= isset($userHobbies[$user->getId()]) ? join(', ',$userHobbies[$user->
↪getId()]) : '' ?></td>
        <td>
            <a href="<?= $this->url('users', ['action' => 'edit', 'id' => $user->
↪getId()]) ?>">Edit</a> |
            <a href="<?= $this->url('users', ['action' => 'delete', 'id' => $user->
↪getId()]) ?>">Delete</a>
        </td>
    </tr>
<?php endforeach; ?>
```

```php
public function indexAction()
{
    $view = new ViewModel();
    $rows = $this->usersTable->getBy();
    $rows->buffer();
    $hobbies = [];

    foreach ($rows as $row) {
        $results = $this->userHobbiesTable->getByUserId($row->getId());
        foreach ($results as $hobby) {
            $hobbies[$row->getId()][] = $hobby->getHobby();
        }
```

```
    }
    $view->setVariable('userHobbies', $hobbies);
    $view->setVariable('userRows', $rows);
    return $view;
  }
```

To get a list of hobbies for each user, we have to iterate all the records and execute a method `getByUserId()`, after which we need to fill a related record with a key `userId` in `$hobbies` array. In the view we use `join()` PHP function that will display an array as a string separated by comas between the elements.

## CHAPTER 11

Creating a comics list with pagination

In this chapter we are going to create a list of cartoon comics with a limit to only two positions per page. We will look into a view helper in order to create our own generating pagination code and we will use a simple example of DB results caching that can be reused instead of requesting queries into the database.

11.1. New controller

We will start with creating a table containing examples of records, so that we have at least 3 pages of pagination for 2 records per page.

```
CREATE TABLE IF NOT EXISTS `comics` (
    `id` int(10) unsigned AUTO_INCREMENT PRIMARY KEY NOT NULL,
    `title` varchar(200) NOT NULL,
    `thumb` varchar(100) NOT NULL
)
```

```sql
INSERT INTO `comics` (`id`, `title`, `thumb`) VALUES
    (1, 'batman', 'bat.png'),
    (2, 'spiderman', 'spider.jpg'),
    (3, 'thor', 'bolt.jpg'),
    (4, 'hulk', 'green.png'),
    (5, 'captain america', 'captain.jpg');
```

For a successful display of the examples we also need photos placed in a *public/uploads* folder (which we have created before and are going to use again in next chapter about images processing). Let's create a minimalistic controller for comics with name `ComicsController`.

```php
namespace Application\Controller;
use Zend\Mvc\Controller\AbstractActionController;
use Application\Model\ComicsTable;
class ComicsController extends AbstractActionController
{
    private $comicsTable = null;
    public function __construct(ComicsTable $comicsTable)
    {
        $this->comicsTable = $comicsTable;
    }
    public function indexAction()
    {
        return [
            'comics' => $this->comicsTable->getBy(['page' =>
↳$this->params()->fromRoute('page')])
        ];
    }
}
```

The only issue worth to mention in this controller is that it passed a parameter 'page' to the model class, which will be defined in declaration routes in the configuration file. A result from `ComicsTable` is automatically returned to the view as variable 'comics'. Analogically to the User controller class, we will define it in configuration file in a moment. *Module.php*:

```php
'ComicsTableGateway' => function ($sm) {
    $dbAdapter = $sm->get('Zend\Db\Adapter\Adapter');
    $config = $sm->get('Config');
    $baseUrl = $config['view_manager']['base_url'];
    $resultSetPrototype = new ResultSet();
```

```
    $identity = new Rowset\Comics($baseUrl);
    $resultSetPrototype->setArrayObjectPrototype($identity);
    return new TableGateway('comics', $dbAdapter, null, $resultSetPrototype);
},

'Application\Model\ComicsTable' => function($sm) {
    $tableGateway = $sm->get('ComicsTableGateway');
    $table = new ComicsTable($tableGateway);
    return $table;
},
```

We need to keep in mind, that to pass a value $baseUrl into a constructor of new Rowset model. Next, we will add a definition of new a controller to the alias 'controllers' (just like for NewsController) and a new rule of address recognizing in key routes. In the new key routes/comics_list/ ↪child_routes we add a section with name paginator; after such operation child_routes should look like the following:

```
'child_routes' => [
    'dodaj' => [
        'type' => 'literal',
        'options' => [
            'route' => '/add',
            'defaults' => [
                'controller' => Controller\ComicsController::class,
                'action' => 'add',
            ],
        ]
    ],
    'paginator' => [
        'type' => 'segment',
        'options' => [
            'route' => '/[page/:page]',
            'defaults' => [
                'page' => 1
            ]
        ]
    ]
]
```

Here we define a new URL parameter with name 'page', which by default will return 1 as an initial page number of results.

We already have an initial definition of our controller and configuration - let's move into a model layer of our application.

11.2. A new model

We start our work with a model by ensuring that Zend Paginator package is available in our installation (we can do that by checking if we have a directory *vendor/zendframework/zend-paginator*). If we don't have that library, we need to add it by Composer in the following way:

```
composer require zendframework/zend-paginator
```

A script will ask if we want to insert a new library record in one of our configurations (we choose option [1], to insert it into *modules.config.php*) and will ask to remember this option for other libraries (we choose Y). Next, we install a Zend Serializer component and repeat just mentioned steps.

```
composer require zendframework/zend-serializer
```

`Paginator` package gives us a functionality to use results pagination, however `Serializer` will be used to convert these results into cached files on the disk in order to create their quicker local versions. We will define a model of type `Rowset` with the following values: `id`, `title` and `thumb` into our new table class:

```
namespace Application\Model\Rowset;

class Comics extends AbstractModel
{
    public $title;
    public $thumb;
    public function exchangeArray($row)
    {
        $this->id = (!empty($row['id'])) ? $row['id'] : null;
        $this->title = (!empty($row['title'])) ? $row['title'] : null;
        $this->thumb = (!empty($row['thumb'])) ? $row['thumb'] : null;
    }
```

```php
    public function getId() {
        return $this->id;
    }
    public function setId($value) {
        $this->id = $value;
    }
    public function getTitle() {
        return $this->title;
    }
    public function getThumb() {
        return $this->thumb;
    }
    public function getThumbUrl() {
        return $this->baseUrl.'public/uploads/'.$this->thumb;
    }
    public function getArrayCopy()
    {
        return [
            'id' => $this->getId(),
            'title' => $this->getTitle(),
            'thumb' => $this->getThumb()
        ];
    }
}
```

Notice that we have declared a method `getThumbUrl()` that uses a base URL address variable and returns a full path to the sent images. Thanks to that we won't need to take care of the proper formatting of address in our view.

Let's finally have a closer look with new `ComicsTable` class:

```php
namespace Application\Model;
class ComicsTable extends AbstractTable
{
    protected $resultsPerPage = 2;
    public function getBy(array $params = array())
    {
        $select = $this->tableGateway->getSql()->select();

        if (!isset($params['page'])) {
            $params['page'] = 0;
        }
        if (isset($params['id'])) {
```

```
            $select->where('id = ?', $params['id']);
            $params['limit'] = 1;
        }
        if (isset($params['title'])) {
            $select->where('title = ?', $params['title']);
        }
        if (isset($params['thumb'])) {
            $select->where('thumb = ?', $params['thumb']);
        }
        if (isset($params['limit'])) {
            $select->limit($params['limit']);
        }
        $result = (isset($params['limit']) && $params['limit'] == 1)
            ? $select->fetchRow()
            : $this->fetchAll($select, ['limit' => $this->resultsPerPage,
↪'page' => $params['page']]);
        return $result;
    }
}
```

The only one `getBy()` class method checks a few parameters that can filter
out results as: id, title or thumb. For the first time we use a method `where()`
from the `getSql->select()` object, which we have already covered in the
previous chapter. It helps us pass the parameters to the query itself and is
later used to pass in more data in `fetchAll()` method. For the `ID` parameter
we additionally set a variable of `$param['limit']` with `1`; and thanks to
that we will be getting just one record back instead of an array of objects.
Exactly this value will choose whether we call a regular `fetchRow()` or
`fetchAll()` with a parameter `Select` object and additional parameters
array. The second argument contains data like actual page number or a limit
of displayed records on the page. Of course, the method `fetchAll()` does
not exist yet, that is why we will define it together with new import cases in
our abstract class `AbstractTable`:

```
use DivixUtils\Zend\Paginator\Paginator as CustomPaginator;
use Zend\Paginator\Adapter\DbSelect;
use Zend\Cache\StorageFactory;

class AbstractTable
{
    protected static $paginatorCache;
    protected $tableGateway;
```

```php
public function __construct(TableGateway $tableGateway)
{
    $this->tableGateway = $tableGateway;
    if (empty(self::$paginatorCache)) {
        // set a cache in form of text files in folder data/cache and
        // apply serialize convertion for storing data
        // our copy will be deleted after 10 minutes (600 seconds)
        self::$paginatorCache = StorageFactory::factory([
            'adapter' => [
                'name' => 'filesystem',
                'options' => [
                    'cache_dir' => 'data/cache',
                    'ttl' => 600
                ]
            ],
            'plugins' => ['serializer'],
        ]);
        CustomPaginator::setCache(self::$paginatorCache);
    }
}
...
protected function fetchAll($select, array $paginateOptions = null)
{
    if (!empty($paginateOptions)) {
        // create first adapter, which we will pass to he paginator
        $paginatorAdapter = new DbSelect(
            $select,
            $this->tableGateway->getAdapter(),
            $this->tableGateway->getResultSetPrototype()
        );
        $paginator = new CustomPaginator($paginatorAdapter);
        // set number of records per pgae
        $paginator->setItemCountPerPage($paginateOptions['limit']);
        // if we are passing page parameter, then we set offset for the results
        if (isset($paginateOptions['page'])) {
            $paginator->setCurrentPageNumber($paginateOptions['page']);
        }
        return $paginator;
    }
    return $this->tableGateway->select();
}
```

Most of our code is closely described in the script, but because there is a lot that happens in these sections, we will describe them further in a moment.

Surely it you will be interested in a usage of your own paginator class `CustomPagiantor` from the package `DivixUtils`. It has been written in order to fix an error which at the time of writing this book is still unresolved: *https://github.com/zendframework/zend-paginator/issues/1*. The main error of the original class is due to the usage of function `spl_object_hash()`, which generates a unique hash for objects to create their local ID name of our internal cache. Unfortunately, this function always returns a new value after reloading a page. This is why in the newly created class, which extends the original `Zend\Paginator\Paginator` class, we override a method `_getCacheInternalId()` with usage of `json_encode()` and `get_object_vars()`. Of course, we place our new class in an appropriate place inside `DivixUtils` library: *vendor/divixutils/src/DivixUtils/Zend/↪Paginator/Paginator.php*.

```php
namespace DivixUtils\Zend\Paginator;
class Paginator extends \Zend\Paginator\Paginator
{
    /**
     * Get the internal cache id
     * Depends on the adapter and the item count per page
     *
     * Used to tag that unique Paginator instance in cache
     *
     * @return string
     */
    protected function _getCacheInternalId()
    {
        return md5(
            json_encode(
                get_object_vars($this->getAdapter())
            ) . $this->getItemCountPerPage()
        );
    }
}
```

We have specified a phpdoc documentation declaration, so that our editor displays an information about the new method properly.

Let's go back to `AbstractTable`. In a constructor we have written a line checking settings of a static class variable `$paginatorCache`, which will store an object of class Zend Cache. Of course, we could skip this whole condition and initialize `StorageFactory` object every time, but this would be a waste of our memory and it might cause a slowdown of a script loading, if we called this method in many places at the same time.

```
self::$paginatorCache = StorageFactory::factory([
    'adapter' => [
        'name' => 'filesystem',
        'options' => [
            'cache_dir' => 'data/cache',
            'ttl' => 600
        ]
    ],
    'plugins' => ['serializer'],
]);
CustomPaginator::setCache(self::$paginatorCache);
```

We use a factory solution expecting a settings array with keys `'adapter'` and `'plugins'`, which relate to defining a type of storing copies in the system files and a way of compressing them. In this example we used a plugin called `'serializer'`, which simply serializes objects the same as with the usage of a function `serlize()`. Additionally, in adapter parameter we have set where the generated file copies are created (taking into account that the main folder is *htdocs/zend3/*) and how long those copies will be maintained before they would update into a new data (600 seconds is 10 minutes in our scenario). `fetchAll()` method itself is creating a new `Zend\Paginator\Adapter\DbSelect` object, into which we pass our `Zend\Db\Select` object and the actual adapter along with the type of objects returned, in sequence: `getAdapter()` and `getResultSet` ↪`Prototype()`. A later step is to create a paginator object, which will already has a results caching mode set in a constructor by `CustomPaginator::setCache()` and a setup number of records per page `setItemCountPerPage()`. The last steps are passing currently displayed page number of results and returning the paginator object. Everything is wrapped inside an if statement when there is some information passed about the pagination via `$paginateOptions`. In other case we call a default class method of `TableGateway`, so-called `$this->tableGateway->select()`.

Now our class model will get results for single page from the database, then it will store them in text files in folder *data/cache/zfcache-[number]*, and at the very end it will return these sets. Thanks to that, other calls for the same page results will be grabbed from the temporary files instead of database queries within the next 10 minutes. This built-in function of Zend Paginator is without any doubt very useful and is very easy to configure and use, ignoring of course that one error in the library.

There is no obstacle to taking care of the last part of the application, in other words views, which we will split to make it easier to use them later in other application's modules.

11.3. A new view

It's time to take a look at the view of displaying a list of comics together with their thumbnails – in this case we will create a file *index.phtml* in a newly entered folder *view/application/comics/*.

```
<div class="jumbotron">
    <h1><span class="zf-green">Comics</span></h1>
    <table class="table">
        <tr>
            <th>Id</th>
            <th>Title</th>
            <th>Cover</th>
        </tr>
        <?php foreach ($comics as $rowModel): ?>
            <tr>
                <td><?= $rowModel->getId() ?></td>
                <td><?= $rowModel->getTitle() ?></td>
                <td><img src="<?= $rowModel->getThumbUrl() ?>" /></td>
            </tr>
        <?php endforeach; ?>
    </table>

    <?= $this->paginationControl(
        $comics,
        'Sliding',
        'pagination_search',
        ['route' => 'comics/paginator']
```

```
    ) ?>
  </div>
```

We display a list of comics in a regular way, by iterating a foreach loop, then we call a view helper method with name `paginationControl`, which takes four arguments: a list of objects, pagination type, a name of a view file to display and additional address later added to our paged links. Available pagination types are as follows:

  ▪ Sliding – sets a basic pagination style with numbers as links, where an actual selected page is centered (similar to the mechanism used by Yahoo!);

  ▪ All – returns all the pages at once; quite often we can see a solution of that type for pagination in drop down lists;

  ▪ Elastic – pagination similar to the Google one; it enlarges itself once we go further into pages;

  ▪ Jumping – when a user is scrolling pages, a number of another pages are properly enlarged to allow "jumping" between bigger amount of pages.

By the way, we will add a few new definitions of CSS selectors, which will highlight our graphical result in a pleasing to the eye format. In this case we add the following lines at the end of the *public/css/style.css* file:

```
.comicsList img {
    width: 75px;
    margin: 4px 0 11px 10px;
}
.comicsList th {
    width: 75px;
}
.paginationControl {
    margin-top: 22px;
    font-size: 17px;
}
.paginationControl select {
    padding: 10px;
```

```
}
```

Of course, our view does not work just yet, since we do not have a view with name *pagination_search.phtml*.

11.4. Pagination

We could define pagination views in the same folder as *comics/*, but we wouldn't be able to reuse them in other module view files. For that reason we will create a new shared folder called *_shared* in folder *view/application*. That's where we will put new files: *pagination_search.phtml*, *pagination_* ↪*dropdown.phtml* and *pagination_item.html*. All these define a different display format of pagination apart from style. Before we create them, we have to first inform Zend that we have a new folder *_shared*, which should be included during a search of pagination availability. Let's do this in *module.config.php* file inside a key `view_manager/tempalate_path_` ↪`stack`. We add a new element with location of our new folder in there, as a result of which our configuration should look like:

```
'template_path_stack' => [
    __DIR__ . '/../view',
    __DIR__ . '/../view/application/_shared'
],
```

From now on, whenever Zend is looking for view files, it will include a directory *application/_shared*. Of course, such solution entails little problems, mainly regarding the same view names inside a given module. This is why our pagination files have a prefix of `pagination_`, to minimize an unintentional name duplication.

We are now able to create pagination files – for starters a default view *pagination_search.phtml*:

```
<?php if ($this->pageCount): ?>
    <div class="paginationControl">
        <!-- Previous page -->
        <?php if (isset($this->previous)): ?>
```

```
            <a href="<?= $this->url($this->route, ['page' => $this->previous]); ?>">
                &lt; Previous
            </a> |
        <?php else: ?>
            <span class="disabled">&lt; Previous</span> |
        <?php endif; ?>

        <!-- Page numbers -->
        <?php foreach ($this->pagesInRange as $page): ?>
            <?php if ($page != $this->current): ?>
                <a href="<?= $this->url($this->route, ['page' => $page]); ?>">
                    <?= $page; ?>
                </a> |
            <?php else: ?>
                <?= $page; ?> |
            <?php endif; ?>
        <?php endforeach; ?>

        <!-- Next page -->
        <?php if (isset($this->next)): ?>
            <a href="<?= $this->url($this->route, ['page' => $this->next]); ?>">
                Next &gt;
            </a>
        <?php else: ?>
            <span class="disabled">Next &gt;</span>
        <?php endif; ?>
    </div>
<?php endif; ?>
```

Before any testing we just copy the contents of a folder *public/uploads* into our application, in order to correctly display our sample images.

Comics

Id	Title	Cover
1	batman	
2	spiderman	

< Previous | 1 | 2 | 3 | 4 | Next >

Image 11.1.

In order to generate a link to a previous or next page we call to the properties previous or next, which returns us a given page number. After checking if the value is not empty, we execute a helper method $this->url, by passing an initial address returned by an object variable 'route' and a 'page' parameter to generate a proper link address. A property pagesInRange returns a pagination number available in actual range, which we can also control. By checking an actual page number via $this->current, we are able to differentiate and delete a link to not reload a page for the same result unnecessarily.

Another pagination formatting is to display it into a form of a drop down list in <select>, so *pagination_dropdown.phtml*:

```php
<?php if ($this->pageCount): ?>
    <div class="paginationControl">
        Page:
        <select id="paginationControl" size="1">
            <?php foreach ($this->pagesInRange as $page): ?>
                <?php $selected = ($page == $this->current) ?
↳' selected="selected"' : ''; ?>
                    <option value="<?= $this->url($this->route, ['page' => $page]);?>
↳"<?= $selected ?>>
                        <?= $page; ?>
```

```
            </option>
        <?php endforeach; ?>
      </select>
    </div>
<?php endif; ?>

<script type="text/javascript"
src="http://ajax.googleapis.com/ajax/libs/prototype/1.6.0.2/prototype.js">
</script>
<script type="text/javascript">
    $('paginationControl').observe('change', function() {
        window.location = this.options[this.selectedIndex].value;
    })
</script>
```

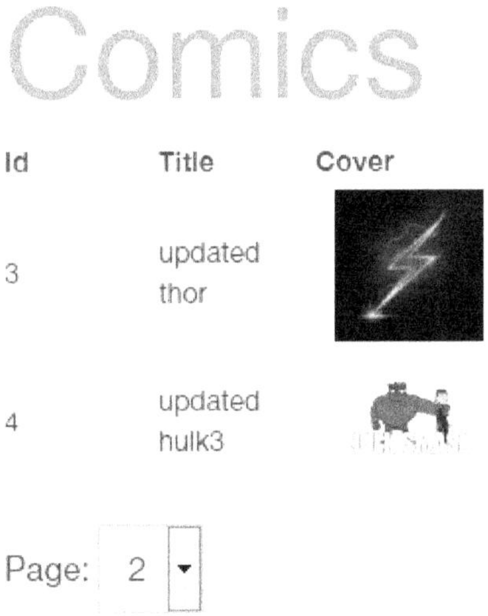

Image 11.2.

Above example uses a JavaScript code, thanks to which we no longer need a button Submit, which will send and parse our request.

The last of our formatting is *pagination_item.phtml*, which displays only the most vital items for pagination, like Current, Next, Previous, First or Last.

```
<?php if ($this->pageCount): ?>
    <div class="paginationControl">
```

```php
        <?= $this->firstItemNumber; ?> - <?= $this->lastItemNumber; ?>
        from <?= $this->totalItemCount; ?>
        <!-- Link to first page -->
        <?php if (isset($this->previous)): ?>
            <a href="<?= $this->url($this->route, ['page' => $this->first]); ?>">
            First
            </a> |
        <?php else: ?>
            <span class="disabled">First</span> |
        <?php endif; ?>

        <!-- Link to previous page -->
        <?php if (isset($this->previous)): ?>
            <a href="<?= $this->url($this->route, ['page' => $this->previous]); ?>">
            &lt; Previous
            </a> |
        <?php else: ?>
            <span class="disabled">&lt; Previous</span> |
        <?php endif; ?>

        <!-- Link to next page -->
        <?php if (isset($this->next)): ?>
            <a href="<?= $this->url($this->route, ['page' => $this->next]); ?>">
            Next &gt;
            </a> |
        <?php else: ?>
            <span class="disabled">Next &gt;</span> |
        <?php endif; ?>

        <!-- Link to last page -->
        <?php if (isset($this->next)): ?>
            <a href="<?= $this->url($this->route, ['page' => $this->last]); ?>">
            Last
            </a>
        <?php else: ?>
            <span class="disabled">Last</span>
        <?php endif; ?>
    </div>
<?php endif; ?>
```

Comics

Id	Title	Cover
5	kapitan ameryka	

5 - 5 z 5 First | < Previous | Next > | Last

Image 11.3.

Take a look, that we have to remember about displaying an inactive function for each option, because we don't want a user to have for example an option to click on Last link when they already are on the last page.

To summarize all available properties of $this object within pagination view, we present them in a table below:

Property name	Type	Description
first	integer	A first page number (usually 1).
firstItemNumber	integer	A number of the first element on this page.
firstPageInRange	integer	A first page in range, returned by scroll style.
current	integer	An actual page number.
currentItemCount	integer	A number of the elements on this page.
currentCountPerPage	integer	A maximum number of elements available on a page.

last	integer	A last page number.
lastItemNumber	integer	A number of the last element on this page.
lastPageInRange	integer	A last page in range, returned by scroll style.
next	integer	Next page number.
pageCount	integer	A number of pages.
pagesInRange	array	An array of pages, returned by scroll style.
previous	integer	A previous page number.
totalItemCount	integer	A total number of elements.

We are going to come back again to the pagination subject in a chapter where we will create an administrator panel. Then we will modify our views by passing extra parameters, so that the pagination would look a bit different and it would gain an additional functionality, such as AJAX results.

CHAPTER 12.
Apigility

In this chapter we are going to add a system that will help us generate and quickly write an API layer, so-called Apigility. Apigility is a production of Zend Framework authors. Its initial draft was built in the framework itself in 2.0 version. Eventually it has been moved as an independent and separate tool for defining an endpoint of the API level. API, that is Application Programming Interface, describes a WWW address, which returns or properly parses input parameters sent to it. Thanks to such interface it is possible to create requests like AJAX that would return an expected data format like JSON, XML or CSV. Mobile applications also will be using those interfaces to communicate with functions on the server side. Each unique WWW address, which processes or returns the data, is called an endpoint. Of course, we could also secure our single endpoints by OAuth 1.0 or 2.0 authorization, so that our application or single website has an exclusive access to our resources.

12.1. Setting an environment

First, download Apigility code with the administration panel into our Zend Framework 3 application. It's important to pay attention to the version of Apigility we download. The support for ZF3 was added since 1.3 version, however the last updates have been pushed with another release, so 1.4, that is why we should use this command:

```
composer require "zfcampus/zf-apigility:~1.4"
```

As in the previous examples, we start with adding a configuration to *modules.config.php*. We will now add a graphical user interface of Apigility to generate our endpoint – this package has been granted support to Zend Framework 3 only in 1.5.0. But the current stable version is 1.5.10 and we will be using exactly this version here.

```
composer require –dev "zdcampus/zf-apigility-admin:~1.5.10"
```

At the end we add a ZF Development Mode library in version 3.0, which would be used to turn on and off of the administration panel.

```
composer require --dev "zfcampus/zf-development-mode:~3.0"
```

If we have not got `Zend\InputFilter` in our configuration yet, we need to install it via below line by adding its definition into *modules.config.php*.

```
composer require zendframework/zend-inputfilter
```

We just need one more manager for CSS and JS files that must be generated for the graphical interface of Apigility. For this purpose we can select the AssetManager from package rwoverdijk – by adding it via:

```
composer require --dev "rwoverdijk/assetmanager:~1.7"
```

Optionally we can also add a package which generates a full documentation of our Apigility services:

```
composer require zfcampus/zf-apigility-documentation
```

The next step will be to add new modules into *development.config.php.dist* and *development.config.php*:

```
'modules' => [
    'ZF\Apigility\Admin',
    'ZF\Apigility\Admin\Ui',
    'ZF\Configuration',
    'AssetManager'
],
```

From now on, the UI graphical version of Apigility administration panel is from now on available under the address *apigility/ui*, however this won't be functional just yet. For the successful working state of the interface we also have to install a few modules via NPM. The NPM is a system run from the command line level (similar to Composer), managing external tools. It comes by default together with NodeJS application, which we will install on our computer. For this purpose we open a website *http://nodejs.org* and download a Current version. Next, we install it and restart our computer in order to refresh the XAMPP SHELL configuration. After the restart we run XMAP SHELL window and test a new module by typing npm. We should get a result visible on the image 12.1.

If we get a message about an unrecognized command, we need to double check our environment variable and the location referring to something like *C:\Program Files\nodejs*.

Now we are going to use an instruction for setting up an environment from the GitHub side. We will begin from doing an initial installation of autoinit:

```
npm install –g npm-autoinit
```

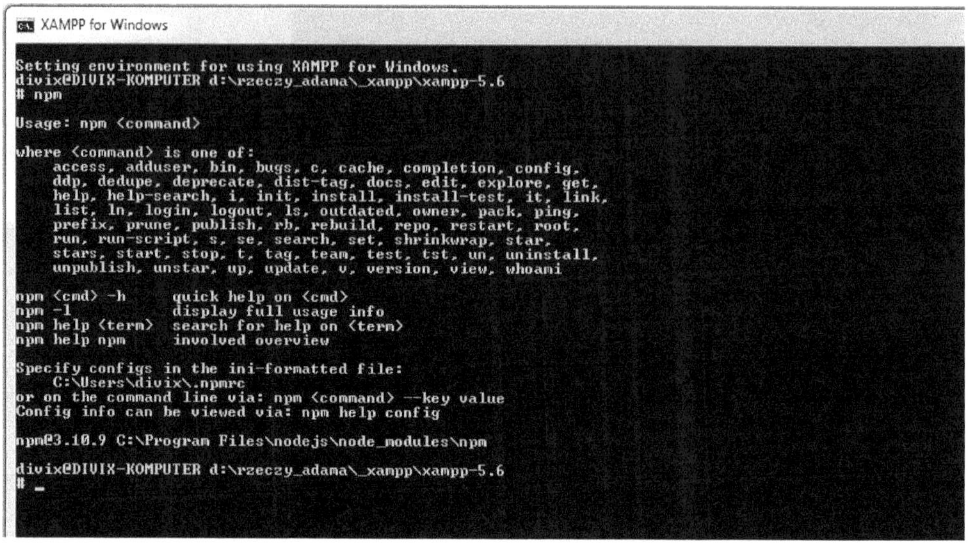

Image 12.1.

Next, we will add the following tools like grunt or bower:

```
npm install –g grunt
npm install –g bower
```

Before running the bower command we would need a GIT support in our command line interface, this is why we download and install Git related to our platform (in my case it's Git for Windows), which additionally will also have a built-in graphical interface from the website: *https://git-for-windows.github.io*. Remember to restart our computer after above mentioned activities.

Now let's add a new module that will be taking care of API layer of our application only; we will call it ApplicationApi. The file is available and ready to download from the catalogue: *module_chapter12*. We place it of course in the same folder as Application, that is *module/*. Then, we add a definition about the autoloader, which declares that the same as for `Application`, `ApplicationApi` it will be implemented according to PSR-4 standards in *composer.json* file:

```
"autoload": {
    "psr-4": {
```

196

```
    "Application\\": "module/Application/src/",
    "ApplicationApi\\": "module/ApplicationApi/src/",
    "DivixUtils\\": "vendor/divixutils/src/DivixUtils"
  }
},
```

In order for the changes to be confirmed, we call a command: `composer update`.

Afterwards, we add ApplicationApi into a module list in: *modules.config.php*.

Optionally, if we want to convert our module into a compatible with Apigility one, we can use the automatic tool, which will be used when we call the following request via some request builder tool, for instance Postman Launcher:

```
PUT http://localhost/zend3/apigility/api/module.enable HTTP/1.1
Accept: application/json
Content-Type: application/json

{"module":"ModuleName"}
```

To check if our example module ApplicationApi works as expected, we will navigate into the address: *http://localhost/zend3/apigility/api/module/↪ApplicationApi*. If we got a JSON response, everything is setup properly.

Finally, we can navigate to the URL *http://localhost/zend3/apigility/ui*, which should display a welcome page of Apigility Admin UI:

Image 12.2.

In order to be able to create our own services in Apigility, we have to add Zend modules responsible for validations and filters. For this purpose we use a composer in the command line to get Zend Validator, Zend Filter, Zend InputFilter, Zend Code and Zend Hydrator into our application:

```
composer require zendframework/zend-validator
composer require zendframework/zend-filter
composer require zendframework/zend-inputfilter
composer require zendframework/zend-code
composer require zendframework/zend-hydrator
```

We just need to check out if we have all the new modules in our modules.config.php file (apart from `Zend\Code`). If not, we add them into correct places, for instance: `'Zend\\Filter'` etc.

12.2. UI Administration Panel

Obviously, we didn't have to copy the folder *ApplicationApi* into our application and use a *New Api* button. But then we wouldn't learn how to add an Api module from the other project into ours. We have chosen the longer route, but learned how to add an external libraries of Apigility type into our Zend 3 project.

Apigility describes endpoints as services, that is API locations, and splits them into RPC (Remote Procedural Code) and REST (Representational State Transfer).

RPC is an endpoint type, which does not have specified principles or rules to keep. Services of such type are mainly used for the single AJAX requests from the website frontend level, which apply to the small service matters, as logging, sending flags of the read message or account activation.

REST differs from RPC mainly by having a defined a set of rules, which describe how the naming convention should look like and allocation of services based on the request type. Let's focus on a set of services that communicate with an `Users` model – in this case there will be the endpoints as: *users/get/[id]*, *users/edit/[id]*, *users/delete/[id]* etc. The request type has a big meaning in defining a service. For example, every GET request type should only return data from the object or database, it should not however in any way modify other data in the system. In the Users case, GET requests types are: *users/get*, *users/getBy*, *users/getCount* etc. If we want to implement a service *users/update/[id]*, we should expect a `PUT` request type. Analogically, for the `DELETE` request we need to use a service *users/delete/[id]*. On the other hand, if we want to create a user or pass a flag like in RPC, we should use a `POST` type of request: *users/create*, *users/markMessage/[id]/* .

The top navigation in UI Administration Panel are: *Content Negotation, Authentication, Database, Documentation, Package and About*. The first link describes a display type, view and model, which the view would use for rendering. By default there are 2 built-in types: `JsonModel` and `HalJsonModel`. We have an ability to modify the existing types or to create our custom selectors. The link *Authentication* sets the way of authentication for services; here we can also add an access adapter, like HTTP Basic, HTTP Digest, OAuth 2.0, PDO or Mongo – image 12.3.

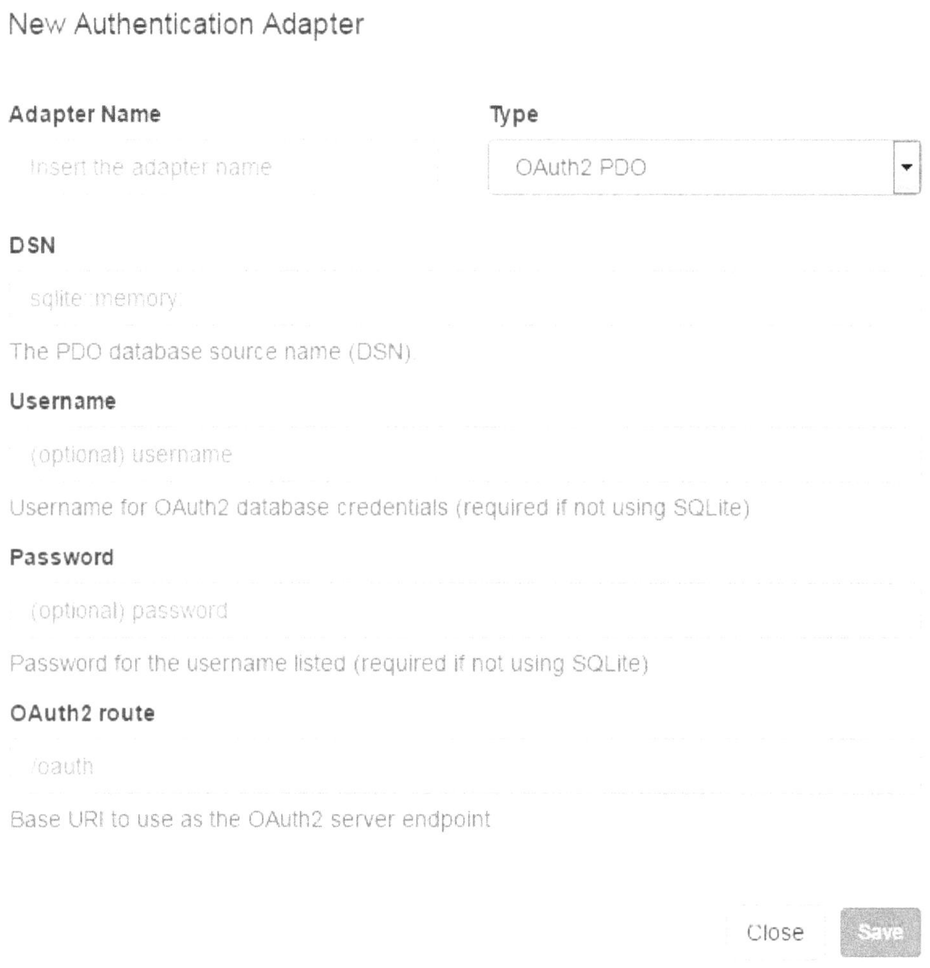

New Authentication Adapter

Adapter Name

Insert the adapter name

Type

OAuth2 PDO ▾

DSN

sqlite:memory

The PDO database source name (DSN)

Username

(optional) username

Username for OAuth2 database credentials (required if not using SQLite)

Password

(optional) password

Password for the username listed (required if not using SQLite)

OAuth2 route

/oauth

Base URI to use as the OAuth2 server endpoint

Close   Save

Image 12.3.

Database manages the connections with data bases that are supported in Zend Framework 3. A link *Documentation* returns a full documentation about the existing API and the services themselves, regarding sample requests and responses. The penultimate option *Package* is a tool allowing to build a self-implemented API file in any format: ZIP, TAG, TGZ and ZPK. The last link *About* informs us about available features of Apigility together with links to the related and used tools with solutions.

As we can see, since 1.4 version Apigility uses a Bootstrap framework to generate HTML and CSS codes together with AngularJS for AJAX calls and

JavaScript. Thanks to that the panel becomes more responsive and mobile friendly for users.

12.3. Creating RPC services

Let's create then a first very easy service of RPC type, which will serve us for encrypting strings. We click on *New Service*, then we select tab *RPC*, and in a new window we enter Encryption as the service name and */encrypt* as *Route to match* - the address of our endpoint execution – image 12.4.

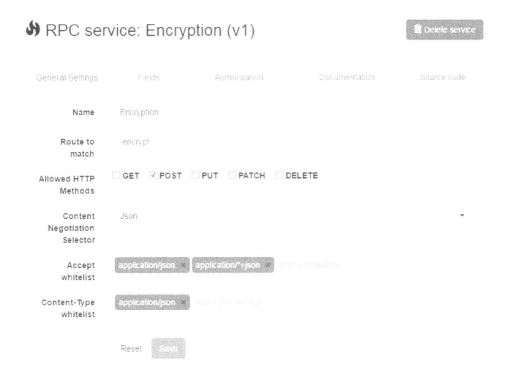

Image 12.4.

At this stage we are able to set an acceptable request types, but for this example we will leave only one available option POST. A section *Content Negotiation Selector* describes the type of returned information format – we leave the safer option Json here. An accept whitelist informs which values are available in the header of *Content-Type*. The main difference between Accept and Content-Types is that the first one sets the format in which the request will accept our response, whereas the Content-Type sets an actual type of returned information. From both options we have deleted the first value, which would will not come handy in this service. We save all data by pressing *Save* button.

Let's move into *Fields* tab that defines available parameters passed to the specific services. By pressing a button *New Field*, we fill a dialog modal as on the image 12.5.

As we can notice, we define a parameter with name input, which is a required string type. Additionally, we could select options like: *File upload?* used for sending files, *Allow Empty* to pass empty values or *Continue if Empty*, which gives us an option to ignore a parameter if it's missing. Our next step is to add one validator: `Zend\I18n\Validator\Alnum` in order to get characters only from the range A-Z and then two filters `Zend\Filter\StringTrim` and `Zend\Filter\StringToLower`.

The last thing to do in the administration panel is to move to the *Documentation* tab and enter a relative information which then will be available in public for external developers.

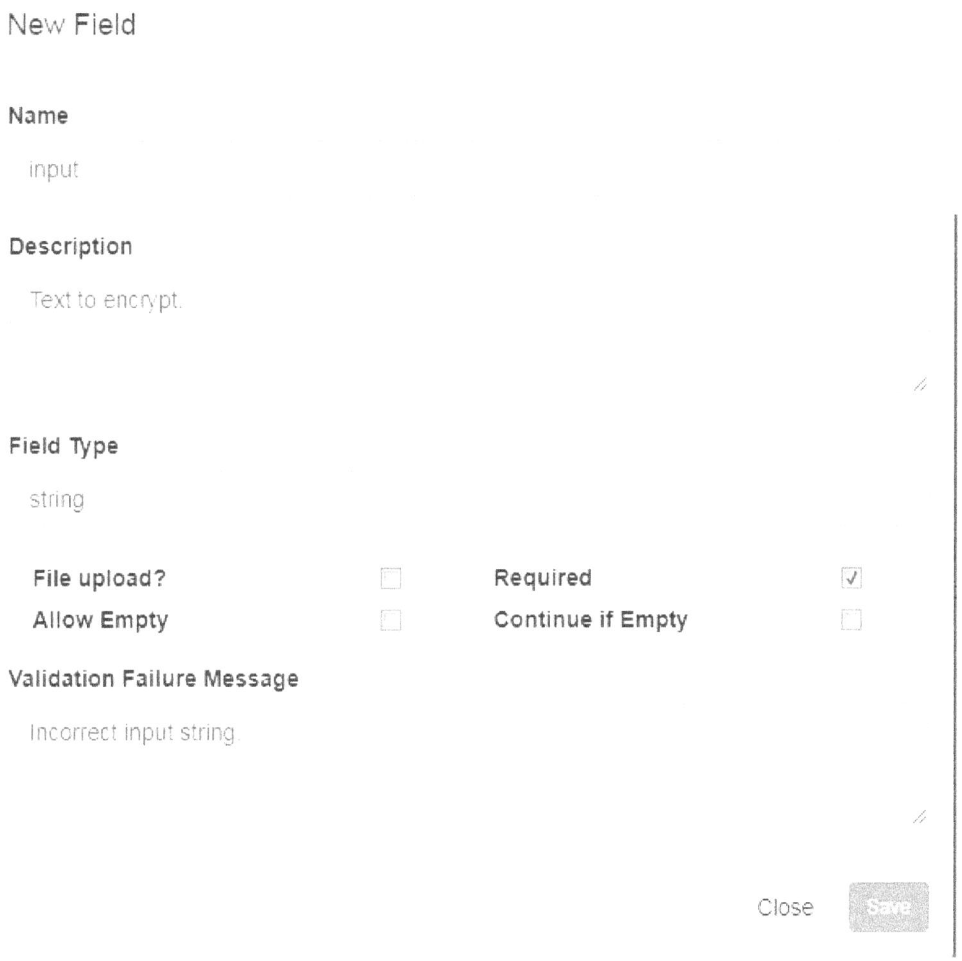

New Field

Name

input

Description

Text to encrypt.

Field Type

string

File upload?	☐	Required	☑
Allow Empty	☐	Continue if Empty	☐

Validation Failure Message

Incorrect input string

Close Save

Image 12.5.

Image 12.6.

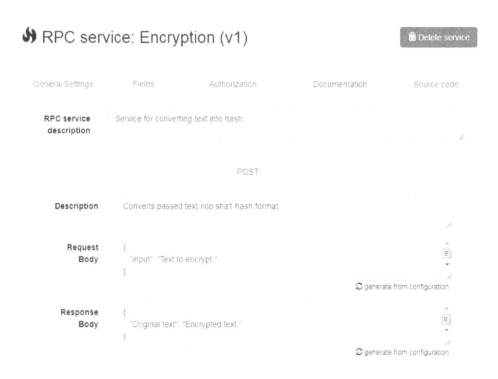

Image 12.7.

A tab *Source* code shows currently self-generated service files, like *EncryptionController.php* or *EncryptionControllerFactory.php*, where the first service is passing dependencies for the first class. We modify the first file in our editor in the following way:

```php
namespace ApplicationApi\V1\Rpc\Encryption;
use Zend\Mvc\Controller\AbstractActionController;
use ZF\ContentNegotiation\ViewModel;

class EncryptionController extends AbstractActionController
{
    public function encryptionAction()
    {
        $event = $this->getEvent();
        $inputFilter = $event->getParam('ZF\ContentValidation\InputFilter');
        $input = $inputFilter->getValue('input');
        return new ViewModel([
            $input => sha1($input)
        ]);
    }
}
```

We have added a few lines of code responsible for grabbing a variable `'input'` and using it to display a result. `AbstractActionController` class, which we extend in controller file, offers an access to an actual request event. Thanks to `$event` object we are able to get an instance of `InputFilter` that already has a full access to the variables passed into services. By using a method `getValue([name])`, we receive a filtered and validated value of the parameter. For comparison, we can get the original value of a parameter by calling:

```php
$inputFilter->getRawValue('input');
```

If however we need to display all the passed and formatted values, we should use:

```php
$inputFilter->getValues();
```

We will finally test our service in the browser. For endpoint testing it is best to use external applications or browser plugins, such as RESTClient or

HTTPie. I would surely recommend Postman Launcher - an extension to the Chrome browser. We just need to type down a plugin name in Chrome store *https://chrome.google.com/webstore/category/extenstions*, install it and click on the icon appearing on the top right corner of the browser window. Our first request will be looking like on the image 12.8.

Image 12.8.

First, we have entered a service address, after which we changed the request type to POST, then we opened a *Headers* view on the right, to display the options of entering custom headers, like *Accept* or *Content-Type*. Let's check if our endpoint works as expected. This is where a small surprise appears:

```
{
    "validation_messages": {
        "input": [
            "Invalid input string."
        ]
    },
    "type": "http://www.w3.org/Protocols/rfc2616/rfc2616-sec10.html",
    "title": "Unprocessable Entity",
    "status": 422,
    "detail": "Failed Validation"
}
```

The application informs us about an invalid parameter "input". Notice that Apigility has generated a full JSON object together with status, error title and specific error message regarding given parameter and error type with the URL address. If we typed headers other than expected, we would get other message from *encrypt*:

```
"detail": "Cannot honor Accept type specified"
```

or

```
"detail": "Invalid content-type specified"
```

To pass a variable into our services according to the specified JSON format, we need to click the raw button next to form-data and enter a value there:

```
{
    "input": "aBc     "
}
```

After submitting another request, response below from the encrypt service should be presented:

```
{
    "abc": "a9993e364706816aba3e25717850c26c9cd0d89d"
}
```

It's noteworthy that our original value (a key) has been filtered out, allowing us to delete space characters and change the uppercase letters into the lowercase ones. A value of the `"abc"` key is a hash generated by `sha1()` function. If you want to check the correctness of validators, you can pass the parameter like `"input"` with any given number or a special character. Both these character types are forbidden and they should display an information about the invalid input string.

In order to display all available options of our service, we can execute a request to *encrypt* with `OPTIONS` type. Thanks to that we will know which request formats are supported at that particular moment.

```
Allow → POST
Connection → Keep-Alive
Content-Length → 0
Content-Type → text/html; charset=UTF-8
Date → Sat, 26 Nov 2016 23:25:04 GMT
Keep-Alive → timeout=5, max=100
```

Server → Apache/2.4.10 (Win32) OpenSSL/1.0.1i PHP/5.6.3
X-Powered-By → PHP/5.6.3

Remember to click *Headers (8)* tab, just above the response window.

A full documentation can now be previewed by going back to the Apigility administration panel by clicking a *Documentation* link, where all the information needed to prepare a request as the guides of external interfaces would display.

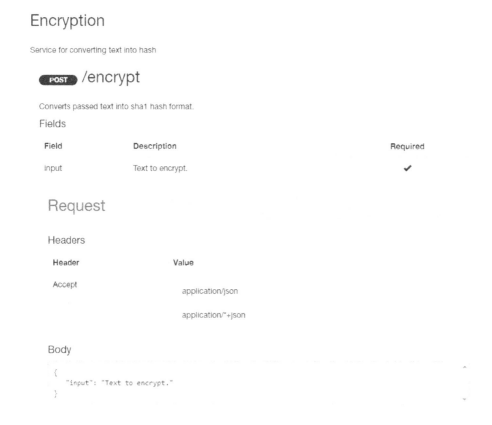

Image 12.9.

12.4. Creating REST services

In this section we will take care of creating services of REST type for our comics items. In this case we will be able to return a single object representation as well as the collection of objects according to our own defined helper classes. Having selected an API: `ApplicationApi`, we click on *New Service* and add a new service of REST type called `Comics`. On the first screen we should see the settings; the same or very similar are pictured below (see image 12.10).

Route matches is one of important fields; it allows us to determine, which address our service will be replying to. A mark `[/:comics_id]` states that after / char there is an option to send another variable, for instance when we want to get a single record or update it. Names `comics_id` and `[/:comics_id]` must match, otherwise they won't be treated as an Entity class identifier. Next, the *Hydrator Service Name* determines the way values of classes will be converted into a service result; in our example we leave a default setting `ArraySerializable`. We also change the *Entity Class* into an already existing `Application\Mode\Rowset\Comics`, in order not to duplicate a code.

209

Image 12.10.

It's worth noting that it is a good idea only when we can make all the object information of `Comics` public. If however we want to display only a few of them, then we have to create another class or use `ComicsEntity` instead of the one of `Rowset` package.

On the right hand side we have changed an amount of results displayed on the page and we modified available request types: `GET`, `PUT`, `PATCH`, `DELETE` for single record `Entity` and `GET`, `POST`, `POUT`, `PATCH` for the `Colection` of objects. Methods `Http Entity` are used via entering the address *comics/[id]* and information sent in a single JSON object in the case of further modifications of the record. An example is a POST method, which will be creating a new Entity record: `Rowset\Comics`.

However, the methods of `Http Collections` type are performed under address *comics* and they expect a list of JSON objects. We save our settings and go to the *Fields* tab, where we set what is acceptable in our comics service.

We have created three fields here: `id`, `title` and `thumb`; each of them has its own lined validator. The `id` field takes only natural numbers, `thumb` – characters supported in URI standard, and `title` – alphanumeric string with additional flag allowwhitespace set to `TRUE`.

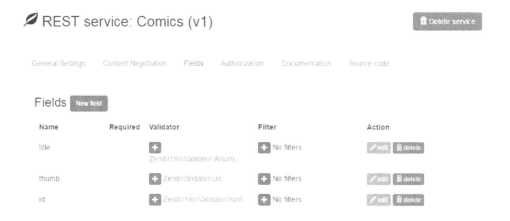

Image 12.11.

Now we can move into a documentation tab and fill up the data about our service.

Let's modify a `ComicsResourceFactory`, which will be responsible for passing an object of `ComicsTable` from the Service Manager, so that we are able to perform operations on the records from comics tbale.

```
namespace ApplicationApi\V1\Rest\Comics;
use Application\Model\ComicsTable;

class ComicsResourceFactory
{
    public function __invoke($services)
    {
        $comicsTableGateway = $services->get(ComicsTable::class);
        return new ComicsResource($comicsTableGateway);
    }
}
```

We also have to change our `ComicsTable` class, so that it is able to fully modify the `Comics` objects:

```
namespace Application\Model;

class ComicsTable extends AbstractTable
{
    protected $resultsPerPage = 2;
    public function getById($id)
    {
        $id = (int) $id;
        $row = $this->getBy(['id' => $id]);
        if (!$row) {
            throw new \Exception('comics not found with id: '.$id);
        }
        return $row;
    }
    public function getBy(array $params = array())
    {
        $select = $this->tableGateway->getSql()->select();
```

```php
        if (!isset($params['page'])) {
            $params['page'] = 0;
        }
        if (isset($params['id'])) {
            $select->where(['id' => $params['id']]);
            $params['limit'] = 1;
        }
        if (isset($params['title'])) {
            $select->where(['title' => $params['title']]);
        }
        if (isset($params['thumb'])) {
            $select->where(['thumb' => $params['thumb']]);
        }
        if (isset($params['limit'])) {
            $select->limit($params['limit']);
        }
        $result = (isset($params['limit']) && $params['limit'] == 1)
            ? $this->fetchRow($select)
            : $this->fetchAll($select, ['limit' => $this->resultsPerPage,
'page' => $params['page']]);
        return $result;
    }
    public function patch($id, $data)
    {
        $passedData = [];
        if (!empty($data['title'])) {
            $passedData['title'] = $data['title'];
        }
        if (!empty($data['thumb'])) {
            $passedData['thumb'] = $data['thumb'];
        }
        $this->tableGateway->update($passedData, ['id' => $id]);
    }
    public function save(Rowset\Comics $comicsModel)
    {
        return parent::saveRow($comicsModel);
    }
    public function delete($id)
    {
        parent::deleteRow($id);
    }
}
```

We have added here a `getById()` method, which in very easy way is using an already existing method `getBy()` and throws an exception when the record is not found. Only `getBy()` gets an additional check, if a key page was not passed and resets it to 0. There is also a new method `patch()` that differs from `save()` mainly because it allows to modify only one class attribute without the need to pass the whole object of `Rowset/Comics` model. The method `delete()` removes an element by a passed id number of comics by executing `deleteRow()` from an abstract class.

Next, we fill in a class: `ApplicationApi\V1\Rest\Comics\Comics` ↪`Resources`, which will be taking care of all request types of our service.

```
namespace ApplicationApi\V1\Rest\Comics;
use ZF\ApiProblem\ApiProblem;
use ZF\Rest\AbstractResourceListener;
class ComicsResource extends AbstractResourceListener
{
    protected $comicsTableGateway;
    public function __construct($comicsTableGateway) {
        $this->comicsTableGateway = $comicsTableGateway;
    }
    public function create($data)
    {
        $arrayData = (array) $data;
        $model = new \Application\Model\Rowset\Comics();
        $model->exchangeArray($arrayData);
        return $this->comicsTableGateway->save($model);
    }
    public function delete($id)
    {
        $this->comicsTableGateway->delete($id);
        return true;
    }
    public function deleteList($data)
    {
        return new ApiProblem(405, 'The DELETE method has not been defined for
↪collections');
    }
    public function fetch($id)
    {
        return $this->comicsTableGateway->getBy(['id' => $id]);
    }
    public function fetchAll($params = [])
    {
```

```php
            return $this->comicsTableGateway->getBy();
    }
    public function patch($id, $data)
    {
        $arrayData = (array) $data;
        return $this->comicsTableGateway->patch($id, $arrayData);
    }
    public function patchList($data)
    {
        $arrayData = (array) $data;
        foreach ($arrayData as $comicsRow) {
            if (empty($comicsRow['id'])) {
                return new ApiProblem(405, 'Invalid ID attribute');
            }
            $result = $this->comicsTableGateway->patch($comicsRow['id'],
↪$comicsRow);
        }
        return $result;
    }
    public function replaceList($data)
    {
        $arrayData = (array) $data;
        foreach ($arrayData as $row) {
            $model = new \Application\Model\Rowset\Comics();
            $model->exchangeArray((array) $row);
            if (empty($model->getId())) {
                return new ApiProblem(405, 'Invalid ID attribute');
            }
            $result = $this->comicsTableGateway->save($model);
        }
        return $result;
    }
    public function update($id, $data)
    {
        $arrayData = (array) $data;
        if (empty($arrayData['id'])) {
            return new ApiProblem(405, 'Invalid ID attribute');
        }
        $arrayData['id'] = $id;
        $model = new \Application\Model\Rowset\Comics();
        $model->exchangeArray($arrayData);
        return $this->comicsTableGateway->save($model);
    }
}
```

I've removed comments before pasting a code here, to save the place a bit, therefore if you want to see a whole class with comments, check a folder *module_chapter12* and `ComicsResource` class. In the constructor we take an instance of `ComicsTable` and store it in a class variable. Let's take a closer look at each method separately, testing its functionality via Postman Launcher plugin at the same time.

12.4.1. create()

A method `create()` creates a new `Comics` object based on passed data in the request. We need to remember that the passed parameters are a standard form of the PHP class object, so it is best to convert the data into a regular array. Notice that we create an object of `Rowset\Comics` and we fill it with an information by calling `exchangeArray()`.

An example usage:

```
POST http://localhost/zend3/comics HTTP/1.1
Accept: application/json
Content-Type: application/json
{
"title": "comics name",
"thumb": "okladka.png"
}
```

Returns:

```
{
    "title": "comics name",
    "thumb": "okladka.png",
    "_links": {
        "self": {
            "href": http://localhost/zend3/comics
        }
    }
}
```

12.4.2. delete($id)

Removes a comics by the a passed id number in URL. Here we return a TRUE value instead of a method $this->comicsTableGateway->delete($id), as in other cases we would get an information about lack of possibility to remove an object.

```
DELETE http://localhost/zend3/comics/6 HTTP/1.1
Accept: application/json
Content-Type: application/json
```

This request returns will return an empty response with a status 204: No Content.

12.4.3. fetch($id)

Returns a single comics element with a full information and a message about an address of this object.

```
GET http://localhost/zend3/comics/3 HTTP/1.1
Accept: application/json
Content-Type: application/json
```

Returns:

```
{
    "id": "3",
    "title": "thor",
    "thumb": "bolt.jpg",
    "_links": {
        "self": {
            "href": http://localhost/zend3/comics/3
        }
    }
}
```

12.4.4. fetchAll()

Returns all the comics with max limit equal to 2, set in Apigility panel.

```
GET http://localhost/zend3/comics HTTP/1.1
Accept: application/json
Content-Type: application/json
```

Returns for example:

```
{"_links":{"self":{"href":"http:\/\/localhost\/zend3\/comics?page=1"},"first":
↪{"href":"http:\/\/localhost\/zend3\/comics"},"last":{"href":"http:\/\/localhost\
↪/zend3\/comics?page=4"},"next":{"href":"http:\/\/localhost\/zend3\/comics?page=2"
↪}},"_embedded":{"comics":[{"id":"1","title":"batman","thumb":"bat.png","_links":{
↪"self":{"href":"http:\/\/localhost\/zend3\/comics\/1"}}},{"id":"2","title":
↪"spiderman","thumb":"spider.jpg","_links":{"self":{"href":"http:\/\/localhost\
↪/zend3\/comics\/2"}}}]},"page_count":4,"page_size":2,"total_items":8,"page":1}
```

12.4.5. patch($id, $data)

Updates one or more attributes of a `Comics` object.

```
PATCH http://localhost/zend3/comics/3 HTTP/1.1
Accept: application/json
Content-Type: application/json
{
"title": "updated thor",
"thumb": "bolt2.png"
}
```

Returns:

```
{
    "title": "updated thor",
    "thumb": "bolt2.jpg",
    "_links": {
        "self": {
            "href": http://localhost/zend3/comics/3
        }
    }
}
```

12.4.6. patchList($data)

Updates one or more attributes of multiple `Comics` objects passed in the list. Additionally, we can check here if every passed record has an id attribute.

```
PATCH http://localhost/zend3/comics HTTP/1.1
Accept: application/json
Content-Type: application/json
[
    {
        "id": 3,
        "title": "updated thor"
    },
    {
        "id": 4,
        "title": "updated hulk3"
    }
]
```

Returns:

```
{
    "_links": {
        "self": {
            "href": http://localhost/zend3/comics
        }
    },
    "_embedded": {
        "comics": [
            {
                "id": 3,
                "title": "updated thor",
                "_links": {
                    "self": {
                        "href": http://localhost/zend3/comics/3
                    }
                }
            },
            {
                "id": 4,
```

```
                    "title": "updated hulk3",
                    "_links": {
                        "self": {
                            "href": http://localhost/zend3/comics/4
                        }
                    }
                }
            ]
        },
        "total_items": 2
}
```

12.4.7. replaceList($data)

Updates all the attributes of multiple passed `Comics` objects in a list. If we missed at least one of the attributes in the request, then these attributes will be reset to their default values in the database. Same as in `patchList()` we also checks here if a passed record contains an id field.

```
PUT http://localhost/zend3/comics HTTP/1.1
Accept: application/json
Content-Type: application/json
[
    {
        "id": 3,
        "title": "updated thor"
    },
    {
        "id": 4,
        "title": "updated hulk3"
    }
]
```

Returns:

```
{
    "_links": {
        "self": {
            "href": http://localhost/zend3/comics
        }
    },
    "_embedded": {
```

```
    "comics": [
        {
            "id": 3,
            "title": "updated thor",
            "thumb": "bolt2.png",
            "_links": {
                "self": {
                    "href": http://localhost/zend3/comics/3
                }
            }
        },
        {
            "id": 4,
            "title": "updated hulk3",
            "thumb": "zielony2.png"
            "_links": {
                "self": {
                    "href": http://localhost/zend3/comics/4
                }
            }
        }
    ]
    },
    "total_items": 2
}
```

12.4.8. update($id, $data)

Updates a single `Comics` object based on an id passed in the address. If we do not pass one of the attributes, it will be reset in the database. Because we have not passed a thumb, our comics object has an empty image in the database.

```
PUT http://localhost/zend3/comics/3 HTTP/1.1
Accept: application/json
Content-Type: application/json
{
    "id": 3,
    "title": "updated thor"
}
```

220

Returns:

```
{
    "id": 3,
    "title": "updated thor",
    "_links": {
        "self": {
            "href": http://localhost/zend3/comics/3
        }
    }
}
```

12.5. Security of the services

It's time to add an authorization to the REST services, which adds, updates or deletes our comics records. It is safer to have endpoints that get or par public data. However, we do not want the data rights management to be assigned to a random person. That's why we should secure our chosen services of PUT, PATCH and DELETE types by Http Basic Authorization. It is a security type based on a browser's user session, which requires a username and a password to enter. Http Basic relies on the Apache server configuration and uses configuration from the *.htpasswd* file, which contains the information about one or multiple users credentials. The passwords are of course encrypted, while the names themselves are just in a plain text format. To create such file we are going to use a command htpasswd of the XAMPP command line. Let's navigate into the folder *htdocs/zend3/data*, where we run the following script:

```
htpasswd -cs comics.htpasswd comicsUser
```

The above command will create a new file (-c) with name *comics.htpasswd*, use a SHA mechanism for password encryption (-s) and will add a first user with name comicsUser. Next, the script will ask about the password of a new user; in my example I used a password: "pass".

```
New password: ****
Re-type new password: ****
Adding password for user comicsUser
```

Let's check the file content comics.htpasswd to see what was added:

comicsUser:{SHA}nU4eI71bcnBGqeO0t9tXvY1u5oQ=

If we want to add another user to the same file, we should call the same line as above, apart from the flag "c", and by typing other username.

Let's add now an authorization type to Apigility, by clicking the top link *Authnetication* and a button *New Adapater* – image 12.12.

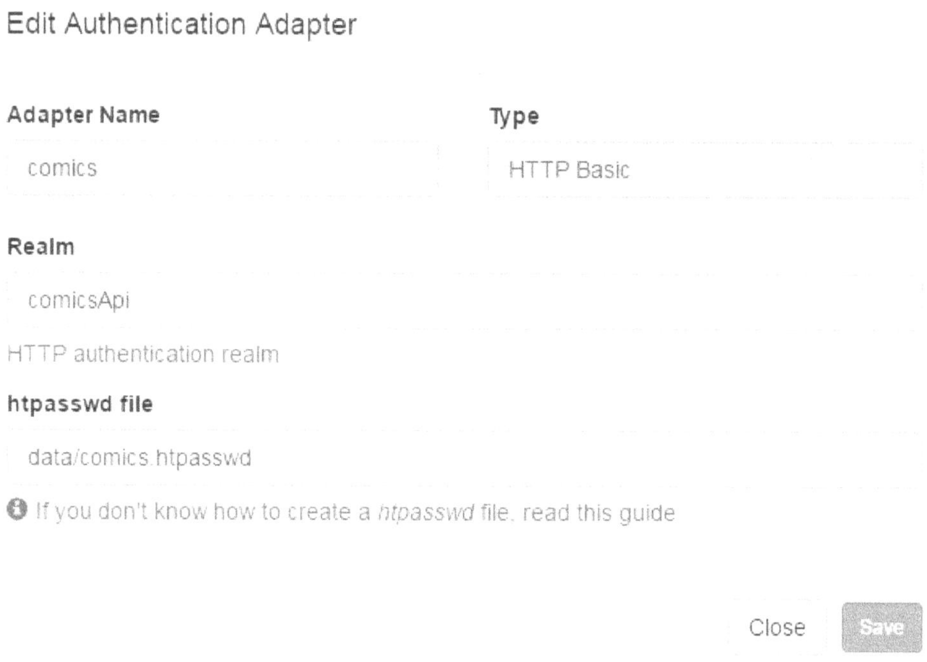

Edit Authentication Adapter

Adapter Name   **Type**

  comics   HTTP Basic

Realm

  comicsApi

HTTP authentication realm

htpasswd file

  data/comics.htpasswd

🛈 If you don't know how to create a *htpasswd* file, read this guide

                                              Close   Save

Image 12.12.

We enter an adapter name: comics, then we choose a type HTTP Basic, after which we set a *Realm*. The realm is a namespace for choosing a group, which will have an access to the particular things. We can for instance have another adapter with the same Realm name, in order to give more permissions for the same users. At the end we set a path to our *.htpasswd* file, but we need to remember that the base folder for Apigility is also a root folder of our application - *htdocs/zend3/*. We save an adapter, which also gives us an adapter definition in the file *config/autoload/local.php*.

```
'zf-mvc-auth' => array(
    'authentication' => array(
        'adapters' => array(
            'comics' => array(
                'adapter' => 'ZF\\MvcAuth\\Authentication\\HttpAdapter',
                'options' => array(
                    'accept_schemes' => array(
                        0 => 'basic',
                    ),
                    'realm' => 'comicsApi',
                    'htpasswd' => 'data/comics.htpasswd',
                ),
            ),
        ),
    ),
),
```

Then we link the authorization with our main API. We do that by clicking on the left hand side in the navigation in `ApplicationApi`, where on the main screen we choose *Set Authentication* type for our newly created adapter comics (basic). Here we can also save a setting; we move into Comics REST service and enter into the *Authorization* tab.

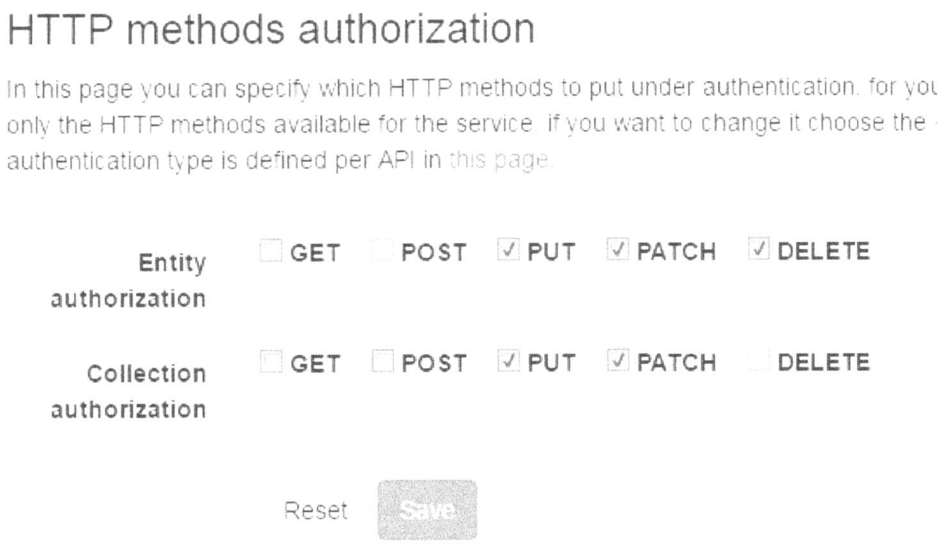

HTTP methods authorization

In this page you can specify which HTTP methods to put under authentication. for you
only the HTTP methods available for the service. if you want to change it choose the
authentication type is defined per API in this page.

	GET	POST	PUT	PATCH	DELETE
Entity authorization	☐	☐	☑	☑	☑
Collection authorization	☐	☐	☑	☑	☐

Reset   Save

Image 12.13.

223

As in the image above, we select available types of the request: PUT, PATCH and DELETE for both methods. Now, when we try for instance to execute a PATCH operation with address *comics/3*, we would get a proper information about the lack of authorization:

```
{
    "type": "http://www.w3.org/Protocols/rfc2616/rfc2616-sec10.html",
    "title": "Forbidden",
    "status": 403,
    "detail": "Forbidden"
}
```

From now on, we need to pass an information about the authorization together with the request, so our call would look like:

```
PATCH http://localhost/zend3/comics/3 HTTP/1.1
Accept: application/json
Content-Type: application/json
Authorization: Basic Y29taWNzVXNlcjpwYXNz
{
    "title": "updated thor",
    "thumb": "bolt2.png"
}
```

Surely you are thinking what a generated hash passed after a word Basic is. Well, it's a string of [username]:[password] encrypted via base64 method. In our example it's comicsUser:pass. To quickly create our hash we use an interactive PHP mode in Shell. Let's go back to the command line and enter php -a. When it opens an insert text mode, we type:

```
<?php
echo base64_encode('comicsUser:pass');
```

We click Enter, and soon after that Ctrl + C to stop and execute a script. The script should return a value 29taWNzVXNlcjpwYXNz, like on the image below:

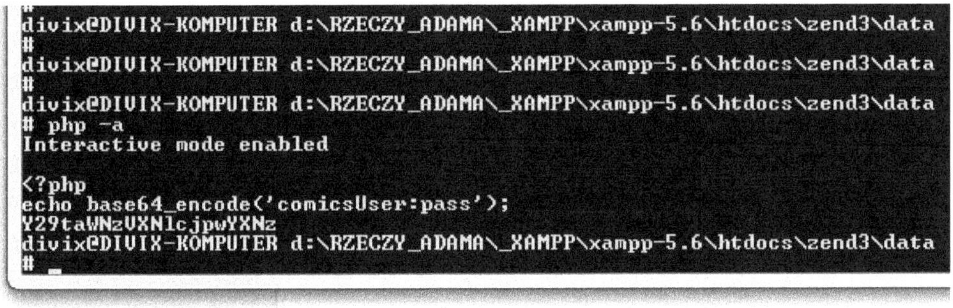

```
divix@DIVIX-KOMPUTER d:\RZECZY_ADAMA\_XAMPP\xampp-5.6\htdocs\zend3\data
#
divix@DIVIX-KOMPUTER d:\RZECZY_ADAMA\_XAMPP\xampp-5.6\htdocs\zend3\data
#
divix@DIVIX-KOMPUTER d:\RZECZY_ADAMA\_XAMPP\xampp-5.6\htdocs\zend3\data
# php -a
Interactive mode enabled

<?php
echo base64_encode('comicsUser:pass');
Y29taWNzVXNlcjpwYXNz
divix@DIVIX-KOMPUTER d:\RZECZY_ADAMA\_XAMPP\xampp-5.6\htdocs\zend3\data
#
```

Image 12.14.

There are also two other methods of authorizations in Apigility: *Http Digest Authorization* and *OAuth 2.0*, however they are more advanced and complex to use.

CHAPTER 13.

Creating a dynamic poll

In this chapter we are going to focus on the implementation of a module that will dynamically gather the data via an API service and store the data based on a response of the current active poll in a text file. The file will be in XML form, so we would use a Zend Xml2Json package that will help us a file conversion into JSON format. Additionally, we are going to secure sending results once per user and by the CSRF field, so that we force the form submission (voting) to be performed only on our website. However, we are going to begin from defining an abstract controller, which would set related variables in each controller. Initially controller will be taking care of setting up a simple navigation situated in our template file, *layout.phtml*. In chapter 20, we will upgrade this simple navigation into Zend Navigation, which will later support generating breadcrumbs, site maps and links.

13.1. New controller

We start our wok from a new abstract controller called AbstractController, which we should place in the same folder as the rest of controllers. Unfortunately, Zend Framework in versions 2 and 3 has removed the `init()` method, which previously was used to initialize the logic and variables. Inside `Zend\EventManager\AbstractAction` ↪`Controller` exists one more method, which is executed a bit sooner than the previous one from Zend 1, but we can reuse it and override as needed:

```
public function onDispatch(MvcEvent $e)
{
    //our init logic
    return parent::onDispatch($e);
}
```

It's worth to keep an eye on the event parameter `MvcEvent` that we pass over and return a result of a base class `onDispatch()`.

To make our solution fully configurable and dynamic, we need to use Event Manager, by which we will pass our action in the form of an anonymous function.

```
public function setEventManager(EventManagerInterface $events)
{
    parent::setEventManager($events);
    $controller = $this;
    $events->attach('dispatch', function ($e) {
        $controllerClass = $e->getRouteMatch()->getParam('controller', 'index');
        $e->getViewModel()->setVariable('controller', $controllerClass);
    }, 100);
}
```

An access to the manager we obviously gain by the `setEventManager()` method, which offers us a variable `$events` and to which we register logic for dispatch action. Primarily, inside the callback we get a controller's class name by using a `getParam()` method from the `Route Match` object. Next, we set a variable with name controller with our grabbed `$controllerClass` value as a view variable, by getting a view mode from the template by `getBiewModel()`.

Another task is to use a newly assigned variable in the template file. Thanks to that we are able to control a display class active for the currently selected subpage in the navigation.

```
<ul class="nav navbar-nav">
    <li <?php if ($this->controller === Application\Controller\IndexController:
↪:class): ?>class="active"<?php endif; ?>><a href="<?= $this->url('home') ?>
↪">Home Page</a></li>
    <li <?php if ($this->controller === Application\Controller\UsersController:
↪:class): ?>class="active"<?php endif; ?>><a href="<?= $this->url('users') ?>"
↪>Users</a></li>
    <li <?php if ($this->controller === Application\Controller\NewsController:
↪:class): ?>class="active"<?php endif; ?>><a href="<?= $this->url('news') ?>
↪">Articles</a></li>
    <li <?php if ($this->controller === Application\Controller\ComicsController:
↪:class): ?>class="active"<?php endif; ?>><a href="<?= $this->url('comics') ?>
↪">Comics</a></li>\
    <li <?php if ($this->controller === Application\Controller\PollingController:
↪:class): ?>class="active"<?php endif; ?>><a href="<?= $this->url('polling') ?>
↪">Poll</a></li>\
</ul>
```

As the variable $this->controller returns a full class package together with the filename, we are able to call ::class of the controller class. Of course it is the simplest way of making a dynamic navigation on a site. If, however, we are looking for something more advanced and functional, we can move into chapter 20.

Let's go back to creating a page of managing polls, which will be handled by the Apigility service and saved in the XML file. First, add a new module for converting XML contents into JSON format.

```
composer require zendframework/zend-xml2json
```

We set a new controller in the configuration file *module.config.php* by the standard item in the routes key, similar to the Users module. Soon after that, we add a new record into controllers.

```
'polling' => [
    'type' => Segment::class,
    'options' => [
        'route' => '/polling[/:action][/:id]',
        'defaults' => [
            'controller' => Controller\PollingController::class,
            'action' => 'index',
        ],
    ],
```

```
]
Controller\PollingController::class => function($sm) {
    return new Controller\PollingController($sm->get(\DivixUtils\Polls\Polls::class));
}
```

We can easily observe that we reused a `Polls` class from the `DivixUtils\Polls` package, which will be presented in a moment. At this moment you need to pay attention that the new class does not take any arguments and that we register it to Service Manager in *Module.php* inside the factories key:

```
'factories' => array(
    ...

    \DivixUtils\Polls\Polls::class => InvokableFactory::class
```

I called our controller a `PollingController` instead of `PollsController` on purpose because the second name was already used as a service controller in Apigility. Thanks to that, a `PollingController` controller looks like below:

```
namespace Application\Controller;
class PollingController extends AbstractController
{
    private $pollsLibrary;
    public function __construct($pollsLibrary)
    {
        $this->pollsLibrary = $pollsLibrary;
    }
    public function indexAction()
    {
    }
    public function manageAction()
    {
        return [
            'polls' => $this->pollsLibrary->getAll()
        ];
    }
    public function viewAction()
    {
        $pollForm = $this->pollsLibrary->getForm();
        $viewParams = [
```

```
            'poll' => $this->pollsLibrary->getActive(),
            'form' => $pollForm
        ];
        return $viewParams;
    }
    public function activateAction()
    {
        $id = $this->params()->fromRoute('id');
        $this->pollsLibrary->activate($id);
        $this->redirect()->toRoute('polling', ['action' => 'manage']);
    }
}
```

In our default action index we only display two links: one to manag polls, and another one to display an active poll.

```
<div class="jumbotron">
    <a href="<?= $this->url('polling', ['action' => 'manage']) ?>"
↪class="btn btn-default">Manage polls</a>
    <a href="<?= $this->url('polling', ['action' => 'view']) ?>" class="btn
↪btn-default">Active poll</a>
</div>
```

Another step will be to add a few CSS selectors into the file *public/css/style.css*, in order to make our form look like a real poll for the user end in the view file:

```
.pollsContainer label {
    display: block;
}
.pollsContainer form {
    border: 1px solid #9d9d9d;
    padding: 7px;
    border-radius: 4px;
    width: 300px;
}
```

Next, in the manage action we have a list of all polls together with an option to activate them.

```
<div class="jumbotron">
    <h1><span class="zf-green">Available polls</span></h1>
    <table class="table">
```

```php
    <tr>
        <th>Id</th>
        <th>Question</th>
        <th>Answers</th>
        <th>Activate</th>
    </tr>
    <?php foreach ($polls as $row): ?>
    <tr>
        <td><?= $row['id'] ?></td>
        <td><?= $row->question ?></td>
        <td>
            <?php foreach ($row->answers->answer as $answer): ?>
                <?= $answer.' ('.$answer['votes'].')' ?><br />
            <?php endforeach; ?>
        </td>

        <td>
            <?php if ($row['active'] == 'true'): ?>
                <b>Active</b>
            <?php else: ?>
                <a href="<?= $this->url('polling').'/activate/'
↪.$row['id']; ?>">Activate</a>
            <?php endif; ?>
        </td>
    </tr>
    <?php endforeach; ?>
</table>
</div>
```

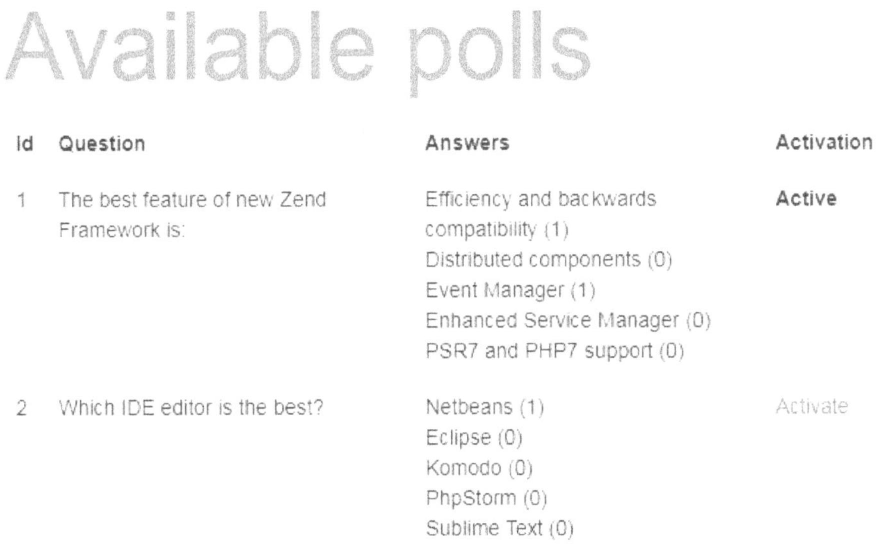

Available polls

Id	Question	Answers	Activation
1	The best feature of new Zend Framework is:	Efficiency and backwards compatibility (1) Distributed components (0) Event Manager (1) Enhanced Service Manager (0) PSR7 and PHP7 support (0)	**Active**
2	Which IDE editor is the best?	Netbeans (1) Eclipse (0) Komodo (0) PhpStorm (0) Sublime Text (0)	Activate

Image 13.1.

`activate` action calls a method activate from the `DivixUtils` library, after which it redirects back to the manage view. The most happens in the view action, which takes an actual active poll and the form to display it.

Additionally, we add an AJAX handlers to the form and triggers when the response comes back from the service.

```
<div class="jumbotron">
    <h1><span class="zf-green">Active poll</span></h1>
    <div class="pollsContainer">
        <?php
        echo $this->form()->openTag($form);
        echo $this->formHidden($form->get('csrf_field'));
        echo $poll->question;
        echo $this->formRow($form->get('answer'));
        echo $this->formSubmit($form->get('submit'));
        echo $this->form()->closeTag();
        ?>
    </div>
    <script>
        $(function() {
```

```
$('#poll').submit(function() {
    var answer = $(this).find('input[type="radio"]:checked'),
    csrf = $(this).find('#csrf_field').val();

    if (answer.length != 1) {
        alert('Select answer');
    return false;
    }
    $.post({
        url: '/zend3/polls',
        data: JSON.stringify({
            answer: answer.val(),
            csrf: csrf
        }),
        headers: {
            'Accept': 'application/json',
            'Content-Type': 'application/json'
        }
    }).done(function(response) {
        if (response.success === true) {
            alert('Vote has been submitted.');
        } else if (response.message) {
            alert(response.message);
        }
    });
    return false;
    });
    });
    </script>
</div>
```

Everything, what JavaScript does is to register an event of the form submission, gets a value of csrf and the user's answer itself and passes it back in a form of the JSON characters together with the required headers.

13.2. A new library

Let's take a look at the `DivixUtils\Polls` library, which will be directly modifying and reusing the data from the poll file in XML. The file *polls.xml* itself will be created in the already existing folder *data/*. Its example content will be presented on the another page.

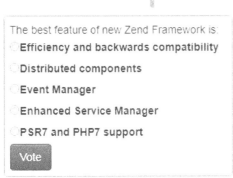

Image 13.2.

```xml
<?xml version="1.0" encoding="UTF-8"?>
<polls>
    <poll id="1" active="true">
        <question>The best feature of new Zend Framework is:</question>
        <answers>
            <answer votes="1">Efficiency and backwards compatibility</answer>
            <answer votes="0">Distributed components</answer>
            <answer votes="0">Event Manager</answer>
            <answer votes="0">Enhanced Service Manager</answer>
            <answer votes="0">PSR7 and PHP 7 support</answer>
        </answers>
    </poll>

    <poll id="2" active="false">
        <question>Which IDE is the the best?</question>
        <answers>
            <answer votes="1">Netbeans</answer>
            <answer votes="0">Eclipse</answer>
            <answer votes="0">Komodo</answer>
            <answer votes="0">PhpStorm</answer>
```

```
            <answer votes="0">Sublime Text</answer>
        </answers>
    </poll>
</polls>
```

By default we only have two polls: the first about the Zend Framework 3 and the second about an IDE selection. Each of them has 5 available answers (of course there can be more or less of them; our poll handles every amount of the answers). We can freely add or remove new polls to a file, we just need to remember to assign an unique ID number for each of them. An additional information about actual active polls is stored in the active attribute, which is set as TRUE for the active element. A number of given votes is stored in the attribute votes="0", available for each of the answers.

If we already have a XML file in the *data/* folder, we can add a library for managing it – for starters a Form class, which will be displaying a structure for the response in a Radio Buttons form and a CSRF field.

```
namespace DivixUtils\Polls;
use Zend\Form\Element;

class Form extends \Zend\Form\Form
{
    public function __construct(array $answers)
    {
        parent::__construct('poll');
        $this->add([
            'name' => 'csrf_field',
            'type' => 'csrf',
            'options' => [
                'salt' => 'unique',
                'timeout' => 300 //5 minutes
            ],
            'attributes' => array(
                'id' => 'csrf_field'
            )
        ]);

        $this->add(array(
            'name' => 'answer',
            'type' => Element\Radio::class,
            'options' => array(
                'value_options' => $answers
```

```
        ),
        'attributes' => array(
            'required' => 'required'
        )
    ));

    $this->add([
        'name' => 'submit',
        'type' => 'submit',
        'attributes' => [
            'value' => 'Vote',
            'id' => 'vote',
            'class' => 'btn btn-primary'
        ]
    ]);
    $this->setAttribute('method', 'POST');
    }
}
```

Our form is named via calling a constructor of the base class together with an actual name as a first argument; in our example it is poll. Next, we attach a hidden CSRF element with the name csrf_field, which is generated via 'unique' salt, and we set its time limit to 300 seconds. The salt in such example is the way of generating a hash, which will be used as a value of the CSRF filed. It's important to remember that if we want to use the CSRF field in two places on the same page, the best practice is to generate a field name in a way it will be unique for every form instance. The next step is to add an answer element that will display single selection fields of available answers. At the end we add a submit button Vote, which additionally gets an ID attribute – we will use it in JavaScript.

Let's have a look now at *Poll.php* class that combines everything together. There is a lot to describe, hence I've split that class into a few parts.

```
namespace DivixUtils\Polls;
class Polls
{
    private $xmlPolls;
    private $xmlPath = 'data/polls.xml';
    private $cache;
    private $message;
    private $form;
```

```
const CACHE_KEY = 'poll_voters';

public function __construct()
{
    $this->xmlPolls = new \SimpleXMLElement(file_get_contents($this->xmlPath));
    $this->cache = \Zend\Cache\StorageFactory::factory(array(
        'adapter' => array(
            'name' => 'filesystem',
            'options' => array(
                'cacheDir' => 'data/cache'
            )
        ),
        'plugins' => array(
            //do not throw exceptions, when a cache key is unrecognized
            'exception_handler' => array(
                'throw_exceptions' => false
            )
        )
    ));

    //let's initialize an empty object as our starting cache, if cache does not exists yet
    if (!$this->cache->getItem(self::CACHE_KEY)) {
        $this->cache->setItem(self::CACHE_KEY, '{}');
    }
}
```

We have over five class variables and one constant with name CACHE_KEY
that stores a key, under which we saved our data about the votes in the cache
text file. In sequence: $xmlPolls stores an XML file content in the
SimpleXML form. $xmlPath is a path to the XML file with polls. $cache is
on the other hand a local memory of Zend\Cache based on text files saved
on the disk at *data/cache*. $message contains the last information about the
error or issue resulting from getting or submitting a new vote. The last
variable, $form, stores a form instance of the DivixUtils\Polls\Form to
check its correctness. In in the last configuration lines of the constructor we
set a silent script work in order not to receive exceptions. We do that because
of another line that initializes an empty cache if it doesn't exists yet.

```
public function getAll()
{
    return $this->xmlPolls;
}
```

238

```php
public function getActive($getIndex = false)
{
    $index = 0;
    foreach ($this->xmlPolls as $poll) {
        if ($poll['active'] == 'true') {
            return $getIndex ? $index : $poll;
        }
        $index++;
    }
    throw new \Exception('active poll has not been found');
}

public function getActiveInJson()
{
    return \Zend\Xml2Json\Xml2Json::fromXml($this->getActive()->asXML(), false);
}
```

First methods return a full list of available polls and a currently active one. An argument `$getIndex` determines if the method should return just the index of the found poll TRUE, or by default the whole object of SimpleXMLElement. In case the poll is not created yet, we display an exception about it missing. The method `getActiveInJson` returns a currently active poll in JSON format via newly attached Zend component: Xml2Json. An optional second parameter additionally determines if the attributes of each element should be returned (FALSE) or ignored (default TRUE).

```php
public function activate($id)
{
    $found = false;
    foreach ($this->xmlPolls as $poll) {
        if ($poll['id'] == $id) {
            $poll['active'] = 'true';
            $found = true;
        } else {
            $poll['active'] = 'false';
        }
    }

    if (!$found) {
        throw \Exception('poll with id not found: '.$id);
    }
    //save a data into file
```

```php
            $this->save();
    }

    public function canVote($givenAnswer)
    {
        $poll = $this->getActive();
        $result = $this->findAnswer($poll, $givenAnswer);
        $votersCache = json_decode($this->cache->getItem(self::CACHE_KEY), true);
        $ip = $this->getUserIp();

        if (!$result) {
            $this->message = 'Invalid answer';
            return false;
        }
        if (isset($votersCache[$ip])) {
            if ($votersCache[$ip] < time()) {
                //limit expired, so delete a record from the cache
                unset($votersCache[$ip]);
                $this->cache->setItem(self::CACHE_KEY, json_encode($votersCache));
            } else {
                $this->message = 'You have already voted';
                return false;
            }
        }
        return true;
    }
```

An activate method takes care of marking a new poll as an active one, and at the same time it resets all other pols by setting them as inactive. At the end it updates an XML file by `save()` method. A function `canVote()` is more interesting – it checks if there is a possibility to submit a vote of a given answer as `$givenAnswer`. Here we execute a range of the condition checks to validate the correctness of a specific answer and if it exists in given poll. We begin from checking if the given answer exists in the active poll at all: `findAnswer()`. Then we grab a local cache of voters and convert it into a regular array, and we grab their IP address used to vote. Our cache stores voters' IPs and timestamps of a last vote. If the voting time is shorter than an actual time (the limit exceeded), we modify a cache and delete this record from the local file. Otherwise we display an error message that the user had already voted. If, however, an IP address of a voter is not found in the file, we return `TRUE`.

```php
public function addVote($givenAnswer)
{
    $pollIndex = $this->getActive(true);
    $index = 0;
    foreach ($this->xmlPolls->poll[$pollIndex]->answers->answer as $answer) {
        if ($answer->__toString() === $givenAnswer) {
            //add a vote
            (int) $this->xmlPolls->poll[$pollIndex]->answers->
↪answer[$index]['votes'] += 1;
            //save user details in cache
            $votersCache = json_decode($this->cache->getItem(self::CACHE_KEY),
↪true);
            $votersCache[$this->getUserIp()] = strtotime('+1 day');
            $this->cache->setItem(self::CACHE_KEY, json_encode($votersCache));
            //store data into file
            $this->save();
            return;
        }
        $index++;
    }
    throw new \Exception('vote was not added');
}
```

Our main method is obviously `addVote()` that adds a vote to the poll itself. In this method, however, we do not check the form validation or the answer – we have already done it in the previous method `canVote()`. By iterating all available answers, we check if a given answer equals to the already existing ones. If so, we add a vote by adding another vote into an existing number. Next, we add the user into a local cache file that stores all the voters together with IP and timestamp (date + time) which is 24 hours ahead of the current date. At the very end we store those details back to the file and break the foreach loop. If, however, our loop does not stop, we need to display an exception about not added vote in a poll.

```php
public function getMessage()
{
    return $this->message;
}

public function getForm()
{
    if (!$this->form) {
        $answers = [];
```

```
        foreach ($this->getActive()->answers->answer as $answer) {
            if (empty($answer)) {
                continue;
            }
            $answer = (string) $answer;
            $answers[$answer] = $answer;
        }
        $this->form = new \DivixUtils\Polls\Form($answers);
    }
    return $this->form;
}
```

In our library we use access methods such as `getMessage()` so that we can control the information and isolate a value of our message to the class itself. The `getForm` method returns only a single instance of the `Form` form, which will contains an actual answers from the active poll. All the empty values are ignored before adding them to the form.

```
private function findAnswer($poll, $givenAnswer)
{
    $found = false;
    if (empty($givenAnswer)) {
        return false;
    }
    foreach ($poll->answers->answer as $answer) {
        if ($answer->__toString() === $givenAnswer) {
            $found = true;
            break;
        }
    }
    return $found;
}

private function save()
{
    file_put_contents($this->xmlPath, $this->xmlPolls->asXML());
}

private function getUserIp()
{
    if (!empty($_SERVER['HTTP_CLIENT_IP'])) {
        $ip = $_SERVER['HTTP_CLIENT_IP'];
    } elseif (!empty($_SERVER['HTTP_X_FORWARDED_FOR'])) {
        $ip = $_SERVER['HTTP_X_FORWARDED_FOR'];
```

```
    } else {
        $ip = $_SERVER['REMOTE_ADDR'];
    }
    return $ip;
}
```

Three last methods: `findAnswer()`, `save()` and `getUserIp()` are marked as private and they should not be available in the public. This is due to the forcing the control of the XML file format for the two first methods, however the last one isolates obtained values of the IP address from the request.

13.3. New API endpoints

In order to make our JavaScript layer have an ability to contact with our poll via AJAX calls, we have to add a few services of type RPC called *Polls* in Apigility.

We begin by creating such RPC service with value route: */polls* and available methods HTTP: GET and POST. In the *Fields* tab we add two parameters: `answer` and `csrf`. Each of them will have just one validator: `Zend\I18n\Validator\Alnum` and with value `allowwhitespace` together with the filter `Zend\Filter\StringTrim`; of course each of them is also a required attribute. To create a controller `Polls` service, we would need just a single class object of `DivixUtils\Polls\Polls`, which we would get from Service Manager:

```
namespace ApplicationApi\V1\Rpc\Polls;
class PollsControllerFactory
{
    public function __invoke($controllers)
    {
        return new PollsController($controllers->get(\DivixUtils\Polls\Polls::class));
    }
}
```

However, the class `PollsController` in package `ApplicationApi`, looks like so:

```
namespace ApplicationApi\V1\Rpc\Polls;
use Zend\Mvc\Controller\AbstractActionController;
use ZF\ContentNegotiation\ViewModel;

class PollsController extends AbstractActionController
{
    private $pollsLibrary;

    public function __construct($pollsLibrary)
    {
        $this->pollsLibrary = $pollsLibrary;
    }
    public function pollsAction()
    {
        if ($_SERVER['REQUEST_METHOD'] === 'GET') {
            exit($this->pollsLibrary->getActiveInJson());
        }
        $inputFilter = $this->getEvent()->getParam('ZF\ContentValidation\
↪InputFilter');
        $answer = $inputFilter->getValue('answer');
        $csrf = $inputFilter->getValue('csrf');
        $response = false;
        $message = null;
        $pollForm = $this->pollsLibrary->getForm();
        $pollForm->setData(['answer' => $answer, 'csrf_field' => $csrf]);

        if (!$pollForm->isValid()) {
            $message = 'Incorrectly completed form';
        } else {
            if ($this->pollsLibrary->canVote($answer)) {
                $this->pollsLibrary->addVote($answer);
                $response = true;
            } elseif (!is_null($this->pollsLibrary->getMessage())) {
                $message = $this->pollsLibrary->getMessage();
            }
        }
        return new ViewModel([
            'success' => $response,
            'message' => $message
        ]);
    }
}
```

In the only action `pollAction`, we do a request type check. If it is a regular GET, then we return a current active poll, otherwise we treat the request as POST. The first thing is to grab the value of `$answer` and `$csrf`, which we pass to the form via a call `setData()`. Then we check the correctness of the form data by `isValid()` method. If something is wrong with the values, then we return an output as FALSE together with the error message. Otherwise, by using `canVote()` method from the library, we check if the user have not already voted on the same day. We also get a message about the error from the library itself by the `getMessage()`. If, however, the user is able to make a vote, then we execute `addVote()` method together with the response, after which we set an output as TRUE, to inform JavaScript about the successful request.

## CHAPTER 4

Registration and login

In chapter number 14 we are going to take care of the most fundamental feature of each web service - registration and login of the users. Our freshly registered user will be automatically signed in based on the provided credentials like an email and password, then we will create a session that will remember the user's account data. We will present the login as a displayed form that will take an email address and password just like before, so that the already added to the system user is able to login back on his account. After the successful login we should replace the register and login links with a link to the user's profile page and a logout link in the website header.

14.1. Users registration

We will begin our fun with the registration by adding missing dependences from the *vendor/* folder. If you walked over all the previous chapters, then we only need to add a single library Zend Captcha, which we will use in a moment. It is a component that generates an image with random text on it, which a user had to rewrite in order to prove that he is not a spam bot. Let's open XAMPP Shell and attach that new dependency:

```
composer require zendframework/zend-captcha
```

As a standard, we first set a router configuration and `RegisterController` controller itself in the *module.config.php* file.

```
'register' => [
    'type' => Literal::class,
    'options' => [
        'route' => '/register',
        'defaults' => [
            'controller' => Controller\RegisterController::class,
            'action' => 'index',
        ],
    ],
],
```

At the beginning we set a registration controller into a single address */register* without segmental checking other actions. To create our new controller we however need a few extra classes in addition to `UsersTable` for user authentication.

```
Controller\RegisterController::class => function($sm) {
    return new Controller\RegisterController(
        $sm->get(Model\UsersTable::class),
        $sm->get(\DivixUtils\Security\Authentication::class),
        $sm->get(\DivixUtils\Security\Helper::class)
    );
},
```

We have added a new sub package with the name `Security` to our own `DivixUtils` package, in which there are such classes as: `Adapter`, `Authentication` or `Helper`. We set their definitions in Service Manager in the *Module.php* file like below:

```
\DivixUtils\Security\Authentication::class => function($sm) {
    $auth = new \DivixUtils\Security\Authentication($sm->get(\
↪Zend\Db\Adapter\Adapter::class));
    return $auth;
},
\DivixUtils\Security\Helper::class => InvokableFactory::class,
```

Let's get familiar with their contents. `Security\Adapter` is so far only an empty class, which extends `Zend\Authentication\Adapter\DbTable\`

↪CredentialTreatmentAdapter. A base class sets an authentication based on the provided plain user information from the database and through built-in hash RDBMS functions, like MD5() or SHA1() in MySQL. Another option is use of the CallbackCheckAdapter class, in which instead of using a function from databases for hashing and verification, we execute our own provided callback function. However, if you already used the class Adapter\DbTable before, then it needs replacing with CredentialTreatmentAdapter, which works in the very similar way.

Another class from the DivixUtils\Secrutiy package is: Authnetication:

```php
namespace DivixUtils\Security;
class Authentication {
    protected $adapter;
    protected $dbAdapter;
    public function __construct($dbAdapter) {
        $this->dbAdapter = $dbAdapter;
        $this->adapter = new Adapter(
            $this->dbAdapter,
            'users',
            'email',
            'password',
            'SHA2(CONCAT(password_salt, "'.Helper::SALT_KEY."', ?), 512)'
        );
    }

    public function authenticate($email, $password) {
        if (empty($email) || empty($password)) {
            return false;
        }
        $this->adapter->setIdentity($email);
        $this->adapter->setCredential($password);
        $result = $this->adapter->authenticate();
        return $result;
    }

    public function getIdentity() {
        return $this->getAdapter()->getResultRowObject();
    }

    public function getIdentityArray()
    {
```

```
        return json_decode(json_encode($this->adapter->getResultRowObject()), true);
    }

    public function getAdapter() {
        return $this->adapter;
    }
}
```

In the above class we define in what way Zend should map our table, column names, email and password. Additionally, for the purpose of this chapter we will create a system that uses the strongest one-way encryption option available in MySQL 5, so-called SHA512 and a salt. MySQL offers many password hashing options, for instance SHA1(), MD5() or SHA2(). All of these mechanisms prevent from password leakages when our if or server is be hacked. Additionally, the salt is an element of hashing mechanisms, which increases the password security level. Salt value can be dynamic or static. In the code fragment:

```
'SHA2(CONCAT(password_salt, "'.Helper::SALT_KEY.'", ?), 512)'
```

you can easily get wrong with assuming that we are using an SHA2 algorithm. The second parameter of this method explains however that we are using a 512-bits variation of this function. The first argument of this function is connected by MySQL CONCAT function, which takes two or more arguments to merge everything into one string. In above example we get a column value of password_salt that we add to the table in a second, then we get a static key from the DivixUitls\Security\Helper class, and at the end we attach a plain password input by the user. Such generated hash would need 128 characters to be stored in the password column – this also needs to be modified in the database table itself.

A method: authenticate() executes a whole jigsaw; it gets values of email and password, sets them properly to the already created adapter and executes the same method on it, then it returns a result. The helper class itself looks like below:

```
namespace DivixUtils\Security;
class Helper
{
    const SALT_KEY = 'FG%7h62CXhi9@zq';
```

```php
/**
 * Generates password of type: sha512 and with passed salte for hashng.
 *
 * @param string $phrase plain password
 * @param string $salt optional salt
 *
 * @return string
 */
public function sha512($phrase, $salt = null)
{
    $result = array();
    if ($salt == null) {
        $salt = $this->generatePassword(8);
    }
    $result['salt'] = $salt;
    $result['hash'] = hash('sha512', $salt.self::SALT_KEY.$phrase);
    return $result;
}

/**
 * Generates a random password
 *
 * @param int $maximumLength max length of the password
 *
 * @return string
 */
public function generatePassword($maximumLength = 14)
{
    $chars = 'qwertyuipasdfghjkzxcvbnm23456789QWERTYUPASDFGHJKCVBNM';
    $shuffle = str_shuffle($chars);
    return substr($shuffle, 0, rand(4, $maximumLength));
}
}
```

Apart from the class constant SALT_KEY, we have two methods here: sha512() that returns an array with two elements (a hash and salt), and generatePassword(), which on the other hand generates a password based on the given length data. An advantage of the second method is the lack of letters and numbers, which looks similar for the user, like: l, 1, O or 0. Because it is our helper class, we have added appropriate comments in a dockblock format to it, which is a documentation standard in almost every programming language. Let's go back however to the Register controller class that will be using a new Security package and pass a data from a form to it:

```
namespace Application\Controller;
use Application\Form;
use Application\Model;
use Application\Hydrator;
use Zend\Session;

class RegisterController extends AbstractController {
    protected $usersModel;
    protected $securityAuth;
    protected $securityHelper;

    public function __construct($usersModel, $securityAuth, $securityHelper)
    {
        $this->usersModel = $usersModel;
        $this->securityAuth = $securityAuth;
        $this->securityHelper = $securityHelper;
    }

    public function indexAction() {
        $form = new Form\UserRegisterForm(
            'user_register',
            [
                'dbAdapter' => $this->usersModel->getTableGateway()->getAdapter(),
                'baseUrl' => $this->baseUrl
            ]
        );
        $viewParams = [
            'userForm' => $form
        ];
        if ($this->getRequest()->isPost()) { $form->setData($this->
↪getRequest()->getPost());
            if ($form->isValid()) {
                $rowset = new Model\Rowset\User();
                $hydrator = new Hydrator\UserFormHydrator($this->
↪securityHelper);
                $formData = $form->getData();
                $rowset->exchangeArray($hydrator->hydrate($form));

                //store to database
                $userId = $this->usersModel->save($rowset);
                $rowset->setId($userId);
                //user logging
```

```
            $this->securityAuth->authenticate(
                $rowset->getEmail(),
                $formData[$form::FIELDSET_LOGIN][Form\
↪UserLoginFieldset::ELEMENT_PASSWORD]
            );
            $identity = $this->securityAuth->getIdentityArray();
            if ($identity) {
                //session creation
                exit('user logged in');
            } else {
                throw new \Exception('Something went bad.. Check if
↪the user has been added to db');
            }
        } else {
            $viewParams['messages'] = $form->getMessages();
        }
    }
    return $viewParams;
}
```

A newly used method `$this->getBaseUrl()` has been defined in `AbstarctController` like so:

```
protected $baseUrl;
public function onDispatch(MvcEvent $e) {
    $this->baseUrl = $this->getRequest()->getBasePath();
    return parent::onDispatch($e);
}
```

The only action in the controller, `indexAction()` creates and then generates a registration form with name user_register and, if it is just a GET request, then it only generates a HTML that needs to be added to the folder *view/application/register/index.phtml*:

```
<section class="page-content">
    <div class="container jumbotron">
        <!-- registration -->
        <div class="formContainer">
            <div class="row">
                <div class="col-md-6">
                    <div class="box">
                        <h3><span class="glyphicon glyphicon-user"></span>
↪Registration</h3>
                            <?= isset($messages) ? print_r($messages) : '' ?>
```

```php
                    <?php
                    $userForm->prepare();
                    echo $this->form()->openTag($userForm);
                    echo $this->formRow($userForm->get('user_username')->
↪get('username'));
                    echo $this->formRow($userForm->get('user_login')->
↪get('email'));
                    echo $this->formRow($userForm->get('user_login')->
↪get('password'));
                    echo $this->formRow($userForm->get('confirm_
↪password'));
                    echo $this->formRow($userForm->get('captcha'));
                    echo $this->formHidden($userForm->get('user_login')->
↪get('users_csrf'));

                    echo $this->formSubmit($userForm->get('submit'));
                    echo $this->form()->closeTag();
                    ?>
                </div>
            </div>
            <div class="col-md-6">
                <div class="alert alert-info">
                    Fill all the form fileds, to register as new user to the website.
                </div>
            </div>
        </div>
    </div>
  </div>
</section>
```

Our form will contain a total of 6 fields: user name, email, password, confirm password, captcha and hidden CSRF. The CSRF field is used to make sure that the form has been submitted via our website only and not any external one. If we would try to send a correctly filled form, a controller's fragment will be executed to start the registration process. It's worth to notice that we cannot use the method $form->bind($rowset) here, since our field names have been moved into another objects, so the email field is no longer set via alias email, but user_login[email]. The controller will set the form data to the request one, next it will check the correctness of the data in form. Then it will fill the data of the form into the Rowset\User object. For this purpose, it is best to use a hydrator that would returns the properly processed data – which later we would pass to the exhchangeArray() method. We add our newly created UserFormHydrator to the Application\Hydrator (a folder we need to create ourselves).

```
namespace Application\Hydrator;
use Application\Form;
class UserFormHydrator implements \Zend\Hydrator\Strategy\StrategyInterface
{
    protected $securityHelper;

    public function __construct($securityHelper)
    {
        $this->securityHelper = $securityHelper;
    }

    public function hydrate($form)
    {
        if (!$form instanceof \Application\Form\UserRegisterForm) {
            throw new \Exception('invalid form object passed to the
↪'.__CLASS__);
        }
        $data = $form->getData();
        $hashedPassword = $this->securityHelper->sha512($data[$form:
↪:FIELDSET_LOGIN][Form\UserLoginFieldset::ELEMENT_PASSWORD]);
        return [
            'username' => $data[$form::FIELDSET_USERNAME][Form\
↪UsernameFieldset::ELEMENT_USERNAME],
            'email' => $data[$form::FIELDSET_LOGIN][Form\
↪UserLoginFieldset::ELEMENT_EMAIL],
            'password' => $hashedPassword['hash'],
            'password_salt' => $hashedPassword['salt']
        ];
    }

    public function extract($array)
    {
        return $array;
    }
}
```

We also pass an object of `Security\Helper` to our hydrator, which will be used to generate a `SHA512` password. A basic hydrator of type `StrategyInterface`, which we have used above, requires two methods: `hydrate()` and `extract()`. In the first method we add the logic, however the second method will only return a passed table. At the very beginning of the `hydrate()` method we check the type of a passed form. If it is not as expected (`UserRegisterForm`), then we throw an exception about this message. Next lines of the code are correlated to creating and returning the prepared array, so that it is properly interpreted by the `UserTableRowset` object.

We can store such prepared and set `Rowset` object into a database by calling:

```
$userId = $this->usersModel->save($rowset);
$rowset->setId($userId);
```

together with that we set its newly created id number from the database table and execute a login bit:

```
$this->securityAuth->authenticate(
$rowset->getEmail(),
$formData[$form::FIELDSET_LOGIN][Form\UserLoginFieldset::ELEMENT_PASSWORD];
$identity = $this->securityAuth->getIdentityArray();
```

Keep in mind that we cannot pass a value of `$rowset->getPassword()`, as the data in `$rowset` object is just a hash with salt of the `sha512()` function. If we want to check if passed data is actually linked with the user in the database, we need to call `getIdentityArray()`, which will return an array with values from the users table. At the very end we will create a new user session, however the session concept itself will be described and implemented in another subsection of logging process. We will finish an actual subsection with explaining the way our new registration form looks and the way we have modified the rest of the forms.

`UserRegisterForm` has caused a small revolution in our previous forms. It is inevitable in order to not repeat the same elements in many form objects at the same time. Above it all, we have moved the username element into its own class `Form\UsernameFieldset`, and elements such as `email` and `password` into `Form\LoginFieldset`; thanks to that we are able to use the same field validators in different places on the site. A second big advantage of such refactoring is a relatively short class `UserRegistrationForm` that looks like this:

```
namespace Application\Form;
use Zend\Form\Element;
```

```php
class UserRegisterForm extends \Zend\Form\Form implements
\Zend\InputFilter\InputFilterProviderInterface
{
    const TIMEOUT = 300;
    const ELEMENT_PASSWORD_CONFIRM = 'confirm_password';
    const ELEMENT_CAPTCHA = 'captcha';
    const FIELDSET_USERNAME = 'user_username';
    const FIELDSET_LOGIN = 'user_login';

    public function __construct($name = 'register_user', $params)
    {
        parent::__construct($name, $params);
        $this->setAttribute('class', 'styledForm');
        $this->add([
            'type' => UsernameFieldset::class,
            'name' => self::FIELDSET_USERNAME
        ]);

        $this->add([
            'type' => UserLoginFieldset::class,
            'name' => self::FIELDSET_LOGIN,
            'options' => $params
        ]);

        $this->add([
            'name' => self::ELEMENT_PASSWORD_CONFIRM,
            'type' => Element\Password::class,
            'options' => [
                'label' => 'Repeat password',
            ],
            'attributes' => [
                'required' => true
            ],
        ]);

        $this->add([
            'name' => self::ELEMENT_CAPTCHA,
            'type' => Element\Captcha::class,
            'options' => [
                'label' => 'Rewrite Captcha text:',
                'captcha' => new \Zend\Captcha\Image([
                    'name' => 'myCaptcha',
                    'messages' => array(
                        'badCaptcha' => 'incorrectly rewritten image text'
```

```php
            ),
            'wordLen' => 5,
            'timeout' => self::TIMEOUT,
            'font' => APPLICATION_PATH.'/public/fonts/arbli.ttf',
            'imgDir' => APPLICATION_PATH.'/public/img/captcha/',
            'imgUrl' => $this->getOption('baseUrl').'/public/img/captcha/',
            'lineNoiseLevel' => 4,
            'width' => 200,
            'height' => 70
        ]),
    ]
]);

$this->add([
    'name' => 'submit',
    'type' => 'submit',
    'attributes' => [
        'value' => 'Register',
        'class' => 'btn btn-primary'
    ]
]);

$this->setAttribute('method', 'POST');
}

public function getInputFilterSpecification()
{
    return [
        [
            'name' => self::ELEMENT_PASSWORD_CONFIRM,
            'filters' => [
                ['name' => \Zend\Filter\StringTrim::class]
            ],
            'validators' => [
                [
                    'name' => \Zend\Validator\Identical::class,
                    'options' => [
                        'token' => ['user_login' => 'password'],
                        'messages' => [
                            \Zend\Validator\Identical::NOT_SAME =>
↪'Passwords are not the same'
                        ]
                    ]
                ]
            ]
```

```
                ]
            ]
        ];
    }
}
```

Notice that we have introduced here a class constants that represent element names of the form itself. Thanks to that, we are able to refer to them from outside of the form class without the need to remember and use the plain static strings. Our form contains a user name and elements of logging of two fieldset classes, an extra field to repeat a password and a `Captcha` element. In order to check if the repeated password is the same as the previous field, we should use a validator of: `Zend\Validator\Identical` and pass an array of error messages, which potentially could be displayed in the form.

We pass quite a large configuration to our `Captcha` element. An advantage of it is that the keys of configuration have not changed at all since Zend Framework 1. Here are a few described keys:

- `wordLen` – a length of characters to rewrite;

- `timeout` – a time which sets a lifecycle of our single captcha instance;

- `font` – an optional parameter that sets a path to the used custom font (we have to of course have a font in format *.ttf*);

- `imgDir` – an absolute location of where the generated `captcha` images will be placed;

- `imgUrl` – an URL address of a image;

- `lineNoiseLevel` – a level of noise in our image;

- `width` – a width of our image in pixels;

- `height` – a height of our image in pixels;

Notice that we have passed a second element in a form of array to our form.

It is a standard way of passing extra dependencies to the forms of fieldsets. To receive an element passed in such way, we call a method `$this->getOption('name')` at any place in the form, for instance in the `imgUrl` alias. In our form we also pass the same option as for the `UserLoginFieldset` element:

```
$this->add([
    'type' => UserLoginFieldset::class,
    'name' => self::FIELDSET_LOGIN,
    'options' => $params
]);
```

`UserLoginFieldset` needs a database adapter in order to verify if the user's passed value of email does not already exist in our database table. The content of that class is presented below:

```
namespace Application\Form;
use Zend\Form\Fieldset;
use Zend\InputFilter\InputFilterProviderInterface;
use Zend\Form\Element;

class UserLoginFieldset extends Fieldset implements InputFilterProviderInterface
{
    const TIMEOUT = 300;
    const ELEMENT_EMAIL = 'email';
    const ELEMENT_PASSWORD = 'password';
    const ELEMENT_CSRF = 'users_csrf';

    public function __construct()
    {
        parent::__construct('user_login');

        $this->add([
            'type' => Element\Email::class,
            'name' => self::ELEMENT_EMAIL,
            'attributes' => [
                'required' => true,
            ],
            'options' => [
                'label' => 'Email'
            ]
        ]);
```

```php
        $this->add([
            'name' => self::ELEMENT_PASSWORD,
            'type' => Element\Password::class,
            'options' => [
                'label' => 'Password',
            ],
            'attributes' => [
                'required' => true
            ],
        ]);

        $this->add([
            'name' => self::ELEMENT_CSRF,
            'type' => Element\Csrf::class,
            'options' => [
                'salt' => 'unique',
                'timeout' => self::TIMEOUT
            ],
            'attributes' => [
                'id' => self::ELEMENT_CSRF
            ]
        ]);
    }

    public function getInputFilterSpecification()
    {
        $validators = [
            [
                'name' => self::ELEMENT_EMAIL,
                'filters' => [
                    ['name' => \Zend\Filter\StringTrim::class]
                ],
                'validators' => [
                    [
                        'name' => \Zend\Validator\StringLength::class,
                        'options' => [
                            'min' => 5,
                            'messages' => [
                                \Zend\Validator\StringLength::TOO_SHORT =>
↪'Minimal length is: %min%'
                            ]
                        ]
                    ],
                    [
```

```php
                        'name' => 'EmailAddress',
                        'options' => array(
                        'messages' => array(
                                \Zend\Validator\EmailAddress::INVALID_FORMAT =>
↪'validator.email.format',
                                \Zend\Validator\EmailAddress::INVALID =>
↪'validator.email.general',
                                \Zend\Validator\EmailAddress::INVALID_HOSTNAME =>
↪'validator.email.hostname',
                                \Zend\Validator\EmailAddress::INVALID_LOCAL_PART =>
↪'validator.email.local',
                                \Zend\Validator\Hostname::UNKNOWN_TLD =>
↪'validator.email.unknown_domain',
                                \Zend\Validator\Hostname::LOCAL_NAME_NOT_ALLOWED
↪=>'validator.email.name_not_allowed'
                            )
                        )
                    ]
                ]
            ],
            [
                'name' => self::ELEMENT_PASSWORD,
                'required' => true,
                'filters' => [
                        ['name' => \Zend\Filter\StringTrim::class]
                ],
                'validators' => [
                        [
                                'name' => \Zend\Validator\StringLength::class,
                                'options' => [
                                        'min' => 5,
                                        'messages' => [
                                                \Zend\Validator\StringLength::TOO_SHORT =>
↪'Minimal length is: %min%'
                                        ]
                                ]
                        ]
                    ]
                ]
            ]
        ];

        //let's add extra DB validator to the register form, ignoring login form
        if (!empty($this->getOption('dbAdapter'))) {
            $validators[0]['validators'][] = [
```

```
            'name' => \Zend\Validator\Db\NoRecordExists::class,
            'options' => array(
                'adapter' => $this->getOption('dbAdapter'),
                'table' => 'users',
                'field' => 'email',
                'messages' => array(
                    \Zend\Validator\Db\NoRecordExists::ERROR_RECORD_FOUND
    ↪=>'Such email address already exists in database'
                )
            )
        ];
    }
    return $validators;
    }
}
```

Apart from the general checking of the minimal amount of characters and email address format, we have a dynamic validator at the end that we append only when we pass a parameter `dbAdapter` to the options list while creating that element. We perform a check of the record in DB via the class `Zend]Validator\Db\NoRecordExists`, which returns `TRUE` when the record is not found. We configure it in a pretty straightforward way by passing an information about the table, column and its own error messages. On the other hand a class `Form\UsernameFieldset` looks very simple and contains only a single element and the validator of the minimal character length. From that reason we would not present it in this chapter in order to save some paper :)

At the end, let's not to forget to modify our users table, which from now on should look like the following:

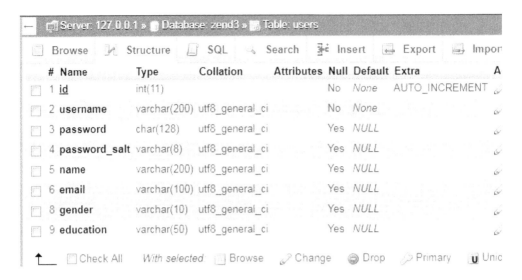

Image 14.1.

After walking through all the steps mentioned in this section, our registration page should look similar to the image below:

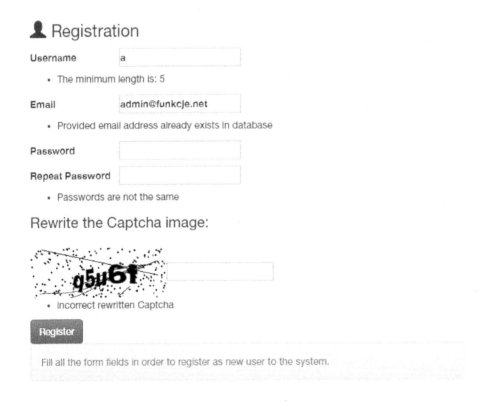

Image 14.2.

14.2. Logging in

Once we have the registration of the new users covered, we should also provide logging to the system based on already processed information by the email and password. This purpose is going to be covered in this section. Again, we begin from defining a configuration of dependencies of the controller and for the new router entries in the *module.config.php* file:

```
controllers' => [
    ...
    Controller\LoginController::class => function($sm) {
        return new Controller\LoginController(
            $sm->get(\DivixUtils\Security\Authentication::class)
        );
    },
    ...
    'routes' => [
        ...
        'login' => [
            'type' => Segment::class,
            'options' => [
                'route' => '/login[/:action]',
                'defaults' => [
                    'controller' => Controller\LoginController::class,
                    'action' => 'index',
                ],
            ],
        ],
```

We have defined a login router as a Segment type; thanks to that in the later stages we will be able to add features like password reminder or logging by Facebook. The login controller itself will contain three main actions:

- indexAction(), which will handle the process of sending a login form;

- `progressUserAction()` for redirecting the user after a successful login;

- `logoutAction()` for logging out an actually logged in user in a current session.

The controller, same as `RegisterController`, will be using a library `DivixUtils\Security\Authentication` to perform an authentication of the user. However, the code for logging in contains much fewer lines because it processes less data passed in the request by the user. Let's have a closer look at it:

```
namespace Application\Controller;
use Application\Model;
use Zend\Session;
use Application\Form;

class LoginController extends AbstractController
{
    protected $securityAuth;

    public function __construct($securityAuth)
    {
        $this->securityAuth = $securityAuth;
    }
    public function indexAction()
    {
        $form = new Form\UserLoginForm();
        if (!$this->getRequest()->isPost()) {
            return [
                'form' => $form
            ];
        }
        $form->setData($this->getRequest()->getPost());

        if (!$form->isValid()) {
            return [
                'form' => $form,
                'messages' => $form->getMessages()
            ];
        }
```

```php
        $auth = $this->securityAuth->authenticate(
            $form->get($form::FIELDSET_LOGIN)->get('email')->getValue(),
            $form->get($form::FIELDSET_LOGIN)->get('password')->getValue()
        );
        $identity = $this->securityAuth->getIdentityArray();
        if ($identity) {
            $rowset = new Model\Rowset\User();
            $rowset->exchangeArray($identity);
            //session creation later in this chapter
            return $this->redirect()->toRoute('login', ['action' => 'progressuser']);
        } else {
            $message = '<strong>Error</strong> Given email address or password is
↪incorrect.';
            return [
                'form' => $form,
                'messages' => $message
            ];
        }
    }

    public function progressUserAction()
    {
        $prefix = $_SERVER['REQUEST_SCHEME'].'://'.$_SERVER['HTTP_HOST'].$this->
↪baseUrl;
        if ($_SERVER['HTTP_REFERER'] !== $prefix.'/register' &&
            $_SERVER['HTTP_REFERER'] !== $prefix.'/login'
        ) {
            return $this->redirect()->toUrl($_SERVER['HTTP_REFERER'], 302);
        }
        $this->redirect()->toRoute('user');
    }

    public function logoutAction()
    {
    }
}
```

In the first place an index action does a check if the request is of a POST type
– if it is not, we return the form data to the view and we stop the whole
action. When, however, the form is submitted and the POST is sent with all
correct details, then we pass the data from a form to the authenticate()
method. We have applied a format with getters ->get(), which returns the
whole element of the form. If, however, we have a form field inside the

nested fieldset, we must first get a group of elements by `$form->get($form::FIELDSET_LOGIN)`, then we can finally refer to the email field by `->get('email')`; and at the end call `getValue()` to display an element value only. If the submitted data is matching with the one in the database, we redirect the user into another action `progressUserAction()`, which is responsible for redirecting it further. A second action method checks if the previous page has not been a registration or login page, as in such example we should redirect the user back to the same page. Having a login form in the page header is a very common feature. Otherwise, we redirect the user to the `UserController` controller that will be created in the next section. Let's have a look at how our newly created `UserLoginForm` form looks like:

```php
namespace Application\Form;

class UserLoginForm extends \Zend\Form\Form
{
    const FIELDSET_LOGIN = 'login_fieldset';

    public function __construct($name = 'login_user')
    {
        parent::__construct($name);
        $this->setAttribute('class', 'styledForm');

        $this->add([
            'type' => UserLoginFieldset::class,
            'name' => self::FIELDSET_LOGIN
        ]);

        $this->add([
            'name' => 'submit',
            'type' => 'submit',
            'attributes' => [
                'value' => 'Login',
                'class' => 'btn btn-primary'
            ]
        ]);
        $this->setAttribute('method', 'POST');
    }
}
```

As we could predict, it only contains a `fieldset` with the data about login and its own button for submitting the form. Notice that we do not pass an `'options'` parameter to the `UserLoginFieldset`; thanks to which we would not need to display an error regarding the already existing user in DB.

Our login view will be as short as the login form itself – apart from the calls to render the `email` and `password` fields, we will also add a `CSRF` element and display an empty array of errors on the top of the form.

```
<section class="page-content">
    <div class="container jumbotron">
        <!-- login -->
        <div class="formContainer">
            <div class="row">
                <div class="col-md-6">
                    <div class="box">
                        <h3><span class="glyphicon glyphicon-lock"></span>
↪Logging</h3>
                        <?php isset($messages) ? print_r($messages) : '' ?>
                        <?php
                        $form->prepare();
                        echo $this->form()->openTag($form);
                        echo $this->formRow($form->get('login_fieldset')->
↪get('email'));
                        echo $this->formRow($form->get('login_fieldset')->
↪get('password'));
                        echo $this->formRow($form->get('login_fieldset')->
↪get('users_csrf'));
                        echo $this->formSubmit($form->get('submit'));
                        echo $this->form()->closeTag();
                        ?>
                    </div>
                </div>
                <div class="col-md-6">
                </div>
            </div>
        </div>
    </div>
</section>
```

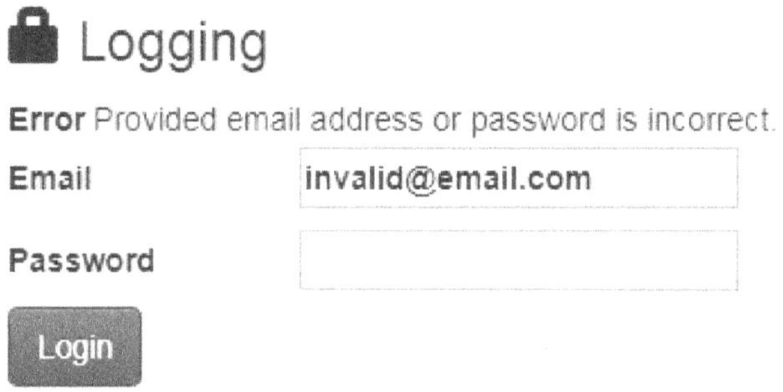

🔒 Logging

Error Provided email address or password is incorrect.

Email   invalid@email.com

Password

[Login]

Image 14.3.

14.3. Session

It's finally time for dessert, which is creating and using the session of the registered and logged in users. A session concept have changed in the new Zend versions in some way. The session is now generated for each guest visiting our page. The only difference between a logged in user and a guest is adding some values to a session, based on which we will be checking the status of such visitor. In Zend Framework 1 the session alone consists of objects of type Zend\Session\Namespace – they have been created to store the specific data in the session. In the new version of Zend that concept has been transformed into Zend\Session\Container, which works similarly to the previous versions. Creating a session alone has changed a lot. The usage of Service Manager and lack of the *Bootstrap.php* file have required another approach to the session subject in Zend 3. This is why we would share a new method onBootstrap() in the *Module.php* file – we can override a default function with our own code implementation, which we would call every time our site is requested. Be careful not to place large code chunks in this fragment, as it would affect the performance of our application. Let's modify the *Module.php* file to initialize our session:

```php
public function onBootstrap($e)
{
    $this->bootstrapSession($e);
}

public function bootstrapSession($e)
{
    $serviceManager = $e->getApplication()->getServiceManager();
    $session = $serviceManager->get(SessionManager::class);
    ...
}
```

Our whole code has been separated from the session into a more specific `bootstrapSession()` method, which would do all the session set. First, we get a Service Manager instance, then we grab a session manager, which we will define in the factories key like below:

```php
SessionManager::class => function ($container) {
    $config = $container->get('config');
    $session = $config['session'];
    $sessionConfig = new $session['config']['class']();
    $sessionConfig->setOptions($session['config']['options']);
    $sessionManager = new Session\SessionManager(
        $sessionConfig,
        new $session['storage'](),
        null
    );
    \Zend\Session\Container::setDefaultManager($sessionManager);
    return $sessionManager;
}
```

Take a closer look, at we need a `'use Zend\Session;'` usage at the top of the file. The first new factory definition lines get some data from the config key and another nested key `'session'`. We have added this configuration into a *global.php* file:

```php
'session' => [
    'config' => [
        'class' => \Zend\Session\Config\SessionConfig::class,
        'options' => [
            'name' => 'session_name',
        ],
    ],
```

```
    'storage' => \Zend\Session\Storage\SessionArrayStorage::class,
    'validators' => [
        \Zend\Session\Validator\RemoteAddr::class,
        \Zend\Session\Validator\HttpUserAgent::class,
    ],
]
```

Generally speaking, we have informed Zend about the type of session we want to create. The session class itself is the basic information. In our example we will use a standard `Zend\Session\Config\SessionConfig`, name, a type of the session storage and a list of the session validators, which will make sure that our session has been created by the right user and not the hacker by using a Session Injection.

However, going back to the *Module.php*, we create a `SessionManager` class, which takes exactly the above configuration from the other field, then we describe by `setDefaultManager()` that this is our default manager of all sessions. Thanks to that we will be able to refer to `new Session\Container()` in any other PHP file, which by default is linked to the default application session. Let's finish a `bootstrapSession()` method:

```php
public function bootstrapSession($e)
{
    $serviceManager = $e->getApplication()->getServiceManager();
    $session = $serviceManager->get(SessionManager::class);
    $session->start();
    $container = new Session\Container('initialized');

    //let's check if our session is not already created (for the guest or user)
    if (isset($container->init)) {
        return;
    }

    //new session creation
    $request = $serviceManager->get('Request');
    $session->regenerateId(true);
    $container->init = 1;
    $container->remoteAddr = $request->getServer()->get('REMOTE_ADDR');
    $container->httpUserAgent = $request->getServer()->get('HTTP_USER_AGENT');
    $config = $serviceManager->get('Config');
    $sessionConfig = $config['session'];
    $chain = $session->getValidatorChain();
```

```
foreach ($sessionConfig['validators'] as $validator) {
    switch ($validator) {
        case Validator\HttpUserAgent::class:
            $validator = new $validator($container->httpUserAgent);
        break;
        case Validator\RemoteAddr::class:
            $validator = new $validator($container->remoteAddr);
        break;
        default:
            $validator = new $validator();
    }
    $chain->attach('session.validate', array($validator, 'isValid'));
    }
}
```

We begin with starting the session by a `start()` method, then we create a sample session container, which we call `'initialized'`. If we already have a prepared and validated session in the browser, then we can finish an execution of the method. A condition responsible for handling that is a sample `$container->init` – it is executed later in that method. In order to create a new session, we get a `Request` object, then we generate an id session number and we assign a default variables to the `Container`, like: init, `remoteAddr` and `httpUserAgent`. We retrieve the two latest data from the request object. Then we grab a configuration from the *global.php* file once more by `$servicemanager->get('Config')` in order to get its object and available session validators. Currently, we have two validators: `HttpUserAgent` (verifies a browser used by the user) and `RemoteAddr` (checks an IP address used to connect to the website). If one of these is incorrect or automatically changes itself, we logout the user straight away. At the end, we pass such prepared validator to the event of name `session.validate`, because the above code is executed only once per session.

With such prepared and available session in Bootstrap, we can fill our register and login controllers the way it is showed below:

Register:

```
if ($identity) {
    //session creation
    $sessionUser = new Session\Container('user');
```

```
    $sessionUser->details = $rowset;
    return $this->redirect()->toRoute('login', ['action' => 'progressuser']);
} else {
    throw new \Exception('Something went wrong.. Check if the user has been
↪added tot he database correctly');
}
```

Login:

```
if ($identity) {
    $rowset = new Model\Rowset\User();
    $rowset->exchangeArray($identity);
    $sessionUser = new Session\Container('user');
    $sessionUser->details = $rowset;
    return $this->redirect()->toRoute('login', ['action' => 'progressuser']);
}
```

As we can easily see, in both cases we have created objects of type
Zend\Session\Container with specified name: 'user'. We modify such
created container the same way as any dynamic object, so we set a value by
referring to ->[name]. We set a 'details' variable with $rowset, that is
the Rowset\User object in our examples. Thanks to that, in each available
file, we will be able to return all the data about the logged in user in the
object form, like: getId() or getEmail(). Additionally, we have added a
line for redirecting to the login action of the controller in the registration,
progressUserAction(), so that we are able to display an appropriate page.
Let's fill in an empty method logoutAction() from the login controller, if
we already have a ready session object.

```
public function logoutAction()
{
    $session = new Session\Container('user');
    $session->getManager()->destroy();
    $this->redirect()->toRoute('home');
}
```

We create, just like before, a regular active Session\Container object,
which already exists, then we get a manager object by getManager() and
normally destroy a session by the call of destroy(). At the end, we redirect
the user to the home page.

There is still a need to modify our navigation and add a new

`UserController`. We change the navigation so that it starts displaying links to log out, user panel for logged in users and *Register* and *Login* links for site guests.

```php
<?php if ($this->user): ?>
    <li <?php if ($this->controller === Application\Controller\UserController:
↪:class): ?>class="active"<?php endif; ?>><a href="<?= $this->url('user')
↪?>">My Account</a></li>
    <li><a href="<?= $this->url('login', ['action' => 'logout'])
↪?>">Logout</a></li>
<?php else: ?>
    <li <?php if ($this->controller === Application\Controller\RegisterController:
↪:class): ?>class="active"<?php endif; ?>><a href="<?= $this->url('register')
↪?>">Registration</a></li>
    <li <?php if ($this->controller === Application\Controller\LoginController:
↪:class): ?>class="active"<?php endif; ?>><a href="<?= $this->url('login')
↪?>">Log-in</a></li>
<?php endif; ?>
```

In the above scenario, we use a `$this->user` variable, which has been added in the abstract controller, so that it is available in every possible view file. We have attached a code regarding this variable to the already existing `setEventManager()` method, which we have created for the purpose of passing the controller's name to the view template.

```php
public function setEventManager(EventManagerInterface $events)
{
    parent::setEventManager($events);
    $events->attach('dispatch', function ($e) {
        $controllerClass = $e->getRouteMatch()->getParam('controller', 'index');
        $e->getViewModel()->setVariable('controller', $controllerClass);
        $userSession = new Session\Container('user');
        if ($userSession->details) {
            $e->getViewModel()->setVariable('user', $userSession->details);
        }
    }, 100); // function call will be triggered before controller's action logic
}
```

We configure a router of the newly added controller `User` the same way as for the `LoginController`, with an exception to the route name as `/user/[:action]`. The controller does not require other dependencies yet, thus it is enough to add it into a controller key in the following way:

```
Controller\UserController::class => InvokableFactory::class
```

The controller itself and the view is trivial. `UserController` returns a single session variable to display the information about the user:

```
namespace Application\Controller;
use Zend\Session;

class UserController extends AbstractController {
    public function indexAction() {
        $userSession = new Session\Container('user');
        return [
            'user' => $userSession->details
        ];
    }
}
```

A new view of the controller presents like so in the code format and as output to the user:

```
<section class="page-content">
    <div class="container jumbotron">
        <h2><span class="zf-green">Correctly logged in user with id:
↪<?= $this->user->getId() ?></span></h2>
        <pre><?php print_r($this->user) ?></pre>
    </div>
</section>
```

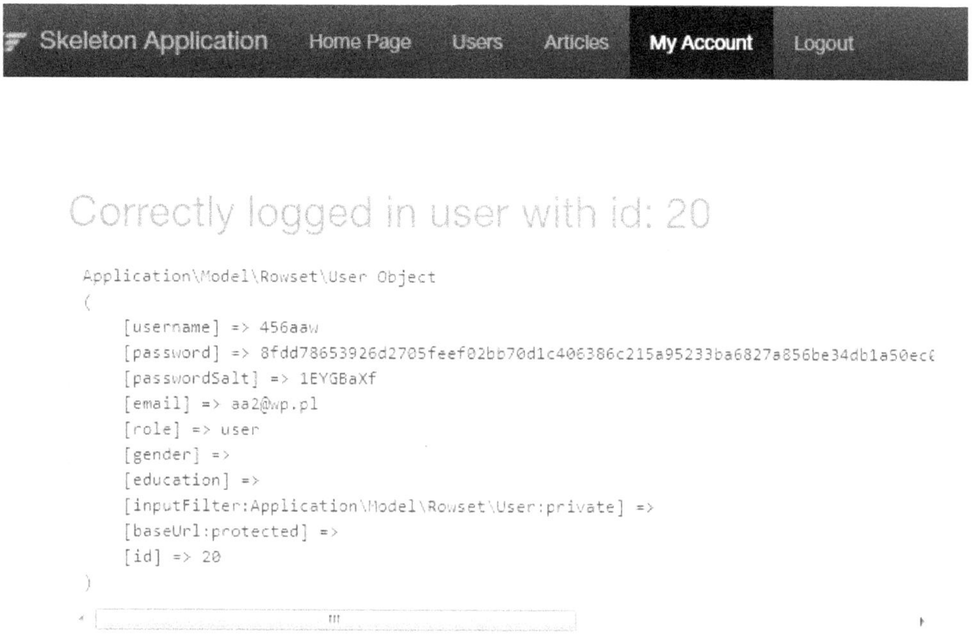

Correctly logged in user with id: 20

```
Application\Model\Rowset\User Object
(
    [username] => 456aaw
    [password] => 8fdd78653926d2705feef02bb70d1c406386c215a95233ba6827a856be34db1a50ec8
    [passwordSalt] => 1EYGBaXf
    [email] => aa2@wp.pl
    [role] => user
    [gender] =>
    [education] =>
    [inputFilter:Application\Model\Rowset\User:private] =>
    [baseUrl:protected] =>
    [id] => 20
)
```

Image 14.4.

CHAPTER 15.

Creating an administration panel and CMS

In this chapter we are going to discuss the managing page for administrators. We will create a completely new module designed exactly for users with admin rights, and we will redirect them into their new panel soon after they have logged in. We will cover a ZFC Admin module, which is a foundation of creating an admin tool in Zend. Thanks to it we will get a generic template with the dynamic menu links and dependencies. At first, we are going to build a sample module for an administrator, allowing to create his own articles and assigning the data stored in HTML format to them by a CKEditor (a free rich editor). Additionally, each article/page will have the multi-language support and META data like: title, description or keywords.

15.1. A new module

We will start our chapter from adding a new clean module named Admin and its setup in the *module/* folder. Its folder structure can be found and downloaded at *https://github.com/ZF-Commons/ZfcAdmin*, however we will modify it according to our needs. A ZfcAdmin is a structure of the directories together with an example controller, template and a view of the administrative panel. This project is supposed to help us create an initial version of a custom panel for managing a site. Once we get files from the ZfcAdmin, we will be able to inspect and modify the initial *Module.php* file.

```php
namespace Admin;
use Zend\Loader;
use Zend\EventManager\EventInterface;
use Zend\Mvc\MvcEvent;
use Zend\Mvc\Router\V2RouteMatch;
use Zend\Router\RouteMatch as V3RouteMatch;
use Zend\Router\Http\Literal;
use Zend\Router\Http\Segment;

class Module
{
    public function getAutoloaderConfig()
    {
        return [
            Loader\AutoloaderFactory::STANDARD_AUTOLOADER => [
                Loader\StandardAutoloader::LOAD_NS => [
                    __NAMESPACE__ => __DIR__,
                ],
            ],
        ];
    }

    public function getConfig()
    {
        $provider = new ConfigProvider();
        return [
            'service_manager' => $provider->getDependencyConfig(),
            'view_manager' => $provider->getViewManagerConfig(),
            'admin' => $provider->getModuleConfig(),
            'controllers' => [
                'factories' => [
                    Controller\AdminController::class => function($sm) {
                        return new Controller\AdminController();
                    },
                ],
            ],
            'navigation' => array(
                'admin' => array(
```

```php
            'home' => array(
                'label' => 'Home Page',
                'route' => 'admin',
            ),
            'logout' => array(
                'label' => 'Logout',
                'route' => 'logout',
            ),
        ),
    ),
    'router' => [
        'routes' => [
            'admin' => [
                'type' => Literal::class,
                'options' => [
                    'route' => '/admin',
                    'defaults' => [
                        'controller' => Controller\AdminController::class,
                        'action' => 'index',
                    ],
                ],
                'may_terminate' => true,
                'child_routes' => [
                ]
            ],
            'logout' => [
                'type' => Literal::class,
                'options' => [
                    'route' => '/login/logout',
                    'defaults' => [
                        'controller' => \Application\Controller\
↪LoginController::class,
                        'action' => 'logout',
                    ],
                ],
                'may_terminate' => true,
            ],
        ],
    ],
];
}

public function onBootstrap(EventInterface $e)
{
```

```
        $app = $e->getParam('application');
        $em = $app->getEventManager();
        $em->attach(MvcEvent::EVENT_DISPATCH, [$this, 'selectLayoutBasedOnRoute']);
    }

    public function selectLayoutBasedOnRoute(MvcEvent $e)
    {
        $app = $e->getParam('application');
        $sm = $app->getServiceManager();
        $config = $sm->get('config');

        if ($config['admin']['use_admin_layout'] === false) {
            return;
        }
        $match = $e->getRouteMatch();
        $controller = $e->getTarget();

        if (!($match instanceof V2RouteMatch || $match instanceof V3RouteMatch)
            || 0 !== strpos($match->getMatchedRouteName(), 'admin')
            || $controller->getEvent()->getResult()->terminate()
        ) {
            return;
        }
        $layout = $config['admin']['admin_layout_template'];
        $controller->layout($layout);
    }
}
```

A `getAutloaderConfig()` is an important piece, which defines a current folder as the place from which it starts to search for package names according to the standard autoloader. A method `getConfig()` is mainly based on the `ConfigProvider` class, which stores the view dependencies and settings of the actual module. In the controllers key we currently have only one controller, `AdminController`, which does not require any dependencies yet. `navigation` defines a list of the elements of our main menu. Each of them requires a name and a URL address. At the moment we only have a link to the homepage and to the logout. All our newly created links to the modules will be placed inside the `admin` key and the `child_router` parameter. An exception to this rule is our link to logout, which redirects only to the existing login controller in the `Application` module and `logout` action.

In order to replace a view template in `onBootstrap()` method, we register a function `selectLayoutOnRoute()` to the event `EVENT_DISPATCH`. Via that method we check an existing configuration around the preference of replacing a view, and we perform a check if an actual address is a child of the *admin* address. If it is, we get a path of the template and we register it by `$controller->layout($layout)`.

Let's have a look at the `ConfigProvider` class itself, placed in the folder *admin/src*. It's worth to mention that we are using a factory class here, which only returns a string of `"admin"`. For the navigation in the panel and inside of `getModuleConfig()` method, we have values to which we refer inside `selectLayoutOnRoute()`, that is the preference of overriding the view template and the path of that view.

```
namespace Admin;
class ConfigProvider
{

    public function __invoke()
    {
        return [
            'dependencies' => $this->getDependencyConfig(),
            'view_manager' => $this->getViewManagerConfig(),
            'admin' => $this->getModuleConfig(),
        ];
    }

    public function getDependencyConfig()
    {
        return [
            'factories' => [
            'admin_navigation' => Navigation\Service\
  ↪AdminNavigationFactory::class,
            ],
        ];
    }

    public function getViewManagerConfig()
    {
        return [
            'template_path_stack' => [
                __DIR__ . '/../view',
            ],
        ];
```

```
    }

    public function getModuleConfig()
    {
        return [
            'use_admin_layout' => true,
            'admin_layout_template' => 'layout/admin',
        ];
    }
}
```

Now, we move into our view file of *view/layout/admin.phtml*, which will control everything on the screen:

```
<?= $this->doctype(); ?>
<html lang="en">
    <head>
        <meta charset="utf-8">
            <?= $this->headTitle('Panel Admina - Zend Framework 3')->setSeparator(' - ')-
>
↪setAutoEscape(false) ?>
            <?= $this->headMeta()
                ->appendName('viewport', 'width=device-width, initial-scale=1.0')
                ->appendHttpEquiv('X-UA-Compatible', 'IE=edge')
            ?>

        <!-- Styles -->
        <?= $this->headLink()
            ->prependStylesheet('//maxcdn.bootstrapcdn.com/
↪bootstrap/3.2.0/css/bootstrap.min.css')
                ->prependStylesheet($this->basePath('css/style.css'))?>

        <!-- Scripts -->
        <?= $this->headScript()
                ->prependFile('//maxcdn.bootstrapcdn.com/
↪bootstrap/3.2.0/js/bootstrap.min.js')
                ->prependFile('https://ajax.googleapis.com/ajax
↪/libs/jquery/1.11.1/jquery.min.js')
                ->prependFile('https://oss.maxcdn.com/respond/1.4.2/respond.min.js',
↪'text/javascript', array('conditional' => 'lt IE 9',))
                ->prependFile('https://oss.maxcdn.com/html5shiv/3.7.2/html5shiv.min.js',
↪'text/javascript', array('conditional' => 'lt IE 9',))
                ->appendFile('//cdn.ckeditor.com/4.6.2/full/ckeditor.js')
            ?>
```

```
    </head>

    <body style="padding-top: 70px;">
        <nav class="navbar navbar-inverse navbar-fixed-top" role="navigation">
            <div class="container">
                <div class="navbar-header">
                    <button type="button" class="navbar-toggle" data-toggle="collapse"
↪data-target=".navbar-collapse">
                        <span class="icon-bar"></span>
                        <span class="icon-bar"></span>
                        <span class="icon-bar"></span>
                    </button>
                    <a class="navbar-brand" href="<?= $this->url('admin') ?>">
↪Administration Panelel</a>
                </div>

                <div class="collapse navbar-collapse">
                    <?= $this->navigation('admin_navigation')
                        ->menu()
                        ->setUlClass('nav navbar-nav')
                        ->setMaxDepth(0)
                        ->setRenderInvisible(false)?>
                </div> <!--/.nav-collapse -->
            </div>
        </nav>

        <div class="container">
            <?php
            $flash = $this->flashMessenger();
            $flash->setMessageOpenFormat('<div%s>
                <button type="button" class="close" data-dismiss="alert" aria-
↪hidden="true">
                    &times;
                </button>
                <div>')->setMessageCloseString('</div></div>');

            $flash->clearMessagesFromContainer();
            echo $flash->renderCurrent('error', array('alert', 'alert-dismissable',
↪'alert-danger'));
            echo $flash->renderCurrent('warning', array('alert', 'alert-
↪dismissable', 'alert-warning'));
            echo $flash->renderCurrent('info', array('alert', 'alert-dismissable',
↪'alert-info'));
            echo $flash->renderCurrent('default', array('alert', 'alert-
```

285

```
↪dismissable', 'alert-warning'));
        echo $flash->renderCurrent('success', array('alert', 'alert-
↪dismissable', 'alert-success'));
        ?>
        <div class="row">
          <?= $this->content ?>
        </div>

        <hr>

        <footer>Administration Panel 2017</footer>
      </div> <!-- /container -->
      <?= $this->inlineScript() ?>
    </body>
</html>
```

A scheme might feel very similar to the `Application` module, however it has some different parts. As an example, to display a top menu we reuse a view helper, which is a `navigation()`, by using the same name as in the `ConfigProvider` file. We set a class for the container consisting of a menu as `nav navbar-nav`, and we set a zero depth nest level of the other elements (all of them will be roots).

A very crucial section of this template is mostly the usage of `FlashMessager`, which takes care of the display of all the data, messages and errors, generated for example by forms. Via `setMessageOpenFormat()` method call, we are able to specify HTML tags that need to wrap each message and its end by `setMessageCloseString()`. Of course, for the purpose of this book, all graphical elements will be integrated with the Bootstrap CSS specifications, thus we attach a button to close each flash message. `FlashMessanger` works using the session, which means that messages are deleted when they are removed or displayed a few times by the user. However, we want to use this plugin only for the currently added messages. Hence we insert a line with a `clearMessageCloseFrom` ↪`Container()` call, which resets all the messages in a session, but leaves them in their object container. `FlashMessenger` offers a couple of different types of displaying like `render()`, or `renderError()`. In our example, however, we will reuse the method: `renderCurrent()`, which returns only the current errors and defines their type based on the first parameter. A second argument is an array of CSS classes that will be attached to the messages container. A place where we put controller's content is of course

`$this->content`, which looks the same as in our previous module.

Although our sample `AdminController` is empty, it extends an abstract class `AbstractController`, which will be used by every other controller in the admin module. Inside that class we set a mechanism that verifies if the user has rights to browse the views designed only for admins. The abstract class presents like below:

```
namespace Admin\Controller;

use Zend\Mvc\MvcEvent;
use Zend\Session;

class AbstractController extends \Zend\Mvc\Controller\AbstractActionController
{
    protected $sessionUser;
    protected $baseUrl;

    public function onDispatch(MvcEvent $e) {
        $this->baseUrl = $this->getRequest()->getBasePath();
        $this->sessionUser = new Session\Container('user');
        $action = $e->getRouteMatch()->getParam('action', 'index');
        $e->getTarget()->layout()->action = $action;

        if ($this->sessionUser->details && $this->sessionUser->details->getRole()
 == 'admin') {
            $e->getViewModel()->setVariable('user', $this->sessionUser->details);
        } else {
            $url = $e->getRouter()->assemble(['action' => 'index'], ['name' =>
'login']);
            $response = $e->getResponse();
            $response->getHeaders()->addHeaderLine('Location', $url);
            $response->setStatusCode(302);
            $response->sendHeaders();
            exit();
        }
        return parent::onDispatch($e);
    }
}
```

Same as in already mentioned examples, we override `onDispatch()` method, which we also use in the parent class at the end, at the same time returning its value. For the obvious reasons, we got an information about the currently logged in user and we assigned it to the class variable $sessionUser, which will be reused in the next controllers for different kinds of checks and reads. We also set a $action variable in order to mark an active option in the additional menu for the given functionality. At the start we do a check if the user has logged in and if he is an administrator. If everything is correct, we pass user object to the view template as well. Otherwise, we redirect such guest back to the login view. Our view in file *view/admin/admin/index.phtml* only displays data of the module, controller and the current action. An access to template variables is occurring by a $this->layout() method.

```
<strong>Module:</strong> Admin &raquo;
<strong>Controller:</strong> Index &raquo;
<strong>Action:</strong> <?= $this->layout()->action ?>
```

15.2. Panel access

Obviously we, are not able to enter into an administrative panel and see it without extra additions in our users table structure. First of all, we add a column called 'role' of type VARCHAR(20) with the default value set to 'user'. Then, we create a new user, this time of 'admin' type for the role column. We also have to update the Application\Model\Rowset\User object with the new role property. We add it into exchangeArray() and getArrayCopy() too and add a getRoles() method. If we did everything well, then an empty admin site under the URL */admin* should appear.

Image 15.1.

15.3. CMS – content management system

Once we have a ready managing panel for a special user, we should also have at least one additional feature for this type of the users. A content management system is perhaps the most popular method available for every administrator, that is why we create such system in our new controller `ArticlesController`. Our initial assumptions are pretty simple: we must have a full control over the content visible on various pages, and administrate a mechanism of linking single content blocks into one page, which then we can reuse as news or articles on a blog. Of course, our content will have different language versions, by default English; but we will be able to add another versions that will be automatically picked up and handled based on the browser language - in chapter number 18. For our CMS system it is necessary to add a list of extra DB tables, which we will present below:

```
CREATE TABLE IF NOT EXISTS `pages` (
    `id` int(10) unsigned NOT NULL,
    `name` varchar(40) CHARACTER SET utf8 NOT NULL,
    `url` varchar(100) CHARACTER SET utf8 DEFAULT NULL,
    `parent_id` int(11) NOT NULL DEFAULT '0',
    `required` tinyint(4) NOT NULL DEFAULT '0'
) ENGINE=InnoDB AUTO_INCREMENT=3 DEFAULT CHARSET=latin1;
```

```
CREATE TABLE IF NOT EXISTS `page_contents` (
    `id` int(10) unsigned NOT NULL,
    `name` varchar(100) CHARACTER SET utf8 NOT NULL
) ENGINE=InnoDB AUTO_INCREMENT=5 DEFAULT CHARSET=latin1;

CREATE TABLE IF NOT EXISTS `page_lang_contents` (
    `id` int(10) unsigned NOT NULL,
    `lang` varchar(2) CHARACTER SET utf32 NOT NULL,
    `content` text CHARACTER SET utf8 NOT NULL,
    `page_content_id` int(11) NOT NULL
) ENGINE=InnoDB AUTO_INCREMENT=8 DEFAULT CHARSET=latin1;

CREATE TABLE IF NOT EXISTS `page_metadata` (
    `id` int(10) unsigned NOT NULL,
    `lang` varchar(3) CHARACTER SET latin1 NOT NULL,
    `title` varchar(100) NOT NULL,
    `description` varchar(100) NOT NULL,
    `keywords` varchar(150) NOT NULL,
    `page_id` int(11) NOT NULL
) ENGINE=InnoDB AUTO_INCREMENT=4 DEFAULT CHARSET=utf8;

CREATE TABLE IF NOT EXISTS `page_to_contents` (
    `id` int(10) unsigned NOT NULL,
    `page_id` int(11) NOT NULL,
    `content_id` int(11) NOT NULL
) ENGINE=InnoDB AUTO_INCREMENT=6 DEFAULT CHARSET=latin1;
--
-- Indexes for the tables
--
ALTER TABLE `pages`
ADD PRIMARY KEY (`id`), ADD KEY `parent_id` (`parent_id`);
ALTER TABLE `page_contents`
ADD PRIMARY KEY (`id`), ADD KEY `name` (`name`);
ALTER TABLE `page_lang_contents`
ADD PRIMARY KEY (`id`), ADD KEY `lang` (`lang`);
ALTER TABLE `page_metadata`
ADD PRIMARY KEY (`id`);
ALTER TABLE `page_to_contents`
ADD PRIMARY KEY (`id`), ADD KEY `page_id` (`page_id`,`content_id`);
```

A base table `'pages'` contains information about pages of an article, news or posts on a blog, which will be available under a URL address from a column of the same table. A column `parent_id` will be pointing a parent page, if we have to nest the pages with each other. A parameter `'required'` defines if a given element is necessary for the proper functioning of the system. An example of the required page might be a footer or header. A table `page_contents` is a simple list of contents with a custom name and linked `ID` number. The information about the current content is placed in the `page_lang_contents`, which links the previous table by `page_content_id` column and a language with the a content entered by us in the editor. Another table `page_metadata` is a set of the data needed to display the page itself, such as: title, description, keywords and page link. All of these are of course located and assigned only to a specific language. The last table `page_to_contents` is a linkage between the sites and the object contents, where a relation of "many to many" exists.

Another issue is the location of the class managing the CMS system. It is really difficult, as it will be used by two modules at the same time. Placing it into a *vendor/* folder is not the best idea, as the class needs an access to the database together with a few tables. In order to simplify its later usage in the default site to maximum, we will create it in the `Application` module inside the *module/admin/ContentManager.php*. In order to make our class communicate efficiently with the DB, we will pass a DB adapter into it, which will be used for creating `Zend\Db\Sql\Sql` object. A header of our class will look like:

```
namespace Application\Model\Admin;

use Zend\Db\Sql\Sql;

class ContentManager
{
    public $metadataTableName = 'page_metadata';
    public $pagesTableName = 'pages';
    public $contentTableName = 'page_contents';
    public $contentPageTableName = 'page_to_contents';
    public $langPageTableName = 'page_lang_contents';
    protected $db;
    protected $adapter;
    protected $lang;

    public function __construct($adapter) {
        $this->db = new Sql($adapter);
        $this->adapter = $adapter;
```

```
    $this->lang = 'en';
}
```

All the table names will be kept in a single place to reuse them easily, when for example we rename our table name. By default, we are also set the language to English and create a `Sql` object. To simplify this class I decided to use the direct queries to database without any pages or contents models. They would bring an unnecessary complexity, and it is not always recommended to use them everywhere.

```
public function getPages()
{
    $select = $this->db->select()
        ->from('pages');
    return $this->executeSql($select);
}

public function getPage($id)
{
    $select = $this->db->select()
        ->from('pages')
        ->where(['id' => $id]);
    return $this->executeSql($select)->current();
}

public function addPage($name, $url, $parentID)
{
    if (!$this->isPageExist($name)) {
        $data = array(
            'name' => $name,
            'url' => $url,
            'parent_id' => $parentID
        );
        $insert = $this->db->insert()
            ->into('pages')
            ->values($data);
        return $this->executeSql($insert);
    } else {
        return false;
    }
}

public function updatePage($pageId, $name, $url, $parentId)
```

```
{
    $data = array(
        'name' => $name,
        'url' => $url,
        'parent_id' => $parentId
    );
    $update = $this->db->update()
        ->table('pages')
        ->set($data)
        ->where(['id' => $pageId]);
    return $this->executeSql($update);
}

public function deletePage ($pageId)
{
    $delete = $this->db->delete()
        ->from('pages')
        ->where(['id' => $pageId]);
    return $this->executeSql($delete);
}
```

The first methods relate to the 'pages' table. Over here we have almost all CRUD methods, such as getting pages: getPages(), getPage(), creating: addPage(), modifying: updatePage() and deleting: deltePage(). It is worth noting that the way of creating checks to the queries of a select() type significantly differs from those in Zend 1. In a newer platform version, to specify two AND conditions, we need to pass a single array to the where() method, where keys are the column names, and values are the phrases to search for. For instance, where(['id' => 2, 'name' => 'some name']) will generate a SQL query of: WHERE id = '2' AND name = 'some name'. A structure of the queries such as insert(), table() or from) with the table name has changed as well. Initially, we were able to pass a table name in the constructor, while now, depending on the query type, we would need to call an extra method: into(), table() or from() with the table name. You can notice that we return each query result by calling an executeSql() function with the SQL object as a parameter. In the new Zend Framework 3 there is no longer a fetchAll() method, thus we have implemented the following required call to the database in the executeSql() method:

```
private function executeSql($sql)
{
```

```
    $statement = $this->db->prepareStatementForSqlObject($sql);
    return $statement->execute();
}
```

In our example there are a few primary methods for returning and editing metadata, together with adding and deleting page contents: addMetadata(), updateMetadata(), addContent(), deleteContent() and addLang ↪Content(). They do not stand out from the previous ones, so we will ignore them for now. Our attention should be paid to an assignContentToPage() method that links the content with a page, the function unlinkContent() that deletes that link, and two other helper methods: isPageExists() and isContentExits():

```
public function assignContentToPage($contentID, $pageID)
{
    $data = array(
        'content_id' => $contentID,
        'page_id' => $pageID
    );
    $insert = $this->db->insert()
        ->into($this->contentPageTableName)
        ->values($data);
    return $this->executeSql($insert);
}

public function unlinkContent($pageID, $contentID)
{
    $delete = $this->db->delete()
        ->from('page_to_contents')
        ->where(['page_id' => $pageID, 'content_id' => $contentID]);
    return $this->executeSql($delete);
}

public function isPageExist($name)
{
    $sql = "SELECT COUNT(DISTINCT id) AS count FROM ".$this->pagesTableName."
↪WHERE name=? LIMIT 1";
    $result = $this->adapter->query($sql, array($name));
    return $result->current()->count > 0;
}

public function isContentExist($name)
{
```

```
    $sql = "SELECT COUNT(DISTINCT id) AS count FROM ".$this->contentTableName."
↪WHERE name=? LIMIT 1";
    $result = $this->adapter->query($sql, array($name));
    return $result->current()->count > 0;
}
```

Two last methods are used for checking if a given page or its content does not already exist in the system, thanks to that we would not create duplicates in the database. For more advanced queries I decided to show the usage of the `query()` method from the adapter object, which takes any SQL value in PDO format and passes back an argument as a second call element. Such returned result is of course a regular object of type: `iterator`, which requires getting a first record, and later the column contents (in our example we return an `'id'` column as `'count'`). We can also convert each `iterator` into a normal associative array. We have performed such conversion in the `getAllPageDetails()` method:

```
public function getAllPageDetails($pageID)
{
    $select = $this->db->select()
        ->from($this->metadataTableName)
        ->where(['page_id' => $pageID]);
    return iterator_to_array($this->executeSql($select));
}
```

The last public methods are used for displaying full pages or particular contents on our websites. They reuse the helper private methods, but pass back other query conditions.

```
public function getAllContentsByPageID($pageID)
{
    $condition = 'p2c.page_id';
    $sqlParameter = $pageID;
    return $this->retrieveAllPageContents($condition, $sqlParameter);
}

public function getStaticContentByPageName($pageName)
{
    $condition = 'p.name';
    $sqlParameter = $pageName;
    return $this->retrieveLangPageContents($condition, $sqlParameter);
}
```

```
public function getArtcileContentByPageName($pageName)
{
    $condition = 'p.name';
    $sqlParameter = $pageName;
    return $this->retrieveArticlePageContents($condition, $sqlParameter);
}

public function getArtcileContentByUrl($url)
{
    $condition = 'p.url';
    $sqlParameter = $url;
    return $this->retrieveArticlePageContents($condition, $sqlParameter);
}
```

We can easily get a page by its id number: `getAllContentsByPageID()`, via the content name: `getStaticContentByPageName()`, get all the data for the whole page article or blog post via: `getArticleContent⤷ByPageName()` or via its URL address: `getArticleContentByUrl()`. The helper private methods looks like:

```
private function retrieveLangPageContents($condition, $parameter)
{
    $select = $this->db->select()
        ->from(array('p2c' => 'page_to_contents'),
            array('content_id', 'page_id'))
        ->join(array('p' => 'pages'),
            'p.id = p2c.page_id')
        ->join(array('c' => 'page_contents'),
            'c.id = p2c.content_id')
        ->join(array('l' => $this->langPageTableName),
            'l.page_content_id = c.id')
        ->where([$condition => $parameter])
        ->where(['l.lang' => $this->lang]);
    $result = $this->executeSql($select);

    $resultNew = array();

    foreach ($result as $counter => $entry) {
        foreach ($entry as $key => $single) {
            $resultNew[$counter][$key] = stripslashes($single);
        }
    }
    return $resultNew;
```

```
}

private function retrieveArticlePageContents($condition, $parameter)
{
    $select = $this->db->select()
        ->from(array('p2c' => 'page_to_contents'),
            array('content_id', 'page_id'))
        ->join(array('p' => 'pages'),
            'p.id = p2c.page_id')
        ->join(array('c' => 'page_contents'),
            'c.id = p2c.content_id')
        ->join(array('l' => $this->langPageTableName),
            'l.page_content_id = c.id')
        ->join(array('m' => 'page_metadata'),
            'm.page_id = p2c.page_id')
        ->where([$condition => $parameter])
        ->where(['l.lang' => $this->lang])
        ->where(['m.lang' => $this->lang]);

    $result = $this->executeSql($select);
    $resultNew = array();

    foreach ($result as $counter =>$entry) {
        foreach ($entry as $key => $single) {
            $resultNew[$counter][$key] = stripslashes($single);
        }
        $counter++;
    }
    return $resultNew;
}

private function retrieveAllPageContents($condition, $parameter)
{
    $select = $this->db->select()
        ->from(array('p2c' => 'page_to_contents'))
        ->columns(array('content_id', 'page_id'))
        ->join(array('p' => 'pages'), 'p.id = p2c.page_id')
        ->join(array('c' => 'page_contents'), 'c.id = p2c.content_id')
        ->where([$condition => $parameter]);

    $result = iterator_to_array($this->executeSql($select));

    foreach ($result as $index => $row) {
        $result[$index]['langs'] = $this->getContentLanguages
```

```
↪($result[$index]['content_id']);
    }
    return $result;
}
```

They mainly differ in linking many tables by a `join()` method and reconverting contents by `stripslashes()`, to get rid of escaping from the dangerous characters. We can freely edit a list of available languages by modifying a static list from the `getLanguageList()` method:

```
public static function getLanguageList()
{
    $list = array();
    $counter = 0;
    $list[$counter]['id'] = 'pl';
    $list[$counter]['name'] = 'Polski';
    $counter++;
    $list[$counter]['id'] = 'en';
    $list[$counter]['name'] = 'English';
    $counter++;
    return $list;
}
```

Since we already found out how our new CMS system class looks like, let's learn how to define it in the *Application/Module.php* file:

```
Model\Admin\ContentManager::class => function($sm) {
    return new Model\Admin\ContentManager($sm-
        >get(\Zend\Db\Adapter\Adapter::class));
},
```

Now let's go back to the Admin module and add a new controller responsible for managing of articles to it: we will call it `ArticlesController`. We will present that file by dividing it into two or three action methods.

```
namespace Admin\Controller;

use Admin\Form;

class ArticlesController extends AbstractController
{
    public function indexAction()
    {
```

```php
        return [
            'pages' => $this->cmsObject->getPages()
        ];
    }

    public function previewAction()
    {
        $pageDetails = $this->cmsObject->getArtcileContentByUrl($this->params()->
↪fromRoute('id'));
        $this->getEvent()->getTarget()->layout()->title = $pageDetails[0]['title'];
        $this->getEvent()->getTarget()->layout()->description =
↪$pageDetails[0]['description'];
        $this->getEvent()->getTarget()->layout()->keywords =
↪$pageDetails[0]['keywords'];
        return [
            'page' => $pageDetails
        ];
    }

    public function seecontentsAction()
    {
        $id = $this->params()->fromRoute('id');
        return [
            'title' => $this->cmsObject->getPage($id)['name'],
            'contents' => $this->cmsObject->getAllContentsByPageID($id),
            'pageID' => $id,
            'availableContents' => $this->cmsObject->getContents()
        ];
    }
```

A default view index contains a list of available pages in the database. A previewAction() method displays a full view of the page based on the passed URL address together with its content and metadata in HTML. We pass the data such as title, description as the view template variables. This is why now we will modify the *admin.phtml* file to make it support these extra values:

```php
<?= $this->headTitle(isset($title) ? $title : 'Admin Panel - Zend Framework 3')->
↪setSeparator(' - ')->setAutoEscape(false) ?>
<?= $this->headMeta()
    ->appendName('description', isset($description) ? $description : 'Default
↪description')
    ->appendName('keywords', isset($keywords) ? $keywords : 'Default key
```

↪names')

A method `seecontentsAction()` displays all linked contents to the given page and gives us an ability to assign more fragments.

Another methods like `addpage`, `editpage` and `delete` accordingly add, modify and remove the given page. Two first actions have a very similar structure and require adding an extra form `AddPage` that, depending on usage, takes one or two arguments: pages list to display as the parent and an object of an array type from the pages table. A second argument is of course used with a method responsible for modification, however we only need a page ID number for deleting.

```
public function addpageAction()
{
    $form = new Form\AddPage($this->cmsObject->getPages());
    $viewParams = ['addPageForm' => $form];

    if ($this->getRequest()->isPost()) {
        $form->setData($this->getRequest()->getPost());

        if ($form->isValid()) {
            $added = $this->cmsObject->addPage($form->get('name')->getValue(),
↪$form->get('url')->getValue(), $form->get('parent_id')->getValue());
            if ($added) {
                $this->flashMessenger()->addSuccessMessage('Page has been added.');
            } else {
                $this->flashMessenger()->addWarningMessage('Page already exists.');
            }
        } else {
            $this->flashMessenger()->addErrorMessage('Incorrectly completed form.');
        }
    }
    return $viewParams;
}

public function editpageAction()
{
    $pageId = $this->params()->fromRoute('id');
    $form = new Form\AddPageDetails($pageId, $this->cmsObject->getLanguageList());
    $pageForm = new Form\AddPage($this->cmsObject->getPages(), $this->cmsObject->
↪getPageByID($pageId));
    $viewParams = [
```

```php
        'addPageDetails' => $form,
        'editPageForm' => $pageForm
    ];

    if ($this->getRequest()->isPost()) {
        if ($this->params()->fromPost('url')) {
            $pageForm->setData($this->getRequest()->getPost());

            if ($pageForm->isValid()) {
                $this->cmsObject->updatePage($pageId, $pageForm->get('name')->
↪getValue(), $pageForm->get('url')->getValue(), $pageForm->
↪get('parent_id')->getValue());
                $this->flashMessenger()->addSuccessMessage
↪($pageForm->completeMessage);
            } else{
                $this->flashMessenger()->addErrorMessage('Incorrectly completed form.');
            }
        } elseif ($this->params()->fromPost('title')) {
            $form->setData($this->getRequest()->getPost());

            if ($form->isValid()) {
                $this->cmsObject->addMetadata(
                    $pageId,
                    $form->get('language')->getValue(),
                    $form->get('title')->getValue(),
                    $form->get('description')->getValue(),
                    $form->get('keywords')->getValue()
                );
                $form->completeMsg;
            } else{
                'form.errors';
            }
        }
    }
    $viewParams['pageMetadata'] = $this->cmsObject->getAllPageDetails($pageId);
    $viewParams['pageId'] = $pageId;

    return $viewParams;
}

public function deleteAction()
{
    $pageId = $this->params()->fromRoute('id');
    $this->cmsObject->deletePage($pageId);
```

```
        return $this->redirect()->toRoute('admin/articles');
    }
```

For the first time, in the `AddPage` form we are using methods `setValue` for entering default form values; additionally we iterate an array of `$pages` to create a simple one-dimensional array to pass as elements to the `Select` factory. Below I present a construction of that form:

```php
const ELEMENT_NAME = 'name';
const ELEMENT_URL = 'url';
const ELEMENT_PARENT_ID = 'parent_id';
const ELEMENT_SUBMIT = 'submit';

public function __construct($pages = array(), $pageDetails = array())
{
    parent::__construct('add_page_form');
    $this->setAttribute('class', 'styledForm');
    $this->add([
        'name' => self::ELEMENT_NAME,
        'type' => Element\Text::class,
        'options' => [
            'label' => 'Name',
        ],
        'attributes' => [
            'required' => true
        ],
    ]);

    $this->add([
        'name' => self::ELEMENT_URL,
        'type' => Element\Text::class,
        'options' => [
            'label' => 'URL Address',
        ],
        'attributes' => [
            'required' => true
        ],
    ]);

    $dropDownElements = ['Root'];

    foreach($pages as $page) {
        if (!empty($pageDetails) && $page['name'] == $pageDetails['name']) {
            continue;
```

```php
        }
        $dropDownElements[$page['id']] = $page['name'];
    }

    $this->add([
        'name' => self::ELEMENT_PARENT_ID,
        'type' => Element\Select::class,
        'options' => [
            'label' => 'Site Parent',
            'value_options' => $dropDownElements
        ],
        'attributes' => [
            'required' => true
        ],
    ]);

    $this->add([
        'name' => 'submit',
        'type' => 'submit',
        'attributes' => [
            'value' => 'Add',
            'class' => 'btn btn-primary'
        ]
    ]);

    if (!empty($pageDetails)) {
        $this->setAttribute('id', 'editPage');
        //fill fileds with the passed in data
        $this->get(self::ELEMENT_NAME)->setValue($pageDetails['name']);
        $this->get(self::ELEMENT_URL)->setValue($pageDetails['url']);
        $this->get(self::ELEMENT_PARENT_ID)->setValue($pageDetails['parent_id']);
        $this->get(self::ELEMENT_SUBMIT)->setValue('Edytuj');
    }
}
```

A method: `showcontents` has a task to display all available content in the database. Simple actions like: `addcontent`, `editcontent` or `deletecontent` look similar to the previous actions of managing pages, but operate on a different form, so we will skip them in this statement. Methods `addlangcontent` or `updatelangcontent`, as we have already mentioned, store a content version for a given language. Additionally, after each editing or adding a feature, we redirect the user back to the contents edit page.

```php
public function addlangcontentAction()
{
    $contentID = $this->params()->fromRoute('id');
    $form = new Form\AddLangContent($contentID, $this->cmsObject->
↪getLanguageList());

    if ($this->getRequest()->isPost()) {
        $form->setData($this->getRequest()->getPost());

        if ($form->isValid()) {
            $this->cmsObject->addLangContent(stripcslashes($form->
↪get('language')->getValue()), $form->get('content')->
↪getValue(), $contentID);
            $this->flashMessenger()->addSuccessMessage($form->
↪completeMsg, true);
            //come back tot he articles page
            $this->redirect()->toRoute('admin/articles', ['action' =>
↪'editcontent', 'id' => $contentID]);
        } else {
            $this->flashMessenger()->addErrorMessage('form.errors');
        }
    }
    return ['addLangContentForm' => $form];
}

public function updatelangcontentAction()
{
    $contentID = $this->params()->fromRoute('id');
    $langContents = $this->cmsObject->getContentLanguages($contentID);
    $id = 0;

    foreach($langContents as $entry) {
        $id = $this->params()->fromPost('langID_'.$entry['lang']);
        $contents = $this->params()->fromPost('contents_'.$entry['lang']);
        $this->cmsObject->updateLangContent($id, $contents);
    }
    //come back to the edit page
    $this->redirect()->toRoute('admin/articles', ['action' => 'editcontent',
↪'id' => $contentID]);
}
```

Two last action methods are responsible for merging and deleting links
between pages and contents.

```php
public function assigncontentAction()
{
    $pageID = $this->params()->fromRoute('id');
    $contentID = $this->request->getPost('selectedContentID');
    $this->cmsObject->assignContentToPage($contentID, $pageID);

    //come back to the articles page
    $this->redirect()->toRoute('admin/articles', ['action' => 'seecontents', 'id'
    ↪=> $pageID]);
}

public function unlinkcontentAction()
{
    $pageID = $this->params()->fromRoute('id');
    $contentID = $this->params()->fromRoute('content_id');
    $this->cmsObject->unlinkContent($pageID, $contentID);

    //go back to the edit page
    $this->redirect()->toRoute('admin/articles', ['action' => 'seecontents', 'id'
    ↪=> $pageID]);
}
```

We will use such added CMS library to display a footer initially. Let's begin by creating a view file *footer.phtml*, inside *Application/src/view/_shared/* and by pasting below contents:

```php
<footer>
    <?php foreach ($footerContent as $row): ?>
        <?= $row['content'] ?>
    <?php endforeach; ?>
</footer>
```

Notice that our contents could be linked with more than just one element, thus we have to iterate a variable `$footerContent`, which we will define in `AbstarctController` in the `Admin` module just under the action variable definition:

```php
$e->getViewModel()->setVariable('footerContent', $this->cmsObject->
↪getStaticContentByPageName('Custom Footer'));
```

Now we just need to attach a footer view file into a view template and take out the previous footer:

```
<?= $this->partial('application/_shared/footer.phtml'); ?>
```

We have added the cut-out footer HTML code to the newly created content of name: 'Footer - Contents', which later we will link with the newly created page called 'Custom Footer', so that it matches to the execution from the abstract controller level. Additionally, we can create another page content, this time a bit longer one, and attach it to the new page, for instance: 'Article Test Page' with the address test_article. Of course, firstly we will have to modify the admin file *Module.php*, to support our new URL address with name content_id. We do that in the following way:

```
'route' => '/articles[/:action][/:id][/:content_id]',
```

Thanks to that, we will be able to enter a site */admin/articles/preview/* ↪*test_article* and see a page with the below sample format in the admin panel:

Article Header

Lorem ipsum dolor sit amet, consectetur adipiscing elit. Fusce tempus molestie metus non fringilla. Phasellus orci velit, dictum sit amet vulputate ullamcorper, semper lacinia nunc. Curabitur tempus est non dolor rhoncus, eu maximus nisi rutrum. Pellentesque non neque enim. Pellentesque venenatis consequat ipsum, lobortis sodales dolor. In nec metus at lorem semper placerat. Nam maximus iaculis sapien, in efficitur orci luctus id. Donec ipsum odio, laoreet at mauris vitae, condimentum interdum tortor. Ut convallis consectetur ligula, nec ullamcorper velit. **Cras sed augue risus.** Nam tempus, mi vel porta mollis, lectus velit placerat justo, vel mollis dui lacus sit amet magna. Ut sed rutrum dui. Sed congue mollis orci, et efficitur est venenatis a. Fusce scelerisque urna id ante blandit consequat.

Nam maximus iaculis sapien, in efficitur orci luctus id. Donec ipsum odio, laoreet at mauris vitae, condimentum interdum tortor. Ut convallis consectetur ligula, nec ullamcorper velit. ~~Cras sed augue risus~~. Nam tempus, mi vel porta mollis, lectus velit placerat justo, vel mollis dui lacus sit amet magna. Ut sed rutrum dui. Sed congue mollis orci, et efficitur est venenatis a. Fusce scelerisque urna id ante blandit consequat.

2017 Zend Framework 3 - Developer's Guide. Adam Omelak.

Image 15.2.

CHAPTER 16.

Implementing an authorization system

In this chapter we are going to learn how to integrate an authorization of the guests and logged in users with the single parts of the system. There are three main options of implementing a managing permissions mechanism (authorization) in Zend Framework 3: via libraries like ZFC RBAC, BjyAuthorize, or via clean Zend ACL package (Access Control List). We will take a look at the first and official version of the engine, which can be hooked into an already existing project very easily. By using `ZFC RBAC`, so-called Role Based Access Controller, we will be able to set permissions for specific groups of users with given controllers, actions or URL addressed. RBAC is of course an official Zend tool based on the Zend ACL engine, which generally operates on text files. In our example we will block an access to all addresses starting with */admin* for all the users who are not admins, and we will limit an access to */user* for logged in users only. The library is available together with the English documentation at: *https://github.com/ZF-Commons/zfc-rbac/*.

16.1. Basic concepts

As we already mentioned, RBAC is an abbreviation of the control system based on the roles (grouped permissions). Thanks to grouping we will get more flexible to use management system. An example of such roles are: admins, blogger, logged in user or guest. In RBAC world every user could have zero or many roles. Roles call permissions, which are assigned to one or more roles. An example of such permission can be an ability to write comments, edit articles, or an access to a premium section. There are two types of the RBAC usages: flat and hierarchical. Flat model is based on the possession of one role per user only, where the role contains a definition of all the permissions. It means that if we have a permission like edit comment, we will need to assign it to a logged in user and to an admin. In the hierarchical model, the user is allowed have many roles, and each role can inherit other roles. By that, if for example an admin role has a nested user rank, then we can define a permission `editComment` only to the logged in user role level. The configuration of the all assignments is defined in the *global.php* file, which later we need to move into a root folder of *config/autoload*. An object stored in authorization service has to be an object of the interface `Zfc\Identity\IdentityInterface`, which requires only one method, `getRoles()`. That function can return a list of the roles as plain strings or as legitimate role objects. Of course, each of the RBAC system elements is fully extendable and it is easy to attach our own role, strategy or policy classes, which we will cover in next sections of this chapter.

16.2. Security

Zend Framework 3 MVC works in a very straightforward way: first, the system searches for a path of the URL address, assigns it to the controller, and then the controller executes a specific action. However, when we implement an authorization system, our execution logic receives additional barriers at every step. Firstly, before finding out a path, the security checks if there is an already defined rule for the given path. If it is, it executes a check if a given user has the appropriate role to view a specific path, and only then the logic goes into the controller's code. On the other hand, if we don't have any linked address security rule defined, then RBAC checks a Protection Policy. It's a mechanism defining a default application behavior of all other unsecured URL addresses. There are two modes available for that policy: POLICY_ALLOW, which gives an access to the resource, and POLICY_DENY, which blocks such access. A default protection policy is set as POLICY_ALLOW.

We define all the security in the configuration file under the alias: 'guards'. As we have already mentioned, we can build a security based on the URL address in the following way:

```
'guards' => [
    'ZfcRbac\Guard\RouteGuard' => [
        'cms*' => ['admin'],
        'login/edit_password' => ['user']
    ]
]
```

A given example will secure all the URL address for users of role admin that begins with cms, such as */cms*, */cms/add* or */cms/add/more*. This ability is available by using a wildcard character at the end of the path name. A second rule, however, secures a single address */login/edit_password*, so that it is the only available for the users with role user. If we would wanted to set one address for all the defined roles, then we would need to pass an array with just a wildcard character as a rule value:

```
'guards' => [
    'ZfcRbac\Guard\RouteGuard' => [
        'home' => ['*']
    ]
]
```

On the other hand, if we want to block a traffic on the given page, we pass an empty array for the given path:

```
'guards' => [
    'ZfcRbac\Guard\RouteGuard' => [
        'beta' => [] //no access Sir!
    ]
]
```

Another security type is `RoutePermissionGuard`, so the extended type of the previous security with extra permissions taken into account, apart from the required role. As an example, to get to the */cms* page, we need an admin role, however, to get to */cms/manage*, we need two extra permissions: cms.update and cms.delete.

```
'guards' => [
    'ZfcRbac\Guard\RoutePermissionGuard' => [
        'cms' => ['admin']
        'cms/manage' => ['cms.update', 'cms.delete']
    ]
]
```

In such case, both of the conditions have to be met in order to get into a specified page. We can however change the condition from AND into OR (the fulfillment of only single permission) by using a static class `GuardInterface::CONDITION_OR`.

```
'guards' => [
    'ZfcRbac\Guard\RoutePermissionGuard' => [
        'cms' => ['admin']
        'cms/manage' => [
            'permissions' => ['cms.update', 'cms.delete'],
            'condition' => GuardInterface::CONDITION_OR
        ]
    ]
]
```

In the above example an user has to have an admin role and permission `cms.update` OR `cms.delete`, to have an access.

Additionally, we can assign controller's actions to the particular roles by using Controller `Guard`, as it is presented below:

```
'guards' => [
    'ZfcRbac\Guard\ControllerGuard' => [
        [
            'controller' => UserControler,
            'actions' => ['read', 'delete'],
            'roles' => ['guest', 'user']
        ]
    ]
]
```

In the given situation, an action: `readAction()` will require the guest role, while a `deleteAction()` they would need a user role. If we skip an optional key `'actions'`, the roles will impact all the actions in the controller. By ignoring actions and using inheritance, we can easily block for instance a single action `deleteAll` for all users, which are not administrators, but continue to offer an access to other actions:

```
'guards' => [
    'ZfcRbac\Guard\ControllerGuard' => [
        [
            'controller' => UserController,
            'roles' => ['guest', 'user']
        ],
        [
            'controller' => UserController,
            'actions' => ['deleteAll'],
            'roles' => ['admin']
        ]
    ]
]
```

The last available type of security is `ControllerPermissionGuard`, which assigns an access to the controller based on the single permissions. Thanks to that we can set a rule for `UsersController`, which does a check if the user has permissions of name: `users.view` and `users.manage`:

```
'guards' => [
    'ZfcRbac\Guard\ControllerPermissionsGuard' => [
        [
            'controller' => UserController,
            'permissions' => ['users.view', 'users.manage']
        ]
    ]
]
```

We can of course use the same configuration possibilities of the security, same as in the Controller `Guard` or `RoutePermissionsGuard`, to change the access logic from AND into OR.

We can also directly manage the access to the particular sections in controllers, models or even views. A mechanism, which we are going to use, is called Authorization Service. It is a service that is an additional layer allowing to throw errors types as `403` (of browser requests). There are available such methods as: `$this->isGranted('permission_name')`, or `$this->hasRole('role_name')`. A sample usage of that service will be:

```php
namespace Application;

use ZfcRbac\Exception\UnauthorizedException;

class CmsController
{
    public function deleteAction()
    {
        if (!$this->isGranted('cms.delete')) {
            throw new UnauthorizedException('Access denied.');
        }
        return true;
    }
}
```

However, in the view we can do a role check in the following way:

```php
<?php if ($this->hasRole('admin')): ?>
    <div>Hello admin!</div>
<?php endif; ?>
```

Without any problems, we can also pass an authorization service to any other object, not just to the model, but also to an external library. All done via the Service Manager. Our authorization is under the key `ZfcRbac\Service\`↳`Authorizationservice`, which we can pass to our classes:

```php
return [
    'factories' => [
        ExternalClass::class => function($sm) {
            $authService = $sm->get(ZfcRbac\Service\AuthorizationService::class);
            return new ExternalClass($authService);
        }
    ]
];
```

16.3. Strategies

The strategies in ZFC RBAC are objects that listen for events called `MvcEvent::EVENT_DISPATCH_ERROR`. They set a logic, which needs to be applied when a request is not authorized. Each of the strategies must be of course registered in the `onBootstrap()` method, where by using a class from the Service Manager we can override a behavior of the `onError()` method. It is called via the event `EVENT_DISPATCH_ERROR` like so:

```
public function onBootstrap(MvcEvent $e)
{
    $app = $e->getApplication();
    $em = $app->getEventManager();
    $sm = $app->getServiceManager();
    $em->attach(
        $e::EVENT_DISPATCH_ERROR,
        function($e) use ($sm) {
            return $sm->get('ZfcRbac\View\Strategy\RedirectStrategy')->onError($e);
        }
    );
}
```

Or alternatively in a shorter way, but more convoluted, by creating a listener and attaching it to the Event Manager object:

```
public function onBootstrap(MvcEvent $e)
{
    $app = $e->getApplication();
    $em = $app->getEventManager();
    $em->attach(MvcEvent::EVENT_DISPATCH, [$this, 'selectLayoutBasedOnRoute']);
    $sm = $app->getServiceManager();
    $listener = $sm->get(\ZfcRbac\View\Strategy\RedirectStrategy::class);
    $listener->attach($em);
}
```

By default there only are two available redirect strategies – used above `RedirectStrategy` and `UnauthorizedStrategy`. `RedirectStrategy` involves redirecting a request of the URL router `'login'` for all not logged in users, who do not have access. However, the logged in users are redirected to the router of `'home'` name. Additionally, for redirecting to the `'login'` router, a variable of name `'redirectTo'` is passed there – this sets a desired page, which blocked an access. As an example, if the user tries to access the blocked part of the system: *http://localhost/zend3/cms/delete/2*, then a `redirectTo` variable: *http://localhost/zend3/login?redirectTo=http://↪localhost/zend3/cms/delete/2* will be passed to */login* address .

Of course all of these values are completely configurable and we can change them in *global.php* file:

```
return [
    'zfc_rbac' => [
        'redirect_strategy' => [
            'redirect_when_connected' => true,
            'redirect_to_route_connected' => 'home',
            'redirect_to_route_disconnected' => 'login',
            'append_previous_uri' => true,
            'previous_uri_query_key' => 'redirectTo'
        ],
    ]
];
```

A key `'redirect_when_connected'` defines if the page guests also should be redirected to the `'login'` page. An alias `'previous_uri_query_key'` gives us an ability to set a custom variable name in the URL address after redirecting.

A second strategy type is `UnauthorizedStrategy`, which integrates with the application in the same way as the previous type, so via `onBootstrap()`, but with the name `ZfcRbac\View\Strategy\UnauthorizedStrategy`. It redirects all unauthorized requests to the specified template in *error/403* path without changing the URL address in the browser. We can also modify a path of the view by overriding it in the configuration:

```
return [
    'zfc_rbac' => [
        'unauthorized_strategy' => [
            'template' => 'error/custom-page-403'
        ],
    ]
];
```

16.4. Authorization system integration

We begin our integration with ZFC RBAC by grabbing a new library in a standard way, so via the composer, and by adding that new module into a list of modules in *modules.config.php*.

```
composer require zf-commons/zfc-rbac
```

Next, we copy a file called *zfc_rbac.global.php.dist* from a newly added library folder into a root directory of Zend Framework 3: *config/autoload*. We also change a filename into *zfc_rbac.global.php*. Another step is to uncomment some of the sections and add a few example roles, like admin and user.

```
return [
    'zfc_rbac' => [
        'guards' => [
            \ZfcRbac\Guard\RouteGuard::class => [
                'admin*' => ['admin']
            ]
        ],

        'role_provider' => [
            'ZfcRbac\Role\InMemoryRoleProvider' => [
                'admin' => [
                    'children' => ['user'],
                    'permissions' => ['delete']
                ],
                'user' => [
                    'permissions' => ['edit']
                ]
            ]
        ],

        'redirect_strategy' => [
            'redirect_when_connected' => true,
            'redirect_to_route_connected' => 'home',
            'redirect_to_route_disconnected' => 'login',
```

```
            'append_previous_uri' => true,
            'previous_uri_query_key' => 'redirectTo'
        ]
    ]
];
```

We also set the strategy type to `Redirect` with specific values for all guests visiting our webpage. We adopted a hierarchical roles model, and these roles can now inherit from each other. In our example the `'admin'` role extends the `'user'` role and receives an additional permission named `'delete'`. The role `'user'` has only one permission - `'edit'`. Just before the declarations of roles we have set an access to the address of *admin* or *admin/* for administrator roles only.

To integrate the authorization we need to modify our authentication class `DivixUtils\Security\Authentication` and its configuration in the *application/src/Module.php* file:

```
\DivixUtils\Security\Authentication::class => function($sm) {
    $auth = new \DivixUtils\Security\Authentication(
    $sm->get(\Zend\Db\Adapter\Adapter::class),
    $sm->get(\DivixUtils\Security\Adapter::class)
    );
    return $auth;
},
```

Note that apart from the DB adapter we also assign an authorization adapter, which we will define in the main configuration file, *config/autoload/global.php*:

```
'service_manager' => array(
    'factories' => array(
        'Zend\\Db\\Adapter\\Adapter' => 'Zend\\Db\\Adapter\\
↪AdapterServiceFactory',
        \Zend\Authentication\AuthenticationService::class => function($sm) {
            return $sm->get(\DivixUtils\Security\Authentication::class);
        },

        \DivixUtils\Security\Adapter::class => function($sm) {
            return new \DivixUtils\Security\Adapter(
                $sm->get(\Zend\Db\Adapter\Adapter::class),
                'users',
                'email',
```

```
                    'password',
                    'SHA2(CONCAT(password_salt, "'.\DivixUtils\
    ↪Security\Helper::SALT_KEY.'", ?), 512)'
                );
            }
        ),
    ),
```

As you can see here, we moved the data of the connection itself into an INI file, because now we can pass the object `DivixUtils\Security\Adapter` under the `Zend\Authnetication\AuthenticationService` key. We have done this because the RBAC module uses this exact service for checking the information about the logged in user. Now, let's register our redirect strategy of the users according to the `RedirectStrategy` type in the *module/Admin/Module.php* file (so in the place where we are currently doing the users checks of the admin role):

```
public function onBootstrap(MvcEvent $e)
{
    $app = $e->getApplication();
    $em = $app->getEventManager();
    $em->attach(MvcEvent::EVENT_DISPATCH, [$this, 'selectLayoutBasedOnRoute']);
    $sm = $app->getServiceManager();
    $listener = $sm->get(\ZfcRbac\View\Strategy\RedirectStrategy::class);
    $listener->attach($em);
}
```

Once we started using this library to check the access, let's remove our previous, very pioneer version of checking the permission from the file *module/Admin/src/Controller/AbstractController*, beginning from `if ($this->sessionUser->details && …)`, together with else and `exit()`; We no longer need to reuse this mechanism ever again. Another task is to add the data about the available user roles into the `Rowset\User` module. We do that by adding the `getRoles()` method and by implementing an interface of `ZfcRbac\Identity\IdentityInterface` via the actual class. `getRoles()` method alone will look like below for a moment:

```
public function getRoles() {
    return [$this->getRole()];
}
```

Let's remember that `getRoles()` has to return an array of role names or just role objects. After the initial changes we have to change the source class of the authorization, which is `DivixUtils\Security\Authnetication`, by adding an extra adapter to the constructor and by changing the name of the method to `auth()` together with calling an `authenticate()` of the class parent, according to its structure. By the way, we also delete a method `getIdentity()`, which is no longer needed or used.

```
namespace DivixUtils\Security;

class Authentication extends \Zend\Authentication\AuthenticationService
{
    protected $adapter;
    protected $dbAdapter;

    public function __construct($dbAdapter, $authAdapter) {
        $this->dbAdapter = $dbAdapter;
        $this->adapter = $authAdapter;
    }

    public function auth($email, $password) {
        if (empty($email) || empty($password)) {
            return false;
        }
        $this->adapter->setIdentity($email);
        $this->adapter->setCredential($password);
        $result = $this->adapter->authenticate();
        $this->authenticate($this->adapter);
        return $result;
    }

    public function getIdentityArray()
    {
        return json_decode(json_encode($this->adapter->getResultRowObject()), true);
    }

    public function getAdapter()
    {
        return $this->adapter;
    }
}
```

The last matter will be an update of the login controller, which need to reflect all the changes we have done for the purpose of this chapter.

```php
namespace Application\Controller;

use Application\Model;
use Zend\Session;
use Application\Form;

class LoginController extends AbstractController
{
    protected $securityAuth;

    public function __construct($securityAuth)
    {
        $this->securityAuth = $securityAuth;
    }

    public function indexAction()
    {
        ...
        if (!$form->isValid()) {
            return [
                'form' => $form,
                'messages' => $form->getMessages()
            ];
        }
        $this->securityAuth->auth(
            $form->get($form::FIELDSET_LOGIN)->get('email')->getValue(),
            $form->get($form::FIELDSET_LOGIN)->get('password')->getValue()
        );
        $identity = $this->securityAuth->getIdentityArray();

        if ($identity) {
            $rowset = new Model\Rowset\User();
            $rowset->exchangeArray($identity);
            $this->securityAuth->getStorage()->write($rowset);

            $sessionUser = new Session\Container('user');
            $sessionUser->details = $rowset;
            $redirectParam = '';

            if (!empty($this->params()->fromQuery('redirectTo'))) {
                $redirectParam = '?redirectTo='.$this->params()->
↪fromQuery('redirectTo');
            }
            return $this->redirect()->toUrl('login/progressuser'.$redirectParam);
```

```
        } else {
            $message = '<strong>Error</strong> Given email address or password is
    ↪incorrect.';
            return [
                'form' => $form,
                'messages' => $message
            ];
        }
    }

    public function progressUserAction()
    {
        $sessionUser = new Session\Container('user');

        if (!empty($this->params()->fromQuery('redirectTo'))) {
            return $this->redirect()->toUrl($this->params()->
    ↪fromQuery('redirectTo'), 302);
        }

        if ($sessionUser->details->getRole() === 'admin') {
            $this->redirect()->toRoute('admin', ['controller' =>
    ↪'IndexController', 'action' => 'index']);
        } else if($sessionUser->details->getRole() === 'user') {
            $this->redirect()->toRoute('user');
        }
    }
}
```

First of all, we have renamed the method name from `authenticate()` to
`auth()`, like it is in authentication class, and soon after that we stored our
user object into an authentication memory by calling a `write($rowset)`
method on the object returned by `getStorage()`. Thanks to that, RBAC will
know that this user is already logged in. Then we created a `$redirectPart`
variable, which I set to `?redirectTo=VARIABLE` when `redirectTo` URL
variable is available. In order to properly redirect the user into such address,
we also changed the `toRoute()` method into `toUrl()` and we passed a new
variable together with the request. In the `progressUserAction()` method
we replace the lines with the calls of the server variables with a simple `if`
condition, which passes our request further if there is a `redirectTo` variable
available. At the very end we just need to use an authorization service in our
`ArticlesController`. To check if our security verifies the roles, we add a
method `deleteAction()`. which will be available only for the users with a

superadmin role:

```php
public function deleteAllAction()
{
    if (!$this->isGranted('super_admin')) {
        throw new UnauthorizedException('An access only for superadmins.');
    }
    //some our logic
    return true;
}
```

Just a small update in *Module.php* in `Admin` package, which sometimes can return `FALSE` for the `getResult()` method:

```php
if (!($match instanceof V2RouteMatch || $match instanceof V3RouteMatch)
    || 0 !== strpos($match->getMatchedRouteName(), 'admin')
    || ($controller->getEvent()->getResult() && $controller->getEvent()->
⤷getResult()->terminate())
) {
    return;
}
```

The end. In such way we have integrated an authorization layer available in our whole application, and we have used its most crucial features in the everyday situations. To get to know all available options of ZFC RBAC library, I suggest you visit its official homepage on the GitHub and check the documentation available here: *https://github.com/ZF-Commons/zfcrbac/tree/ ⤷master/docs*.

## CHAPTER 17

Creating debugs and logs module

In this chapter we are going to discuss subjects such as application debugging and storing logs of WWW websites. At the same time we will learn about Zend classes like `Logger`, `Writers`, `Filters` or `Debug` for a custom debugging and external library Whoops, which will make our error pages more attractive and allow us to place any additional data about an occurred exception on that page.

17.1. Custom debug module

Before showing a code of our new class, we will learn a bit more about the subject of `Zend\Log` package and its linked components. A log component is used for logins or for saving all kinds of data in various places, such as databases, system files or emails. This module will contain a base class: `Logger`, which is a primary object – we can assign an additional features here. The `Logger` class alone allows most of all adding messages to a channel where other already stored messages are. For this purpose there is a method `log()` that has three parameters. First parameter is a priority number, second - messages and the last one - an array of optional options, which will be passed to a `MvcEvent` object. Any number can be a priority variable, however it is recommended to use only class constants from the `Zend\Log\Logger` class, which look like below:

```
const EMERG = 0 – emergency;
const ALERT = 1 – an alert;
const CRIT = 2 – critical error;
const ERR = 3 – regular error;
const WARN = 4 – warning;
const NOTICE = 5 – notice;
const INFO = 6 – information;
const DEBUG = 7 – debugs.
```

All above priority codes are listed from the most important one to the less important. They are defined according to the RFC-3164 standard, thanks to which they should be respected accordingly in every other work environment. The easiest usage of the Logger will look like so:

```
$logger = new Zend\Log\Logger();
$logger->log(Zend\Log\Logger::INFO, 'A message');
```

Unfortunately, above lines will not result in display anywhere on site, due to the fact that we have not defined a helper class for storing, `Writer`, yet. Apart from saving the classes by `Writer`, a `Logger` has an ability to attach other classes to it, for example filters `Filter`, save formatters `Formatter` or processors `Processor` to interfere with a not yet thrown `Event`. All these components of the `Logger` class can be attached by using one of the public methods like: `addWriter()`, `setForamtter()` or `addProcessor()`. Storage classes, formatters or processors are added directly to the `Logger` class, however we add filter classes directly to the storage classes. Optionally, we can attach additional components to the `Logger` class by passing a configuration array to the constructor. Notice that all methods like `addWriter()` or `addProcessor()` could be executed multiple times in the base object. It means that there is a possibility to add many types of storage mechanisms or processors. On the other hand, `setFormatter()` means that we can specify only one type of a formatter per object.

Classes of `Writer` type give an ability to store such forms as:

- PHP data streams,

- databases based on RDMS,

- FirePHP component,

- email addresses,

- MongoDB,

- Syslog,

- Zend Monitor,

- stubbing out the data (for disabling logging)

- mocking for the test purposes.

As we already mentioned, there is a single `Logger` class which can handle many types of storage types. Thanks to that we can use a single logging class at the same time, for example for application errors to text files, exceptions to databases and debugging data to MongoDB. It gives us powerful possibilities to select, sort related data in various places and get rid of redundant lines.

Filters, however, specify which type of data needs to be stored in particular storage classes. This is why we are not applying them directly to the base Logger class, but to the `Writer` class. If we want for instance to store only regular errors, we should use a filter in the following way:

```
$writer = new Zend\Log\Writer\Stream('/some_path/to/file.log');
$logger->addWriter($writer);
$filter = new Zend\Log\Filter\Priority(Logger::ERR);
$writer->addFilter($filter);
```

Other available filters are:

- `Regex` that filters via regular expressions;

- `Timestamp` that uses data and time to specify a place of storage;

- SuppressFilter for specifying logging of all errors or none at all;

- Validator, which filters only if there is a passed condition in the passed validator object.

Let's move into formatters that define how our stored messages will look like. A default setting is using a Zend\Log\Formatter\Simple, which specifies a simple text format based on a PSR-3 for passing variables. An example formatter could as well be:

```
$format = '%timestamp% %priorityName% (%priority%): %message%' . PHP_EOL;
$formatter = new Zend\Log\Formatter\Simple($format);
$writer = new Zend\Log\Writer\Stream('php://output');
$writer->setFormatter($formatter);
$logger = new Zend\Log\Logger();
$logger->addWriter($writer);
```

Optionally we can use an XML formatting, thanks to Zend\Log\ ↪Formatter\XML or FirePHP for an extension in the Firefox browser; the XML class is placed in the same place.

Processors give us options to pass additional parameters to the Event object, and later to embellish our logs. For example, we can pass an information about backtrace, like file name, line number, class and the method to the event or insert the variable in the PSR-3 format, like below:

```
$logger->addProcessor(new Zend\Log\Processor\PsrPlaceholder());
$logger->warn('Invalid class object: {object}', ['object' =>
'My\CustomClass']);
//will return:
Invalid class object: My\CustomClass
```

There is also a processor type ReferenceId, which is used for entering a custom format identification via the setIdentifier() method of the same processor class. The last option is RequestId. This one is similar to the ReferenceId, but when we do not specify an identification in there, then it will be automatically created based on the provided information from the $_SERVER global array.

326

`Zend\Debug` package is used for displaying all kind of variable types as their equivalents to the plain strings. A Debug class detects a work environment (web or command line), and then it displays messages in HTML format or in a plain text format. A method used to display debugs is `dump()` that, as the first argument takes an object to display, then a flag for prefixing a value and a flag used for displaying a result straightaway on the screen. Additionally, it improves the white space characters, tabs and configures a class for escaping characters. A default escape class is `Zend\Escaper\Escaper`, which formats particular HTML characters, encoding, URL and secures a structure of such languages as JavaScript or CSS.

We have already covered the basis of the logger class itself and its components which fulfil the whole debugging process. It's time to use our knowledge to develop a custom class for debugging. A primary goal of our class will be a simplicity of usage and the availability in every other class, so that we do not need to register it in the Service Manager. We have decided to use a class of name `DivixUtils\Logs\Debug` with the static methods of `dump()` and `displayMessages()` and two other protected methods: `getMediumMessage()` and `getLongMessage()`.

```php
<?php
namespace DivixUtils\Logs;

use Zend\Log\Logger;
use Zend\Log\Writer\Stream;
use Zend\Log\Filter\Priority;

class Debug
{
    protected static $logger;
    /**
     * @var array $debugMessages contains all debug messages
     */
    public static $debugMessages = '';

    /**
     * Stores a message to the global contains with messages
     *
     * @param mixed $var a message to display/store
     * @param array $params available keys:: log:Boolean = false, desc:String = 'short',
     exit:Boolean = false, display:Boolean = true
     *
```

```php
 * @return void
 */
public static function dump($var, $params = [])
{
    if (empty($params['display'])) {
        $params['display'] = true;
    }
    if (empty($params['log'])){
        $params['log'] = false;
    }
    if (empty($params['exit'])) {
        $params['exit'] = false;
    }
    if (empty($params['desc'])) {
        $params['desc'] = 'short';
    }
    $debugBacktrace = debug_backtrace();
    $message = '<hr style="margin: 5px 0 0 0; border-top-color: #bfbfbf" /><hr
↪style="margin: 0 0 3px 0;" />';

    switch ($params['desc']) {
        case 'short':
            $message .= '<strong>'.$debugBacktrace[0]['file'].'</strong>
↪in line <strong>'.$debugBacktrace[0]['line'].'</strong>';
        break;
        case 'medium':
            $message .= self::getMediumMessage($debugBacktrace);
        break;
        case 'long':
            $message .= self::getLongMessage($debugBacktrace);
        break;
        default:
            throw new \Exception('invalid description provided: '.$params
↪['desc']);
    }

    $message .= \Zend\Debug\Debug::dump($var, 'DUMP', false);

    if ($params['display']) {
        self::$debugMessages .= $message;
    }
    if (!isset(self::$logger)) {
        $writer = new Stream(APPLICATION_PATH.'/data/logs/dump.log');
        self::$logger = new Logger();
```

```php
            self::$logger->addWriter($writer);
        }
        if ($params['log']) {
            self::$logger->log(Logger::INFO, strip_tags(html_entity_
↪decode($message, \ENT_QUOTES)));
        }
        if ($params['exit']) {
            exit();
        }
    }


    /**
     * Displays all of the messages inside of the HTML container
     *
     * @return string
     */
    public static function displayMessages()
    {
        if (empty(self::$debugMessages)) {
            return;
        }
        $msgContainer = '<div class="devLoggs" style="text-align: left;
↪background-color: #dfdfdf; font-family: Courier,monospace;
↪font-size: 11px; font-style: normal; font-weight: normal;
↪font-variant: normal; padding: 5px; word-wrap:break-word">';
        $msgContainer .= self::$debugMessages;
        $msgContainer .= '</div>';
        return $msgContainer;
    }


    protected static function getMediumMessage($debugBacktrace)
    {
        $message = '<ol style="margin-bottom: 2px;">';

        foreach ($debugBacktrace as $debug) {
            if (!isset($debug['class'])) {
                $debug['class'] = '';
            }
            if (!isset($debug['type'])) {
                $debug['type'] = '';
            }
            $message .= '<li>';
            $message .= '<strong>'.$debug['class'].$debug['type'].
↪$debug['function'].'</strong>';
```

```php
            $message .= ' – in file '.$debug['file'].' at line '.$debug['line'];
            $message .= ' with '.count($debug['args']).' arguments.';
            $message .= '</li>';
        }
        $message .= '</ol>';
        return $message;
    }

    protected static function getLongMessage($debugBacktrace)
    {
        $message = '<ol style="margin-bottom: 2px;">';

        foreach ($debugBacktrace as $debug) {
            if (!isset($debug['class'])) {
                $debug['class'] = '';
            }
            if (!isset($debug['type'])) {
                $debug['type'] = '';
            }
            $message .= '<li>';
            $message .= 'In file '.$debug['file'].' at line '.$debug['line'];
            $message .= ' executed <strong>'.$debug['class'].$debug['type'].
↪$debug['function'].'</strong>';

            if (count($debug['args']) != 0) {
                $message .= '<ol>';
                $args = [];

                foreach ($debug['args'] as $index => $argument) {
                    if (is_object($argument)) {
                        $argument = get_class($argument);
                    }
                    $args[] = $argument;
                }
                $message .= '<li>'.\Zend\Debug\Debug::dump($args, 'VARS',
↪false).'</li>';
                $message .= '</ol>';
            }
            $message .= '</li>';
        }
        $message .= '</ol>';
        return $message;
    }
}
```

We have created in our new class two static variables, which should be set only once per whole application. A logger variable will store an object of our `Logger`, however `debugMessages` will contain all the messages in a presentation form to display. The main method `dump()`, which will be using, apart from the object has an array of options such as `'display'` (attaching to the rest of messages), `'log'` (storing a message in the file), `'exit'` (stopping a script), or `'desc'` (a way of displaying messages). In here we have a full access to the three possible types of an object display: short for little information, medium for showing backtrace and long for displaying all available variables in every backtrace file. We can notice that the code of two bigger message types is moved over to the separate methods, so that we can decrease the size of the `dump()` method. After selecting a display format to display an object, we call a component `Zend\Debug\Debug` with `DUMP` flag and we assign such presentation to the other messages. At the end phase, we create a single full-fledge logger object and check if we need to store a message in a file of the *cache/logs/dump.log* folder. A method `displayMessages()` takes care of displaying all the gathered messages and wrapping them in a proper `<div>` with specified presentation styles. To integrate our new class, we only need to modify a single file *public/index.php*, by adding to the last lines a call of the method responsible for displaying all the messages:

```
if ($_SERVER['APPLICATION_ENV'] == 'development') {
    echo \DivixUtils\Logs\Debug::displayMessages();
}
```

Now, at any time or in any object, we can call a method `dump()` and expect it to display on the page. For example we will add 3 debug messages to the `IndexController` in the `Application` module in the following way:

```
public function indexAction()
{
    $view = new ViewModel();
    $model = $this->usersTable;
    $row = $model->getById(1);
    $view->setVariable('id', $row->getId());
    $view->setVariable('username', $row->getUsername());
    $view->setVariable('password', $row->getPassword());

    \DivixUtils\Logs\Debug::dump('short message');
    \DivixUtils\Logs\Debug::dump('medium message', ['desc' => 'medium']);
```

```
    \DivixUtils\Logs\Debug::dump('long message', ['desc' => 'long', 'log' =>
↪true]);
    return $view;
}
```

Above change should result in showing the following results in the page footer:

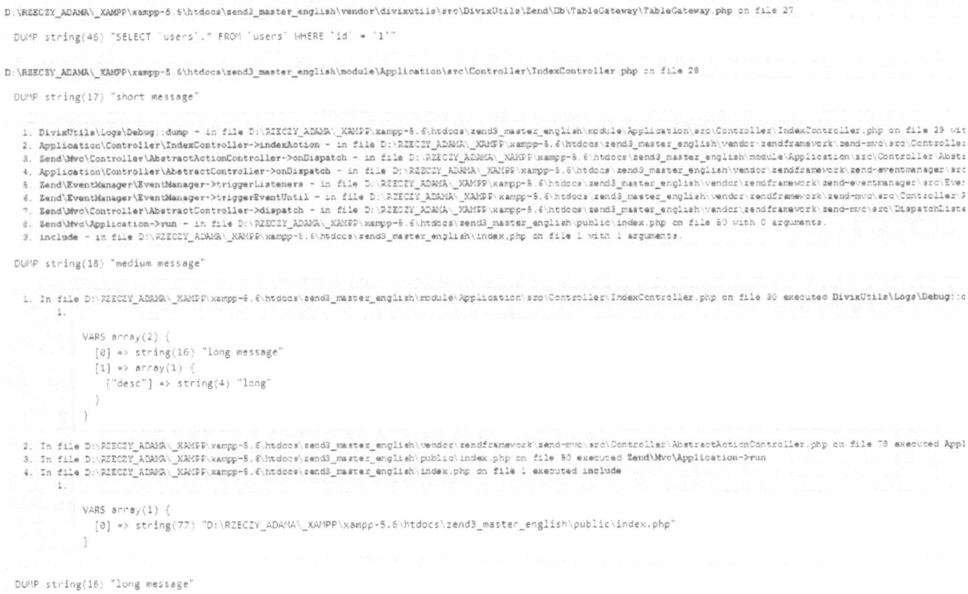

```
D:\RZECZY_ADAMA\_XAMPP\xampp-5.6\htdocs\zend3_master_english\vendor\divixutils\src\DivixUtils\Zend\Db\TableGateway\TableGateway.php on file 27

DUMP string(46) "SELECT `users`.* FROM `users` WHERE `id` = '1'"

D:\RZECZY_ADAMA\_XAMPP\xampp-5.6\htdocs\zend3_master_english\module\Application\src\Controller\IndexController.php on file 28

DUMP string(17) "short message"

1. DivixUtils\Logs\Debug::dump - in file D:\RZECZY_ADAMA\_XAMPP\xampp-5.6\htdocs\zend3_master_english\module\Application\src\Controller\IndexController.php on file 29 wit
2. Application\Controller\IndexController->indexAction - in file D:\RZECZY_ADAMA\_XAMPP\xampp-5.6\htdocs\zend3_master_english\vendor\zendframework\zend-mvc\src\Controlle
3. Zend\Mvc\Controller\AbstractActionController->onDispatch - in file D:\RZECZY_ADAMA\_XAMPP\xampp-5.6\htdocs\zend3_master_english\module\Application\src\Controller\Abstr
4. Application\Controller\AbstractController->onDispatch - in file D:\RZECZY_ADAMA\_XAMPP\xampp-5.6\htdocs\zend3_master_english\vendor\zendframework\zend-eventmanager\src
5. Zend\EventManager\EventManager->triggerListeners - in file D:\RZECZY_ADAMA\_XAMPP\xampp-5.6\htdocs\zend3_master_english\vendor\zendframework\zend-eventmanager\src\Ever
6. Zend\EventManager\EventManager->triggerEventUntil - in file D:\RZECZY_ADAMA\_XAMPP\xampp-5.6\htdocs\zend3_master_english\vendor\zendframework\zend-mvc\src\Controller\A
7. Zend\Mvc\Controller\AbstractController->dispatch - in file D:\RZECZY_ADAMA\_XAMPP\xampp-5.6\htdocs\zend3_master_english\vendor\zendframework\zend-mvc\src\DispatchListe
8. Zend\Mvc\Application->run - in file D:\RZECZY_ADAMA\_XAMPP\xampp-5.6\htdocs\zend3_master_english\public\index.php on file 50 with 0 arguments.
9. include - in file D:\RZECZY_ADAMA\_XAMPP\xampp-5.6\htdocs\zend3_master_english\index.php on file 1 with 1 arguments.

DUMP string(18) "medium message"

1. In file D:\RZECZY_ADAMA\_XAMPP\xampp-5.6\htdocs\zend3_master_english\module\Application\src\Controller\IndexController.php on file 30 executed DivixUtils\Logs\Debug::d
    1.
       VARS array(2) {
         [0] => string(16) "long message"
         [1] => array(1) {
           ["desc"] => string(4) "long"
         }
       }
2. In file D:\RZECZY_ADAMA\_XAMPP\xampp-5.6\htdocs\zend3_master_english\vendor\zendframework\zend-mvc\src\Controller\AbstractActionController.php on file 78 executed Appl
3. In file D:\RZECZY_ADAMA\_XAMPP\xampp-5.6\htdocs\zend3_master_english\public\index.php on file 50 executed Zend\Mvc\Application->run
4. In file D:\RZECZY_ADAMA\_XAMPP\xampp-5.6\htdocs\zend3_master_english\index.php on file 1 executed include
    1.
       VARS array(1) {
         [0] => string(77) "D:\RZECZY_ADAMA\_XAMPP\xampp-5.6\htdocs\zend3_master_english\public\index.php"
       }

DUMP string(16) "long message"
```

Image 17.1.

However our *dump.log* file will contain a single line with information of medium message in the following form:

```
2017-02-02T23:48:53+01:00 INFO (6): DivixUtils\Logs\Debug::dump – in file
↪D:\RZECZY_ADAMA\_XAMPP\xampp-
5.6\htdocs\zend3\module\Application\src\Controller\
↪IndexController.php at line 29 with 2 arguments.Application\Controller\
↪IndexController->indexAction – in file D:\RZECZY_ADAMA\_XAMPP\xampp↪
5.6\htdocs\zend3\vendor\zendframework\zend-mvc\src\Controller\
↪AbstractActionController.php at line 78 z 0 arguments.Zend\Mvc\Controller\
↪AbstractActionController->onDispatch – in file D:\RZECZY_ADAMA\_XAMPP\xampp-
↪5.6\htdocs\zend3\vendor\zendframework\zend-eventmanager\src\EventManager.php
↪at line 179 with 2 arguments.Zend\EventManager\EventManager->triggerEventUntil -
```

↪in file D:\RZECZY_ADAMA_XAMPP\xampp-
5.6\htdocs\zend3\vendor\zendframework\zend-
↪mvc\src\Application.php at line 332 with 2 arguments.Zend\Mvc\Application->run -
↪in file D:\RZECZY_ADAMA_XAMPP\xampp-5.6\htdocs\zend3\public\index.php at line 50
↪with 0 arguments.include - w pliku D:\RZECZY_ADAMA_XAMPP\xampp-5.6\htdocs\
↪zend3\index.php w linii 1 z 1 argumentami.DUMP string(18) "medium message"

Let's move however a bit further and debug all the SQL queries to the database. For this purpose we have to extend a Zend\Db\TableGateway\ ↪TableGateway with our new class, which we will create in the DivixUtils\Zend\Db\TableGateway\ with the same name of TableGteway. We do that to intercept every possible database interaction in the TableGteway method and we will store those information about the query in our Debug class.

```
namespace DivixUtils\Zend\Db\TableGateway;

use Zend\Db\Sql\Select;
use Zend\Db\Sql\Insert;
use Zend\Db\Sql\Update;
use Zend\Db\Sql\Delete;

class TableGateway extends \Zend\Db\TableGateway\TableGateway
{
    protected $platform;

    public function __construct(
        $table,
        \Zend\Db\Adapter\AdapterInterface $adapter,
        $features = null,
        \Zend\Db\ResultSet\ResultSetInterface $resultSetPrototype = null,
        \Zend\Db\Sql\Sql $sql = null
    ) {
        parent::__construct($table, $adapter, $features, $resultSetPrototype, $sql);
        $this->platform = new \Zend\Db\Adapter\Platform\
↪Mysql($this->adapter->driver);
    }

    public function selectWith(Select $select)
    {
        \DivixUtils\Logs\Debug::dump($select->getSqlString($this->platform));
```

```
            return parent::selectWith($select);
    }

    protected function executeInsert(Insert $insert)
    {
        \DivixUtils\Logs\Debug::dump($insert->getSqlString($this->platform),
↪['log' => true]);
        return parent::executeInsert($insert);
    }

    protected function executeUpdate(Update $update)
    {
        \DivixUtils\Logs\Debug::dump($update->getSqlString($this->platform),
↪['log' => true]);
        return parent::executeUpdate($update);
    }

    protected function executeDelete(Delete $delete)
    {
        \DivixUtils\Logs\Debug::dump($delete->getSqlString($this->platform),
↪['log' => true]);
        return parent::executeDelete($delete);
    }
}
```

We have overridden every available methods of interacting with the database, such as `selectWith()` (we are not using a regular `select()` in our classes) for displaying results, `executeInsert()` for inserting queries, `executeUpdate()` for modifying records and `executeDelete()` for removing data. In every of the overridden methods we only add our `Debug` class with the call of `dump()` and we store all query messages (apart from `SELECT`), to the logs files (as after adding, updating or deleting a phase, we redirect a site to the other address, and because of that we won't be able to see those messages on the bottom of the page). Take a close look at the way of getting a query in the plain string form. We use here a method `getSqlString()` with the passed instance of the MySQL adapter platform created in the constructor of our new class. If we do not set a platform object and just call a method without an argument, then Zend Framework will throw an exception of:

Attempting to quote a value without specific driver level support can introduce
↪security vulnerabilities in a production environment.

The platform passed to the `getSqlString()` defines the way the variables passed to the query should be secured. By default `getSqlString()` does not link with the active adapter (which does not have a platform anyway), thus we have to pass our object every time. To start using our new `TableGateway` class, we still need to update a reference in the *Module.php* file in `Application`, by changing a definition of use from:

```
use Zend\Db\TableGateway\TableGateway;
```

to:

```
use DivixUtils\Zend\Db\TableGateway\TableGateway;
```

From now on we should see all the queries of the SELECT type on the page and all others in the logs file. Often we want to split the information about debugs and errors or warnings, so that a single file does not contain too much data at the same time. This is why we will enhance our `Debug` class to make it pass the particular message to two different files: current one *debug.log* for messages and debugs and *errors.log* for all other errors.

```
if (!isset(self::$logger)) {
    $writer = new Stream(APPLICATION_PATH.'/data/logs/dump.log');
    $writer->addFilter(new Priority(Logger::INFO, '>='));

    self::$logger = new Logger();
    self::$logger->addWriter($writer);
    $errorsWriter = new Stream(APPLICATION_PATH.'/data/logs/errors.log');
    $errorsWriter->addFilter(new Priority(Logger::NOTICE));
    self::$logger->addWriter($errorsWriter);

    \Zend\Log\Logger::registerErrorHandler(self::$logger, true);
    \Zend\Log\Logger::registerFatalErrorShutdownFunction(self::$logger);
    \Zend\Log\Logger::registerExceptionHandler(self::$logger);
}
```

Notice that in the first example by using an `addFilter()` method we have passed a second parameter to the `Priority()` constructor with value of `'>='`. A second parameter sets the operator type, which has to be used. By default the operator is `'<='`, so less than or equal, and this is exactly why we have not provided an argument in the second call of `new Priority` for the NOTICE value. To understand that, we will present a hierarchy or all priority error codes.

```
const EMERG = 0;
const ALERT = 1;
const CRIT = 2;
const ERR = 3;
const WARN = 4;
const NOTICE = 5;
const INFO = 6;
const DEBUG = 7;
```

The list is set from the most important, so 0 to the less important DEBUG with the biggest value of 7. This is why we have used an operator of "greater than or equal" for only filtering INFO and DEBUG messages to the *dump.log* file. However, using the NOTICE without an operator has set the message filtering with a "less than or equal" NOTICE priority, thanks to which we have split all potential error priority codes. Of course, nothing stands in our way to specify the particular codes into a single call, but this would work the same as the first call with the >= operator.

```
$writer->addFilter(new Priority(Logger::INFO, '='));
$writer->addFilter(new Priority(Logger::DEBUG, '='));
```

Unfortunately, such usage blocks a potential new priority code greater than 7 (DEBUG), if we create a custom code; this is why it's better to define an operator which handles all those "less important" information.

Three last lines replaced in the dump() method specify that we are registering our logger to store the regular and fatal errors or all thrown exceptions. A second parameter TRUE for the registerErrorHandler() method, defines if there should be displayed an information about the error to the user by default. The default value of this method is set to FALSE, thus we need to change it. A method registerFatalErrorShutdownFunction() works pretty much the same as set_error_handler() in native PHP. Let's test the operation of the filters and logs of the errors; let's add for instance a call of nonExistingMethod(); in the IndexController. For such error our errors.log should contain a line similar to:

```
2017-02-03T00:27:28+01:00 ERR (3): Call to undefined function
↪Application\Controller\nonExistingMethod()
{"file":"D:\\RZECZY_ADAMA\\_XAMPP\\xampp-5.6\\
```

↪htdocs\\zend3\\module\\Application\\src\\Controller\\IndexController.php",
↪"line":31}

17.2. Error handling and a Whoops library

By default Zend Framework 3 comes with two error template types: 404 for
not found pages and 500 for every other thrown application exception. Both
of the view files are placed in the Application module in the folder
view/error, respectively *404.phtml* and *index.phtml* for errors. Two of these
templates look very sterile and contain some basic data. In this subsection we
are going to try to make them look prettier and enhance their functionality
along with explaining each of the error types. Thanks to *Bootsnipp.com* we
have free snippets (so the usage examples of various elements on the site) at
our disposal, like menu, breadcrumbs of forms. From that site we will copy
the styles for our new application's view errors. Let's modify a *404.phtml*
file, changing its initial code until checking the isset($this->reason), in
the following HTML:

```
<div class="error-page">
    <h2>Whoops!</h2>
    <h1 class="error404"> 404 </h1>
    <div class="error-details">
        <h2>Page not found.</h2>
    </div>

    <form class="form-inline">
        <div class="form-group">
            <label for="search">Search</label>
            <input type="text" class="form-control" id="search" placeholder=
↪"Search something else...">
        </div>
        <button type="submit" class="btn btn-primary btn-large">Search</button>
    </form>

    <div class="error-actions">
        <a href="<?= $this->url('home') ?>" class="btn btn-primary btn-lg">
```

```
        <span class="glyphicon glyphicon-home"></span> Take me back to Home
↪Page
    </a>
    <a href="<?= $this->url('home') ?>" class="btn btn-default btn-lg">
        <span class="glyphicon glyphicon-envelope"></span> Report an issue</a>
</div>
```

Of course, we will link the rest of the code with our div container called `error-page` and close that tag at the very last line by `</div>`, so that our new styles would apply to everything. As we can easily notice, the added HTML code contains a few headings with the most vital information for the user; but we also display a form with the search bar, to be able to redirect an user to the search results of a similar issue. The last two links are redirecting to a home page and to a form page where it is possible to report a bug, which (the same as for the search results) we do not have an application yet. The search module or contact form are that simple to implement, by using already covered examples of this book, so we won't cover them here. Though, it is a perfect opportunity for you to do a homework, my Reader, so that you can start writing your own controllers in Zend Framework 3 :).

Let's go back to the error files. We need to add new CSS selectors into the presentation layer; we will use the same CSS code as in the bootsnipp.com in *public/style.css* file:

```
.error-page {padding: 40px 15px;text-align: center;}
.error-actions {margin-top:15px;margin-bottom:15px;}
.error-actions .btn { margin-right:10px; }
h1.error404 { font-size :100px !important; }
```

If we hit our URL address with the not found action of the `Users` controller (for instance */users/invalid*), then we should get the result as below:

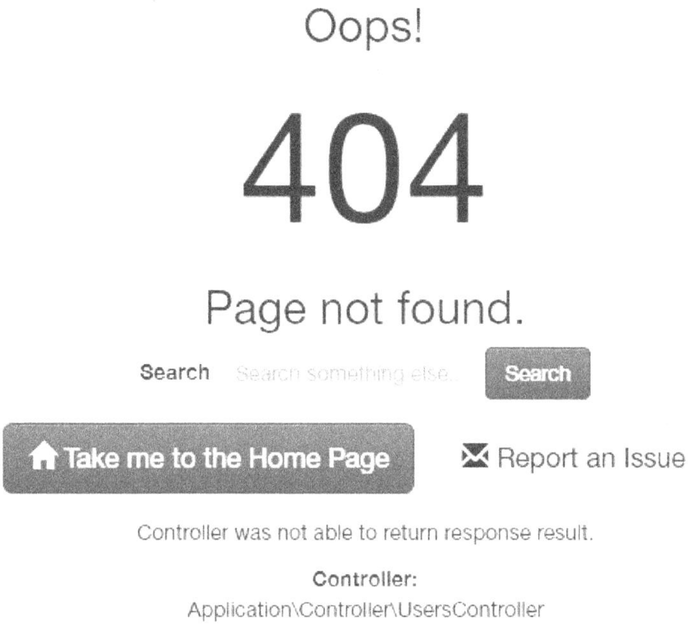

Oops!

404

Page not found.

Search   Search something else...   **Search**

🏠 **Take me to the Home Page**   ✉ Report an Issue

Controller was not able to return response result.

Controller:
Application\Controller\UsersController

Image 17.2.

Let's move into a view responsible for displaying exceptions, so codes of type 500. We will modify an *index.phtml* file the same way as in *404.phtml*, with one difference: we will not add a search form and we will change the top headings into the following ones:

```
<div class="error-page">
    <h2>Error :(</h2>
    <h1 class="error404"> 500 </h1>
    <div class="error-details">
        <h2>An error occurred error during processing, please try again or report
↪a problem.</h2>
    </div>
```

Of course, we altered the labels a bit and we placed an ending tag of </div> at the end. To manually invoke generating a 500 error type, we need to modify our IndexController in the index action, by adding the presented line:

```
throw new \Exception('Our custom exception');
```

Our home page then should look like on the image 17.3.

In this example we have an exception available (or a few previous ones) together with an information about the exceptions and their messages, file names and stack trace. Of course we don't want to display too much detailed data on the production server, but only on the local development one. Therefore we have to ensure that our main file *config/module.config.php* contains a line of view_manager: `display_not_found_reason` and `display_exceptions` set to `FALSE`, and then modify file: *config/autoload/development.local.php and development.local.php.dist* to set the same values to `TRUE`:

```
return [
    'view_manager' => [
        'display_not_found_reason' => true,
        'display_exceptions' => true,
    ]
];
```

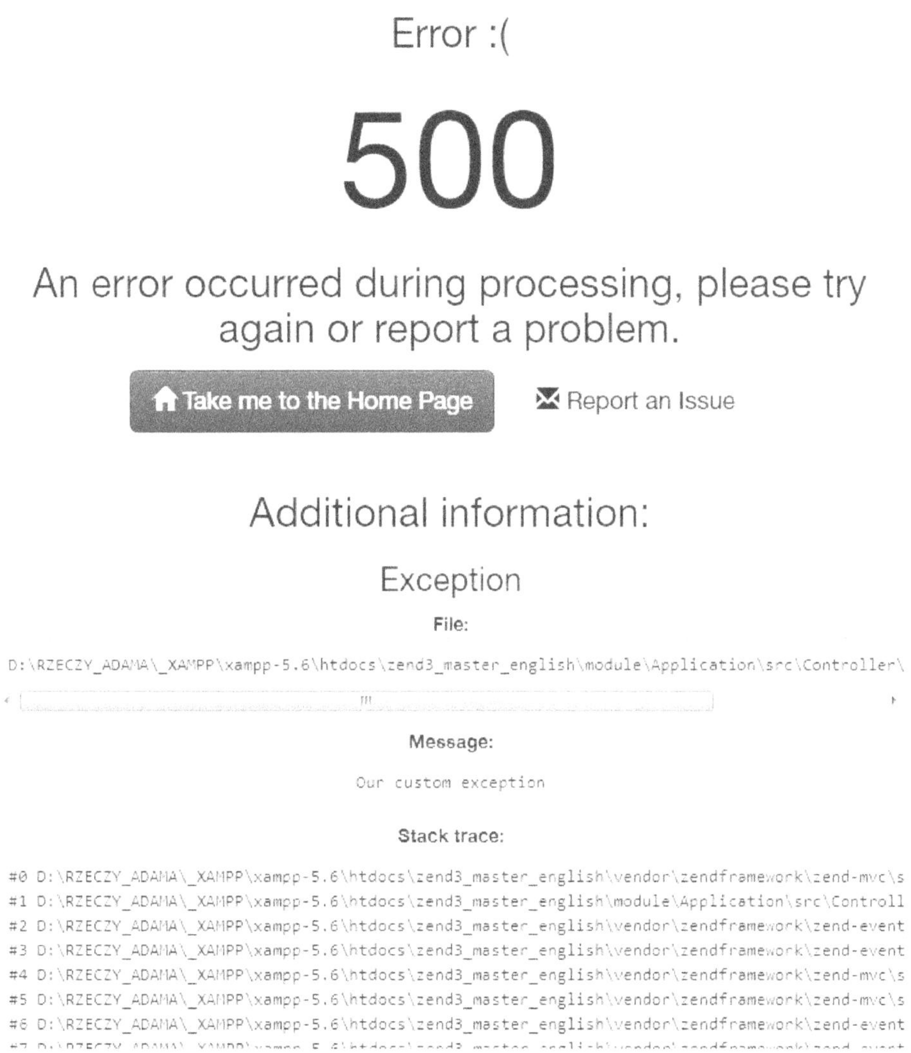

Error :(

500

An error occurred during processing, please try again or report a problem.

🏠 **Take me to the Home Page**   ✉ Report an Issue

Additional information:

Exception

File:

D:\RZECZY_ADAMA_XAMPP\xampp-5.6\htdocs\zend3_master_english\module\Application\src\Controller\

◄ [III   ]   ►

Message:

Our custom exception

Stack trace:

```
#0 D:\RZECZY_ADAMA\_XAMPP\xampp-5.6\htdocs\zend3_master_english\vendor\zendframework\zend-mvc\s
#1 D:\RZECZY_ADAMA\_XAMPP\xampp-5.6\htdocs\zend3_master_english\module\Application\src\Controll
#2 D:\RZECZY_ADAMA\_XAMPP\xampp-5.6\htdocs\zend3_master_english\vendor\zendframework\zend-event
#3 D:\RZECZY_ADAMA\_XAMPP\xampp-5.6\htdocs\zend3_master_english\vendor\zendframework\zend-event
#4 D:\RZECZY_ADAMA\_XAMPP\xampp-5.6\htdocs\zend3_master_english\vendor\zendframework\zend-mvc\s
#5 D:\RZECZY_ADAMA\_XAMPP\xampp-5.6\htdocs\zend3_master_english\vendor\zendframework\zend-mvc\s
#6 D:\RZECZY_ADAMA\_XAMPP\xampp-5.6\htdocs\zend3_master_english\vendor\zendframework\zend-event
#7 D:\RZECZY_ADAMA\_XAMPP\xampp-5.6\htdocs\zend3_master_english\vendor\zendframework\zend-event
```

Image 17.3.

Thanks to that, we can be sure that the detailed error display will be only available in the local environment. We have handled the most popular errors that most often happen after the user interaction with our website. What with the errors in plain PHP or logical errors? Let's take our previous section into an account. In the `TableGateway` file of `DivixUtils` package, we have logged in the all the queries to the log files. If we do a mistake and we do not pass any argument to the method `$select->getSqlString()`, we will end up with a single sentence about the issue:

Notice: Attempting to quote a value without specific driver level support can
↪introduce security vulnerabilities in a production environment. in
↪D:\RZECZY_ADAMA_XAMPP\xampp-5.6\htdocs\zend3\vendor\zendframework\
↪zend-db\src\Adapter\Platform\Sql92.php on line 30

There is not enough information about the error. Of course there is a starting point and we know that we have to start a debugging process in the *Sql92.php* file, but then the debugging has to go up, not down. Without looking into the Zend's code we don't have an information about the place where our application started to cause the problem. This is why we are going to introduce a Whoops library into our 3rd parties, which we could find under the address: *https://github.com/flip/whoops*. The library is available for the frameworks such as: Laravel, CakePHP, Yii or Zend in version 2 and 3. Obviously, as one of decent libraries, it also has different formats of returned messages, like: `PrettyPageHandler` (default HTML format), `PlainTextHandler`, `CallbackHandler`, `JsonResponseHandler` or `XML ResponseHandler`. In our integration with Zend we are going to use a standard and default view type. The library which we will be using will be of course a version `ZF3-Whoops`, available under: *https://github.com/Ppito/zf3-whoops*. We install it by adding a key require with the following value in the *composer.json* file:

```
"ppito/zf3-whoops": "^1.2"
```

Next, we execute composer update in the XAMPP Shell. Then we just need to add a name of the new library into the modules list. We do not do that however in the main *modules.config.php*, but in the *development.config.php* and *.dist*, so that Whoops applies only to the development environment. It's also important to insert a new library as the first record so that it covers more modules:

```
'modules' => [
    'WhoopsErrorHandler',
    'ZF\Apigility\Admin',
    'ZF\Apigility\Admin\Ui',
    'ZF\Configuration',
    'AssetManager'
],
```

If we now visit our homepage again, where previously we have seen a `NOTICE` message, then we should see a completely new error page:

Image 17.4.

From now on, along with the main information about the notice we would also get a preview of the file itself, super global arrays, session, and most of all the full stack trace on the left hand side. A stack trace with the number 14 indicates an exact class of: `TableGateway`, where we have added a malicious code. In easy and convenient way we can localize a main cause of the error in our application.

CHAPTER 18.

Implementing multi-language support

The following chapter will show how to implement a text translating system for multiple languages using Zend\I18n package and an integration with the MVC application by Zend\Mvc\I18n. We will check what formats of translations are available and in what way we can use them. By the way, we will take a closer look at how much the approach to translations of Zend Framework 1 has changed, and what to watch out for when using gettext or INI file types. We will also mention a possibility to increase the performance and about new technique of passing extra parameters to translation. At the end we will present additional helper methods of displaying specific language elements like: currencies, numbers, plurals or filters and validators.

18.1. MvcTranslate object integration

We will begin our integration with ensuring that we have a Zend\I18n and Zend\Mvc\I18n packages. A second step will be quick, easy and pleasant configuration of the translator object in the chosen file: *module.config.php*, inside of one of our modules. We perform that inside the default module called Application. Let's append the below configuration, which is responsible for setting a default language, the way of getting a translation and localization, together with the dynamic file names format.

```
'translator' => [
    'locale' => 'pl_PL',
    'translation_file_patterns' => [
        [
            'type' => 'phparray',
            'base_dir' => 'module/Application/lang',
            'pattern' => '%s.php',
        ],
    ],
]
```

A choice of the type `'phparray'` means that we will be passing our translations in a form of regular PHP arrays, which we will generate in a moment. Let's set our base folder to a path inside the module, as our translations are directly linked with the content of our module. A key `'pattern'` sets a file name for the currently selected alias in `'locale'`. The available names will be: *en_US.php*, *es_ES.php* or as in our example *pl_PL.php* inside the *module/Application/lang* folder. The initial configuration is already done. Now, let's create a directory *Application\lang* and new files within that *location pl_PL.php* with the related contents:

```
<?php

return [
    'abc' => 'translator works in Polish',
    'abc_param' => 'translator %s works in Polish'
];
```

The file format is identical as in Zend 1, where the key is for instance `'abc'`, and the translation is assigned to the value in an array. To check if our translations are available in the view, we just need to use a helper view class `Translate`, which is available under `$this->translate()` and takes three arguments: translation key, category (set by the `Zend\I18n\Translator\`↪`TextDomain`) and language. We need to modify a key `'view_helpers'` or create it in the file *module.config.php*, so that our `Translate` object is used whenever you type `$this->translate()`:

translate:

```
'view_helpers' => [
    'invokables' => [
        'translate' => \Zend\I18n\View\Helper\Translate::class
    ]
],
```

Every one of the translation examples we can execute in any view file inside the Application module. In our example we will modify a default view *index/index.phtml* as follows:

```
<?= $this->translate('abc', 'default', 'pl_PL') ?>
```

Above line should return a first value from the *pl_PL.php* file without any major issues. A second key `'abc_param'`, however, takes one variable to a correct output . To display a value, we have to use a built-in function `sprint()`, which returns a modified and filled string according to the passed variables as a second or any other parameter.

```
<?= sprintf($this->translate('abc_param'), 'super') ?>
```

Because we have called the `sprintf` together with string of `'super'`, our translated string would display: `'translator super works in Polish'`. However, if we want to send and set variables according to the custom order, we have to change the references `%s` to `%1$s` for the first passed variable, `%2$s` for the second and so on. So let's append another variable to our file, so it looks like:

```
'abc_params' => 'translator works %2$s %1$s'
```

Next, let's execute it from the view level and observe the result:

```
<?= sprintf($this->translate('abc_params'), 'first', 'second') ?>
```

```
//will return:
translator works second first
```

In order to increase the performance and to avoid an unnecessary converting of language files like *pl_PL.php*, we will attach a cache method into our `Translate` object. To achieve that, we need to go back to the *module.config.php* file and add the below section to our existing `'translate'` configuration key:

```
'cache' => [
    'adapter' => [
        'name' => 'Filesystem',
        'options' => [
            'cache_dir' => 'data/cache',
            'ttl' => '86400' //24h
        ]
    ],
    'plugins' => [
        [
            'name' => 'serializer',
            'options' => []
        ],
        'exception_handler' => [
            'throw_exceptions' => true
        ]
    ]
],
```

We have set a local cache mode based on the system text files, stored in folder *data/cache*, which will be reloaded only after 24 hours. We also need to set a `'serializer'` plugin, to serialize the object type `Zend\I18n\Translator\TextDomain`. This will create a file with .dat extension, which informs about the converted data. By the way, we set an option `throw_exceptions` to TRUE. If we come across any issues during storing/serliaization of the file, then we should get a proper exception. Our *.dat* file will contain an information similar to those:

C:31:"Zend\I18n\Translator\TextDomain":177:{x:i:0;a:3:{s:3:"abc";s:17:"translator
↪works";s:9:"abc_param";s:20:"translator %s works";s:10:"abc_params";s:28:
↪"translator works %2$s %1$s";};m:a:1:{s:13:" * pluralRule";N;}}

18.2. Available translation formats

Apart from the compatibility with the standard PHP arrays, the translator is compatible with the files of INI and GetText formats. It's worth pointing out that many other formats, which used to be supported in Zend 1, are no longer supported in the latest version of this framework. Another crucial issue is the format change for the INI files, which has become a bit convoluted and it's no longer that simple and elegant as before. Thus, our previous language files would unfortunately require restructuring, so they would function in ZF3.

Let's start from with an example that undoubtedly are new INI files, which from now on should take three lines instead of one:

```
[abc]
message = abc
translation = translator działa ini

[abc_param]
message = abc_param
translation = translator %s działa ini

[abc_params]
message = abc_params
translation = translator działa %2$s %1$s ini
```

Take a look, that from now on a section name is required as the translation key, where two values are nested – the key name and the translation. Above script is a code of a newly generated file in folder *lang/* called *pl_Pl.ini*. To be able to use the new translation source, we have to change the translator configuration into ini type, and file extensions in pattern from *.php* into *.ini*. Of course we can't forget about deleting the cache of our translator object in the *data/cache* folder.

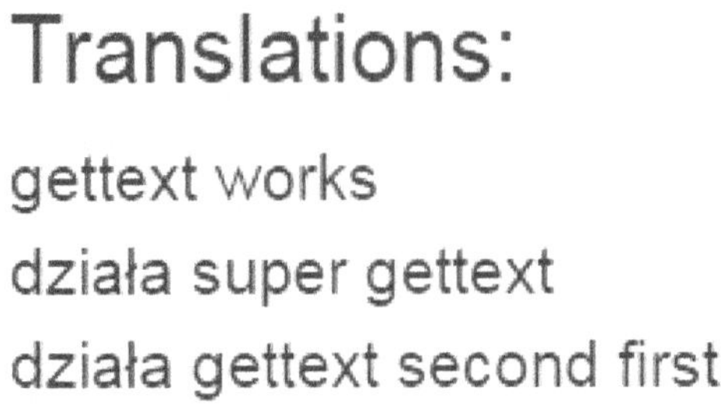

Translations:

gettext works

działa super gettext

działa gettext second first

Image 18.1.

The third and last formatting option of the translation is `GetText`. It's based on the PHP extension and if it's not available, Zend offers a support of that functionality. The extension offers an universal format available in many platforms like C++ or JAVA, but also a built-in function of plurals of each of the translations. More about GetText can be read on the official PHP documentation website: *http://php.net/manual/en/book.gettext.php*. Because GetText goes beyond this book, the only thing we need to know is that files of the GetText type have to be generated. To create such files we can use an official tool, so PoEdit or our own libraries like: *https://github.com/ ↪oscarotero/Gettext*. For the purpose of this section we have decided to self-install an application, which is available for free at: *https://poedit.net*. Before running the application itself, we will explain the different file extensions, on which we will be operating:

PO files (Portable Object) are "project" files of PO Edit – base translations for different files.

POT files (Portable Object Template) these are files containing a translation keys template together with the empty values for the translations.

MO files are files generated based on the PO file together with one or multiple POT files. These are the files we can use in PHP.

We start by creating a template file for translation *.POT*, which we place in the */lang* folder with name *pl_PL.pot*. We set the content of this file as:

```
msgid "abc"
msgstr ""
msgid "abc_param"
msgstr ""
msgid "abc_params"
msgstr ""
```

Let's turn on a PO Edit application and select the *File/New* and accept the selected default language (in my case) Polish. Next, we choose the first option, which states about the chosen *.POT* file. Then we navigate to the created file, thanks to which records for translating will appear. We can update/enter them by an application by using bottom fields:

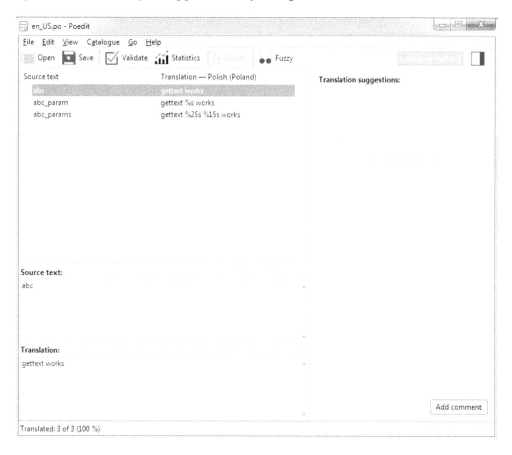

Image 18.2.

We save and export such filled translation file into a *.MO* format by running

File/Compile to MO and we save it under the same name, so *pl_PL.mo*. Next, we go back to the translator configuration in the *module.config.php* file and change the type to gettext together with the file extension of '.*mo'*.

18.3. Additional classes and localization methods

Apart from the default object of string translations, `Zend\I18n` package also contains a few other helper plugins for displaying such things as localized currencies, date formats, numbers or even plurals for a specified language. Each of the plugins must be first registered in the *modules.config.php* file, same as for translate plugin case.

```
'view_helpers' => [
    'invokables' => [
        'translate' => \Zend\I18n\View\Helper\Translate::class,
        'currencyFormat' => \Zend\I18n\View\Helper\CurrencyFormat::class,
        'dateFormat' => \Zend\I18n\View\Helper\DateFormat::class,
        'numberFormat' => \Zend\I18n\View\Helper\NumberFormat::class,
        'plural' => \Zend\I18n\View\Helper\Plural::class,
    ]
],
```

With helper classes set like that, we can begin from the plugin responsible for displaying localized numbers together with values (all of our changes are still located in the view file *index/index.phtml*). This exact formatting class is used also by a `CurrencyFormat` helper, which we will learn about in a second. A signature of this method from the view level looks like below:

```
numberFormat(
    int|float $number [,
    int $formattingStyle = null,
    int $formattingType = null,
    string $locale = null,
    int $decimals = null,
    array $textAttributes = null
) : string
```

First and only required parameter is of course an input number, which by default can be an integer or decimal (float). A parameter `$formattingStyle` defines what is the context of the number – it could be a regular DECIMAL type, PERCENT or DURSTION and ORDINAL from the NumberFormatter class. An information about the available class constants in the NumberFormatter could be found under the address: *http://php.net/manual/en/class.numberformatter.php*.

The third parameter is a formatting type used for specific number parsing like TYPE_DEFAUL, TYPE_DOUBLE and TYPE_INT24. An argument `$decimals` defines how many digits should be displayed after the comma for the given number. If we pass FALSE or NULL, there won't be any visible decimal parts. The last parameter is used for decorating a number in case it's a negative or positive value. Here are a few examples of usage of the formatting number class in the American and Polish formats.

```
<h2>Numbers:</h2>
American format: <?= $this->numberFormat(
    2000.1234560,
    NumberFormatter::DECIMAL,
    NumberFormatter::TYPE_DEFAULT,
    'en_US'
); ?><br />

Polish format: <?= $this->numberFormat(
    2000.1234560,
    NumberFormatter::DECIMAL,
    NumberFormatter::TYPE_DEFAULT
); ?><br />

Polish format without decimals and with negative character on the end: <?= $this->
↪numberFormat(
    -2000.1234560,
    NumberFormatter::DECIMAL,
    NumberFormatter::TYPE_DEFAULT,
    'pl_PL',
    false,
    [
        NumberFormatter::POSITIVE_SUFFIX => ' ^',
        NumberFormatter::NEGATIVE_SUFFIX => ' v'
    ]
); ?><br />
```

```
//will return:
American format: 2,000.123
Polish format: 2 000,123
Polish format without decimals and with negative character on the end: -2 000,123 ∨
```

Notice that not passing a local language results in using a default language set in the configuration of the `'translate'` object.

Another plugin is currency localization via `CurrencyFormat` plugin, which actually uses from `NumberFormat` class, to display appropriate price before or after of the currency sign. The definition usage itself looks like so:

```
currencyFormat(
    float $price,
    string $currency = null,
    bool $decimals = null,
    string $language = null,
    string $pattern = null
) : string
```

The first argument does not require explanations, however, the second parameter is a standard currency code like `PLN`, `GBP`, `USD`, etc. A parameter `$pattern` sets a numbers decoration via custom characters. The rest of the arguments have been already explained in the `NumberFormat` helper example.

```
<h2>Currencies:</h2>
American dolar format: <?= $this->currencyFormat(
    1234.56,
    'USD',
    true,
    'en_US'
); ?><br />

Polish dolar format: <?= $this->currencyFormat(
    1234.56,
    'USD',
    true
); ?><br />

Polish zloty format without decimals: <?= $this->currencyFormat(
    1234.56,
```

354

```
        'PLN',
        false,
        'pl_PL',
        '<#>'
); ?><br />
```

//will return:
American dolar format: $1,234.56
Polish dolar format: 1 234,56 USD
Polish zloty format without decimals: <1235>

The third plugin is `DateFormat`, which formats dates and the full time according to the language.

```
dateFormat(
    mixed $date,
    int $dateType = null,
    int $timeType = null,
    string $language = null
) : string
```

The first argument is an object of `DateTime` type or a string of standard date and time format. Another two arguments define a type of displaying of date and time. Available values are the class constants of `IntlDateFormatter` class, so `FULL`, `LOG`, `MEDIUM`, `SHORT` or `GREGORIAN`. We will present cases of displaying American and Polish dates along with a shorter version of the date only when we do not pass the argument of `$timeType`.

```
<h2>Dates:</h2>
American date format: <?= $this->dateFormat(
    new DateTime(),
    IntlDateFormatter::MEDIUM, //data
    IntlDateFormatter::MEDIUM, //czas
    'en_US'
); ?><br />

Polish date format: <?= $this->dateFormat(
    new DateTime(),
    IntlDateFormatter::LONG,
    IntlDateFormatter::MEDIUM
); ?><br />

Polish shorter date format without time: <?= $this->dateFormat(
```

```
        new DateTime(),
        IntlDateFormatter::SHORT
); ?><br />

//will return:
American date format: Feb 9, 2017, 11:11:40 PM
Polish date format: 9 lutego 2017 23:11:40
Polish shorter date format without time: 09.02.2017
```

The last view plugin is `Plural`, which relates to variations of words in the plural form. In the case of the English language that rule is 1 book and 2 books or 11 books. However, in the Polish language this looks a bit more advanced. Let's have a look at the signature of the method:

```
plural(
    array $varieties,
    int $number
) : string
```

At the beginning we pass a list of word varieties for every rule, which first needs to be established. Next, we pass a number, based on which a proper word variation will be chosen and displayed. A rule has to be declared by us somewhere in the view or in the `onBootstrap()` method if we want to re-use it in more than one file. For the sake of clarity, however, we will set this rule in the view itself.

```
<?php
    //English version
    $this->plugin('plural')->setPluralRule(nplurals=2; plural=(n==0 || n==1 ? 0 : 1)');
    $hours = ['hour', 'hours'];
?>
```

We set the rule via a helper method `setPluralRule()`, which claims that we only have two forms of the word: `'hour'`. Then we perform a check if the number equals `0` or `1`; for those two cases we use a singular form, and for the rest it is a plural form, which we can easily illustrate:

```
<h2>Plural examples:</h2>
English:<br />
<?php
//we set a general rule of the plural in the view file or in onBootstrap() method via Service
Manager
```

```
$this->plugin('plural')->setPluralRule('nplurals=2; plural=(n==0 || n==1 ? 0 :
1)');
$hours = ['hour', 'hours'];
?>

1: <?= $this->plural($hours, 1); ?><br />
2: <?= $this->plural($hours, 2); ?><br />
5: <?= $this->plural($hours, 5); ?><br />

//will return:
1: hour
2: hours
5: hours
```

Things get tough for the irregular languages, and Polish is surely one of them. To begin we have to go into a website with already defined rules or plurals for every language: *https://developer.mozilla.org/en-US/docs/Mozilla/Localization/Localization_and_Plurals*. As we can easily notice, Polish is linked with a rule number 9, which has three possible forms for the every plural word. Based on that we will often have to convert the rules in our plugin. We can also take advantage of the benefits of Zend Framework 1 and the class `Zend\Translate\Plural`: *https://github.com/↳zendframework/zf1/blob/master/library/Zend/Translate/Plural.php* that already contains ready-made rules associated to countries. After a few tweaks, our polonized version of the plural form of the `hour` word will look like so:

```
Polish:<br />
<?php
$this->plugin('plural')->setPluralRule('nplurals=3; plural=((n == 1) ? 0 :
↳(((n % 10 >= 2) && (n % 10 <= 4) && ((n % 100 < 12) || (n % 100 > 14)))
↳? 1 : 2))');
$hours = ['godzina', 'godziny', 'godzin'];
?>

1: <?= $this->plural($hours, 1); ?><br />
2: <?= $this->plural($hours, 2); ?><br />
5: <?= $this->plural($hours, 5); ?><br />

//will return:
Polish
1: godzina
2: godziny
```

At the end of this chapter I also want to mention about the available packages as: `Filter` and `Validator`, which are varieties of the standard components, with the difference that they are linked to a default chosen application language. For the filters it will be: `Alnum, Alpha, NumberFormat` and `NumberParse`, however for the validators: `Alnum, Alpha, IsFloat` and `IsInt`. Their operation and usage is practical the same way as their target equivalents, hence they will not be described further. More information about `Zend\I18n Filter` and `Validator` packages can be found at: *https://docs.zendframework.com/zend-i18n/filters* and *https://docs.↪zendframework.com/zend-i18n/validators*.

CHAPTER 19.

Creating forms based on Bootstrap Twitter CSS structure

In this chapter we are going to present how to create custom helper classes for views, so-called View Helpers, and show how they are configured in our application. We will focus on how an example form is rendered in the CSS Bootstrap v3 library. Our library will be able to generate a HTML code for three types of the forms: vertical, horizontal and in one line, according to the Bootstrap v3 library specifications.

19.1. Preparing a form and a controller

For the uninitiated: Bootstrap 3 is the most recent version of a CSS and JavaScript library, which defines readymade solutions, presentation of particular page elements and their whole structure, by starting with components like Grid 960 and finishing at icons. More information can be found at the URL: *http://getbootstrap.com.*

It won't be a massive surprise if we start by defining a new controller in the `Application` module called `FormsController`, and by adding it to the top navigation on our website. Our very simple controller will only contain the return of the already existing form object of `UserForm` with default call and error display.

```
namespace Application\Controller;

use Application\Form\UserForm;

class FormsController extends AbstractController
{
    public function indexAction()
    {
        $userForm = new UserForm();
        $request = $this->getRequest();

        if (!$request->isPost()) {
            return ['form' => $userForm];
        }
        $userForm->setData($request->getPost());

        if (!$userForm->isValid()) {
            return ['form' => $userForm];
        }
        //some our logic
        return [
            'form' => $userForm
        ];
    }
}
```

Let's modify the form itself, so it doesn't add required HTML attributes for now (this will allow us to see all generated form errors), and let's add an element of `Textarea` type in order to use all most often used form elements. The code of the new element is pasted into `UserInfoFieldset` class at the very end of the constructor.

```
$this->add(array(
    'name' => 'comments',
    'type' => Element\Textarea::class,
```

```
    'options' => array(
        'label' => 'Comments'
    ),
));
```

Additionally, we append the linked validator to a `getInputFilter`
↪`Specification()` method.

```
'comments' => array(
    'required' => true
)
```

We create a view file with the following name *views/forms/index.phtml*,
which will contain the easiest method of displaying a form:

```
<div class="jumbotron">
    <h1><span class="zf-green">Forms in Bootstrap 3 format</span></h1>
    <h2>Vertical format</h2>
    <?= $this->form($form); ?>
</div>
```

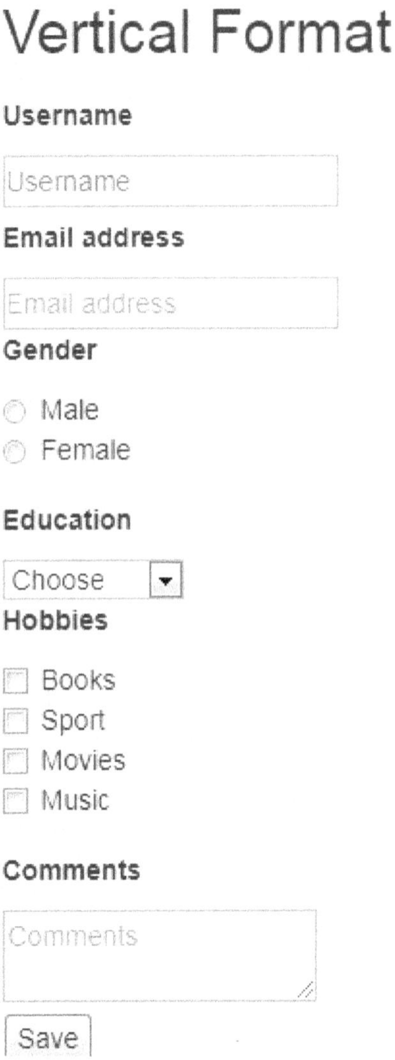

Vertical Format

Username

Username

Email address

Email address

Gender

○ Male
○ Female

Education

Choose ▼

Hobbies

☐ Books
☐ Sport
☐ Movies
☐ Music

Comments

Comments

Save

Image 19.1.

19.2. A form implementation in Bootstrap 3

Once we have an example form with almost all commonly used elements in regular forms, let's take care of "polishing" it to the Bootstrap 3 format. The forms in that library would have to be presented in the following structure and order:

```
<form>
    <div class="form-group">
        <label class="control-label"></label>
        <input class="form-control">
    </div>
</form>
```

Thanks to assigning a specified CSS class to each tag, we will be able to make and modify our presentation without the need to override the previous library styles unnecessarily. As we can easily notice, every of our form elements must be placed inside the `<div>` containing a `form-group` class. However, every label input or `textarea` tag should consist of a `control-label` or `form-control`. Every form in Bootstrap 3 can be presented in three view modes: vertical, horizontal or inline. The vertical view is a default setting, in which the label and form elements appear in two different lines. A horizontal view sets the label on the left of each element. A inline view sets all the elements horizontally in one single line. It is used most often for displaying the narrow login forms in the page heading. Of course, in this chapter we will implement all three view presentation modes of forms in Zend Framework 3.

We will begin our implementation by defining a new helper view class called `bootstrapForm` – which will be responsible for displaying a form, same as the view class form, which we could potentially override also into the custom one. However, we won't be overriding the default logic of displaying regular forms in Zend 3 because we want to have the option to display the standard form or to use it in a new format without affecting other already used form in the old format. To register and attach the new view class, we have to, the same as in previous chapter, modify an array of `view_heleprs` and invokable together with the additional key `'factories'` that defines in what way objects of the given class will be created. The newly generated class will be placed into a `DivixUtils` package inside `Zned\View\Helper\`
↪`BootstrapForm`:

```
'view_helpers' => [
    'invokables' => [
        ...
```

```
        'bootstrapForm' => \DivixUtils\Zend\View\Helper\BootstrapForm::class
    ],
    'factories' => [
        \DivixUtils\Zend\View\Helper\BootstrapForm::class => InvokableFactory::class,
    ]
],
```

By the assigned values `InvokableFactory::class` in the key factories, we set that our new class does not require any additional parameters in the constructor. Let's create the given `bootstrapForm` class with the following code:

```
namespace DivixUtils\Zend\View\Helper;

use Zend\Form\FormInterface;
use Zend\Form\FieldsetInterface;

class BootstrapForm extends \Zend\View\Helper\AbstractHelper
{
    const MODE_INLINE = 'inline';
    const MODE_HORIZONTAL = 'horizontal';
    const MODE_VERTICAL = 'vertical';
    protected $formHelper;

    public function __invoke(FormInterface $form = null, $mode =
↪self::MODE_VERTICAL)
    {
        //$this->formHelper = $this->getView()->plugin('form');
        $this->formHelper = $this->getView()->form();

        if (!$form) {
            return $this;
        }
        return $this->render($form, $mode);
    }

    public function render(FormInterface $form, $mode = self::MODE_VERTICAL)
    {
        if (method_exists($form, 'prepare')) {
            $form->prepare();
        }
        $formContent = '';
        $existingClasses = $form->getAttribute('class');
        //let's make sure that we don't have bootstrap form classes
```

```
        $existingClasses = str_replace('form-horizontal', ",
↪str_replace('form-inline', ", $existingClasses));

        if ($mode == self::MODE_INLINE) {
            $form->setAttribute('class', $existingClasses.' form-inline');
        } elseif ($mode == self::MODE_HORIZONTAL) {
            $form->setAttribute('class', $existingClasses.' form-horizontal');
        }

        foreach ($form as $element) {
            if ($element instanceof FieldsetInterface) {
                $formContent.= $this->getView()->bootstrapFormCollection
↪($element, $mode);
            } else {
                $formContent.= $this->getView()->bootstrapFormRow
↪($element, $mode);
            }
        }
        return $this->formHelper->openTag($form) . $formContent . $this->
↪formHelper->closeTag();
    }
}
```

The presented class, as it is our base helper class, extends only an abstract helper class `Zend\View\Helper\AbstractHelper`. On this level we also define three class constants: `MODE_INLINE`, `MODE_HORIZONTAL` and `MODE_VERTICAL`, which describe the current form display mode. This exact mode is passed to the `invoke()` method that will be called by default when we trigger `$this->bootstrapForm()` from the view level. Obviously, the first argument, as in original class case, will be an optional form – if it is passed, we will execute a `render()` method with the same arguments. Notice that in every such view class we can get other helper classes via two available methods:

```
$this->formHelper = $this->getView()->plugin('form');
```

or:

```
$this->formHelper = $this->getView()->form();
```

They provide the same functionality and can be used interchangeably. A good habit is however to use the second method due to the hints in the IDE editor. The first format can be used for dynamically generated view classes, which come as strings for instance from the configuration.

The `render()` method, as the name explains, is used for generating a proper code for the HTML form. We execute a method `prepare()` in the form, if it exists, to set all the errors and dependencies. We get all existing classes of the form that might be added to the same form file. We reset the previous classes as `form-horizontal` or `form-inline`, which should not be duplicated and shouldn't exist in the same form at the same time. Next, we do a check of the display mode, to apply a new controlling class of the whole form. Another stage is iterating over all the form elements and parsing them properly, if it is a fieldset or a group of elements (`bootstrapForm` ↪`Collection`), or a single element (`bootstrapFormRow`). Both of these calls from `$this->getView()` level require registering two new view classes `bootstrapFormCollection` (instead of `formCollection`) and `bootstrapFormRow` (instead of `formRow`). At the end we return all the generated elements together with the surrounding form tags that already exists in the standard class of `'form'`. Let's create two new additional classes, which of course first we register in the configuration.

```
'view_helpers' => [
    'invokables' => [
        ...
        'bootstrapForm' => \DivixUtils\Zend\View\Helper\BootstrapForm::class,
        'bootstrapFormRow' => \DivixUtils\Zend\View\Helper\
↪BootstrapFormRow::class,
        'bootstrapFormCollection' => \DivixUtils\Zend\View\Helper\
↪BootstrapFormCollection::class
    ],

    'factories' => [
        \DivixUtils\Zend\View\Helper\BootstrapForm::class =>
↪InvokableFactory::class,
        \DivixUtils\Zend\View\Helper\BootstrapFormRow::class =>
↪InvokableFactory::class,
        \DivixUtils\Zend\View\Helper\BootstrapFormCollection::class =>
↪InvokableFactory::class
    ]
],
```

Let's start from a slightly longer class `DivixUtils\Zend\View\`

↪HelperBootstrapFormRow, which will handle the generation of each single form element, such as input field, list of `radio` type or `checkbox`. Because our class only overrides two methods of the already existing class `Zend\Form\View\Helper\FromRow` by using `BootstrapForm`, we will use that as the base class for our view helper.

```php
namespace DivixUtils\Zend\View\Helper;

use Zend\Form\Element\Submit;
use Zend\Form\Element\Checkbox;
use Zend\Form\Element\MultiCheckbox;
use Zend\Form\Element\Radio;
use Zend\Form\Element\MonthSelect;
use Zend\Form\Element\Captcha;
use Zend\Form\Element\Button;
use Zend\Form\ElementInterface;
use Zend\Form\LabelAwareInterface;

class BootstrapFormRow extends \Zend\Form\View\Helper\FormRow
{
    public function render(ElementInterface $element, $labelPosition = null)
    {
        $escapeHtmlHelper = $this->getEscapeHtmlHelper();
        $labelHelper = $this->getLabelHelper();
        $elementHelper = $this->getElementHelper();
        $elementErrorsHelper = $this->getElementErrorsHelper();
        $label = $element->getLabel();
        $inputErrorClass = $this->getInputErrorClass();
        $extraClass = '';
        $extraMultiClassLabel = '';
        $extraMultiClassInput = '';

        if (is_null($labelPosition)) {
            $labelPosition = $this->labelPosition;
        }
        if (isset($label) && '' !== $label) {
            // label translation
            if (null !== ($translator = $this->getTranslator())) {
                $label = $translator->translate($label, $this->
↪getTranslatorTextDomain());
            }
        }
```

Our new class does not override the base method of invoke() because we don't have to make any changes in there. The same as in the BootstrapForm, the method invoke() also calls a method render(), which was presented above. Here we retrieve most of our dependencies of other view classes: escapeHTML, label, element or elementError. They will be useful in generating their HTML code and the further settings. Next, we get a label of the element form and store the $label variable it in. Later, we perform a check if the variable exists, and its translation into a translator view class. Because our BootstrapForm class always calls the render() with a second argument responsible for $labelPosition, a check of is_null above it will not be executed. However, we have left this code from the base class, due to the generic nature of our code. If for instance we want to use the same BootstrapFormRow class without the BootstrapForm, we should set a default label value.

```
$classAttributes = ($element->hasAttribute('class') ? $element->
↪getAttribute('class') . ' ' : '');

// does that element contains errors?
if (count($element->getMessages()) > 0 && !empty($inputErrorClass)) {
    $extraClass .= $inputErrorClass;
}

if ($this->partial) {
    $vars = [
        'element' => $element,
        'label' => $label,
        'labelAttributes' => $this->labelAttributes,
        'labelPosition' => $labelPosition,
        'renderErrors' => $this->renderErrors,
    ];
    return $this->view->render($this->partial, $vars);
}

if ($this->renderErrors) {
    $elementErrorsHelper->setMessageOpenFormat('<div %s>');
    $elementErrorsHelper->setMessageSeparatorString('<br />');
    $elementErrorsHelper->setMessageCloseString('</div>');
    $elementErrors = $elementErrorsHelper->render($element, ['class' =>
↪'help-block']);
}
```

```
if ($label) {
    $element->setAttribute('placeholder', $label);
}
```

Another lines retrieve a `'class'` attribute first to prevent overriding of already existing change, however later we do a check if the given element has any available errors. Next, we append to the `$extraClass` variable a default error class in the string format, retrieved by `$this->getInputErrorClass()`, which we have defined at the end of our new class. A check of the `$this->partial` variable makes sure if the view file for generating a special element was passed. It comes from the base class of `Zend\FormView\Helper\FromRow` of `invoke()` method, which looks like:

```
public function __invoke(ElementInterface $element = null, $labelPosition = null,
↪$renderErrors = null, $partial = null)
{
    if (!$element) {
        return $this;
    }
    if (is_null($labelPosition)) {
        $labelPosition = $this->getLabelPosition();
    }
    if ($renderErrors !== null) {
        $this->setRenderErrors($renderErrors);
    }
    if ($partial !== null) {
        $this->setPartial($partial);
    }
    return $this->render($element, $labelPosition);
}
```

Going back to the previous code of our new class, at the end we check if the flag displaying errors is set on TRUE. It is also a default value of this variable, thus we don't have to additionally pass it over. The last check adds a placeholder attribute to the element, which displays a value of each empty element in a browser.

```
if ($element instanceof Submit) {
    $element->setAttribute('class', 'btn btn-default');
} elseif ($element instanceof Checkbox || $element instanceof
↪MultiCheckbox) {
    $element->setAttribute('class', 'checkbox');
```

```
    } else {
        $element->setAttribute('class', 'form-control');
    }

    $elementString = $elementHelper->render($element, $labelPosition);
    // hidden elements does not need <label> tag
    $type = $element->getAttribute('type');

    if (isset($label) && " !== $label && $type !== 'hidden') {
        $markup = '<div class="form-group '.$extraClass.'">';
        $labelAttributes = ['class' => 'control-label'];

        if ($element instanceof LabelAwareInterface) {
            if ($labelPosition == BootstrapForm::MODE_HORIZONTAL) {
                $labelAttributes['class'] .= ' col-sm-2';
                $extraMultiClassLabel = 'col-sm-2';
                $extraMultiClassInput = 'col-sm-10';
            }
            array_merge($labelAttributes, $element->getLabelAttributes());
        }

        if (! $element instanceof LabelAwareInterface || ! $element->
    ↪getLabelOption('disable_html_escape')) {
            $label = $escapeHtmlHelper($label);
        }

        if (empty($labelAttributes)) {
            $labelAttributes = $this->labelAttributes;
        }
```

Going further, we add the HTML classes, retrospectively: `btn btn-default` for every button of the form submission according to the Bootstrap library specification, and `form-control` for every other element. We generate an element code in the `$elementString` variable, and then perform a check if the label is not empty or the element is not a hidden form element. For such cases we add a tag `<div>` with class `form-group`, which will contain exactly that label with the element. Next, we check if the horizontal mode has been selected; if so, then we have to use classes for setting tags next to each other according to the Grid960 grid. In such definition a single row has the maximum of 12 available `<div>` tags with classes of `col-sm-*`. A number after each of such class name defines how long the element should be. In our example 2 places should cover a label, however the rest (10 places) will be filled by the form element. Next, we merge two arrays of label classes into one and reuse an `escapeHtml` class, which handles and properly reformats the passed in HTML code as the label name.

```
// Elements Multicheckbox must be handled separatly,
// as HTML standard does not allow for the nested labels.
// An approriate replacement here is a fieldset tag
if ($type === 'multi_checkbox'
    || $type === 'radio'
    || $element instanceof MonthSelect
    || $element instanceof Captcha
) {
    $classMapping = [
        'radio' => 'radio',
        'multi_checkbox' => 'checkbox'
    ];

    $markup .= sprintf(
        '<label class="control-label %s">%s</label><div class="%s
↪%s">%s</div>',
        $extraMultiClassLabel,
        $label,
        $classMapping[$type],
        $extraMultiClassInput,
        $elementString
    );
```

As the comment indicates, we perform a check of the element type, if it is radio or `multi_checkbox`, month selection or `captcha`. We treat the same all of these elements; we append and display a class `control-label` first, and later we pass the classes `radio` or `checkbox`, depending on the actually parsed element, to an additional `<div>` element, which will contain the form element itself.

```
    } else {
        // If the element has id attribute, it will display a separate label and element
        if ($element->hasAttribute('id')
            && ($element instanceof LabelAwareInterface && !$element->
↪getLabelOption('always_wrap'))
        ) {
            $labelOpen = '';
            $labelClose = '';
            $label = $labelHelper->openTag($element) . $label .
```

```php
↪$labelHelper->closeTag();
        } else {
            $labelOpen = $labelHelper->openTag($labelAttributes);
            $labelClose = $labelHelper->closeTag();
        }

        if ($label !== '' && (!$element->hasAttribute('id'))
            || ($element instanceof LabelAwareInterface && $element->
↪getLabelOption('always_wrap'))
        ) {
            $label = '<span>' . $label . '</span>';
        }

        //Button Element is a special case, where label is always displayed inside
        if ($element instanceof Button) {
            $labelOpen = $labelClose = $label = '';
        }
        if ($element instanceof LabelAwareInterface && $element->
↪getLabelOption('label_position')) {
            $labelPosition = $element->getLabelOption('label_position');
        }

        switch ($labelPosition) {
            case self::LABEL_PREPEND:
                $markup .= $labelOpen . $label . $labelClose .
↪$elementString;
                break;
            case BootstrapForm::MODE_HORIZONTAL:
                $markup .= $labelOpen . $label . $labelClose .
↪'<div class="col-sm-10">'. $elementString .'</div>';
                break;
            case self::LABEL_APPEND:
            default:
                $markup .= $labelOpen . $label . $labelClose .
↪$elementString;
                break;
        }
    }

    if ($this->renderErrors) {
        $markup .= $elementErrors;
    }

    $markup .= '</div>';
```

```
    } else {
        if ($labelPosition === BootstrapForm::MODE_HORIZONTAL && $element
↳instanceof Submit) {
            $elementString = '<div class="form-group"><div class="col-sm-10
↳col-sm-offset-2">'.$elementString.'</div></div>';
        }
        if ($this->renderErrors) {
            $markup = $elementString . $elementErrors;
        } else {
            $markup = $elementString;
        }
    }
    return $markup;
    }

    public function getInputErrorClass() {
        return 'has-error';
    }
}
```

In all other cases of other elements, we check if the element contains an id
attribute. If so, then we have to keep those two elements separately,
otherwise our label would contain the element itself. Another checks reset the
values of the buttons of Button type and get a position of the label in the
variable $labelPosition form the element itself. In that part of the code a
verification of the display mode and an adequate result are checked. Notice
that LABEL_PREPEND and LABEL_APPEND are the same; I wanted to set them
separately, to make them easier to change later in the code. We add a code
responsible for errors to the result and check if there is an exception in the
horizontal mode, in which a button should have an artificial left margin,
because it does not have its own. At the end we override the
getInputErrorClass() method, which we have used at the top of the
render() method – we return a has-error class together with the
Bootstrap standard here.

It's time for our last class responsible for handling a group of elements,
which undoubtedly is BootstrapFormCollection. Relax, it's not as long
as the previous one :)

```
namespace DivixUtils\Zend\View\Helper;

use Zend\Form\ElementInterface;
```

```
use Zend\Form\Element\Collection as CollectionElement;
use Zend\Form\FieldsetInterface;
use Zend\Form\LabelAwareInterface;

class BootstrapFormCollection extends \Zend\Form\View\Helper\FormCollection
{
    protected $defaultElementHelper = 'bootstrapFormRow';

    public function __invoke(ElementInterface $element = null, $labelPosition =
↪$null, wrap = false)
    {
        if (!$element) {
            return $this;
        }
        $this->setShouldWrap($wrap);
        return $this->render($element, $labelPosition);
    }
```

The same as in the previous example, we use only an existing class of
`Zend\Form\View\Helper\FormCollection` here, but we extend it. At the
start however, we define a key of the default elements helper:
`$defaultElementHelper`, which should point at the newly created class
handling single elements, that is a `bootstrapFromRow`. In this however
example we override the `invoke()` method, which from now on has a label
setting as the second argument, however the previous value is just moved to
the third place. By default a `FormCollection` class did not take a label
position, hence we needed to override that a bit.

```
public function render(ElementInterface $element, $labelPosition = null)
{
    $renderer = $this->getView();

    if (!method_exists($renderer, 'plugin')) {
        //Hold off rendering, if the plugin method does not exists
        return '';
    }
    $markup = '';
    $templateMarkup = '';
    //$this->setDefaultElementHelper('bootstrapFormRow');
    $elementHelper = $this->getElementHelper();
    $fieldsetHelper = $this->getFieldsetHelper();

    if ($element instanceof CollectionElement && $element->shouldCreate
```

```
↪Template()) {
        $templateMarkup = $this->renderTemplate($element);
    }
    $this->shouldWrap = false;

    foreach ($element->getIterator() as $elementOrFieldset) {
        if ($elementOrFieldset instanceof FieldsetInterface) {
            $markup .= $fieldsetHelper($elementOrFieldset,
↪$this->shouldWrap());
        } elseif ($elementOrFieldset instanceof ElementInterface) {
            $markup .= $elementHelper($elementOrFieldset, $labelPosition);
    }
}
```

The beginning of our `render()` method is practically the same as in the base
class - we get a dependencies and check if the element has its own template
for decorating. Next, we set a value of `$this->shouldWrap` to `TRUE`, thanks
to which our element groups will be covered by `FIELDSET` or other proper
style with label for each of them.

```
    // each collection of elements is palced according to the specified style
    if ($this->shouldWrap) {
        $attributes = $element->getAttributes();
        unset($attributes['name']);
        $attributesString = count($attributes) ? ' ' . $this->
↪createAttributesString($attributes) : '';
        $label = $element->getLabel();
        $legend = '';

        if (!empty($label)) {
            if (null !== ($translator = $this->getTranslator())) {
                $label = $translator->translate(
                    $label,
                    $this->getTranslatorTextDomain()
                );
            }

            if (! $element instanceof LabelAwareInterface ||
↪! $element->getLabelOption('disable_html_escape')) {
                $escapeHtmlHelper = $this->getEscapeHtmlHelper();
                $label = $escapeHtmlHelper($label);
            }
            $legend = sprintf(
                $this->labelWrapper,
```

```
                    $label
                );
            }

            $markup = sprintf(
                $this->wrapper,
                $markup,
                $legend,
                $templateMarkup,
                $attributesString
            );
        } else {
            $markup .= $templateMarkup;
        }
        return $markup;
        }
    }
```

The majority of the bottom part of this code was not changed, comparing to
the original version. Here we perform some checks of the label existence of
the whole group, its translations and escaping of the HTML code. Almost the
same as in the previous `BootstrapFromRow` case. At the end we get a format
of `$this->wrapper` and fill it with obtained variables.

That's it! From now on, in order to start using our new forms and enjoy them,
we just need to use our new view plugin instead of the previous `form()`
method. In the following way we will be able to display all three formats of
the form:

```
<div class="jumbotron">
    <h1><span class="zf-green">Forms in Bootstrap 3 format</span></h1>
    <h2>Vertical Format</h2>
    <?= $this->bootstrapForm($form, 'vertical'); ?>
    <br />
    <h2>Horizontal Format</h2>
    <?= $this->bootstrapForm($form, 'horizontal'); ?>
    <br />
    <h2>Single-line Format</h2>
    <?= $this->bootstrapForm($form, 'inline'); ?>
</div>
```

And here are our visual results:

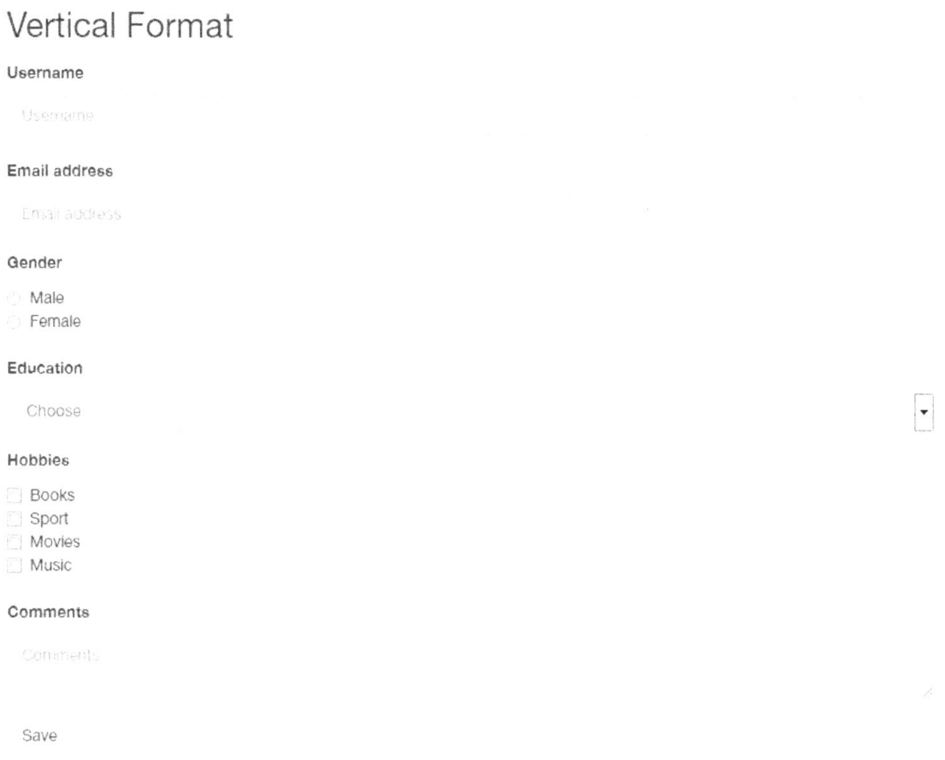

Vertical Format

Username

Username

Email address

Email address

Gender

○ Male
○ Female

Education

Choose ▾

Hobbies

☐ Books
☐ Sport
☐ Movies
☐ Music

Comments

Comments

Save

Image 19.2.

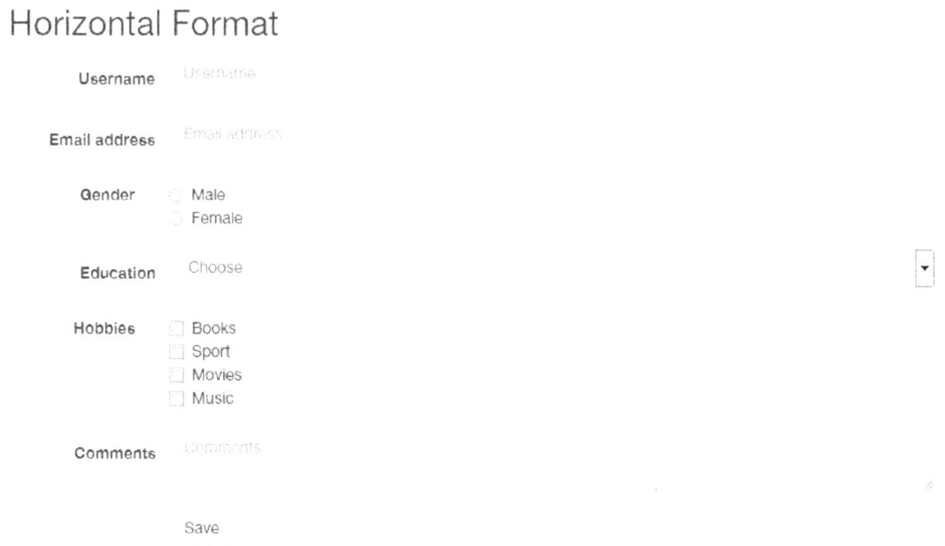

Horizontal Format

Username   Username

Email address   Email address

Gender   ○ Male
       ○ Female

Education   Choose ▾

Hobbies   ☐ Books
       ☐ Sport
       ☐ Movies
       ☐ Music

Comments   Comments

       Save

Image 19.3.

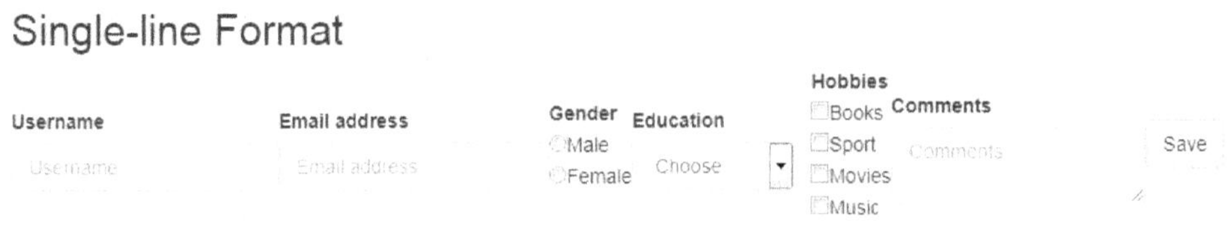

Single-line Format

Username	Email address	Gender	Education	Hobbies	Comments	Save
Username	Email address	○Male ○Female	Choose ▾	☐Books ☐Sport ☐Movies ☐Music	Comments	

Image 19.4.

CHAPTER 20.

Creating a custom navigation and a sitemap

In this chapter we are going to discover the secrets of building a main menu based on the `Zend\Navigation` component and we will find out how much it helps us with placing in the central point next to the page menu elements such as sitemap, breadcrumb or links in HTML tags, `HEAD`. We are going to take a closer look at creating dynamic site maps, which will contain not only our menu links, but also all articles created by the `CmsManager` object covered in chapter 15.

20.1. Updating a navigation

First, let's find out if our project already contains a `Zend\Navigation` package. We can do that by navigating into the folder *vendor\zendframework\zend-navigation*. If we don't have it, we can attach it, the same as other packages, via the composer:

```
composer require zendframework/zend-navigation
```

Let's begin from changing our navigation code from the *layout.phtml* to the configuration file. We can choose any config file, however it is recommended to keep them in the *config/autoload/global.php*. `Zend\Navigation` is a component based on two primary components: Containers and elements inside the containers called Pages. Each page (`Zend\Navigation\AbstractPage`) defines a link to the address, which is described by attributes like label or title. The container (`Zend\Navigation\`↪`AbstractContainer`) however defines a single group of page elements in an easy to iterate interface, and allows the connection with plugins of sitemaps, menus or links. An only possible usage of those plugins for displaying and returning results is using them in the view itself, not in the controllers or models.

Let's go into a template file *layout.phtml* and begin our work! Our current navigation is not scalable and does require a HTML code repetition to check a successful page position every time.

```
<ul class="nav navbar-nav">
    <li <?php if ($this->controller === Application\Controller\IndexController:
↪:class): ?>class="active"<?php endif; ?>><a href="<?= $this->url('home')
↪?>">Home Page</a></li>
    <li <?php if ($this->controller === Application\Controller\UsersController:
↪:class): ?>class="active"<?php endif; ?>><a href="<?= $this->url('users')
↪?>">Users</a></li>
    <li <?php if ($this->controller === Application\Controller\NewsController:
↪:class): ?>class="active"<?php endif; ?>><a href="<?= $this->url('news')
↪?>">Articles</a></li>
    <li <?php if ($this->controller === Application\Controller\ComicsController:
↪:class): ?>class="active"<?php endif; ?>><a href="<?= $this->url('comics')
↪?>">Comics</a></li>
    <li <?php if ($this->controller === Application\Controller\PollingController:
↪:class): ?>class="active"<?php endif; ?>><a href="<?= $this->url('polling')
↪?>">Poll</a></li>
    <?php if ($this->user): ?>
        <li <?php if ($this->controller === Application\Controller\UserController:
↪:class): ?>class="active"<?php endif; ?>><a href="<?= $this->url('user')
↪?>">My Account</a></li>
        <li><a href="<?= $this->url('login', ['action' => 'logout'])
↪?>">Logout</a></li>
    <?php else: ?>
        <li <?php if ($this->controller === Application\Controller\
↪RegisterController::class): ?>class="active"<?php endif; ?>><a href="<?=
```

```
↪$this->url('register') ?>">Registration</a></li>
        <li <?php if ($this->controller === Application\Controller\LoginController:
↪:class): ?>class="active"<?php endif; ?>><a href="<?= $this->url('login')
↪?>">Login</a></li>
    <?php endif; ?>
    <li <?php if ($this->controller === Application\Controller\FormController:
↪:class): ?>class="active"<?php endif; ?>><a href="<?= $this->url('forms')
↪?>">Forms</a></li>
</ul>
```

Right now we can notice that the code of this section seems unnecessary and enormous in the case of many menu elements. This is why all of these elements will be moved according to the `Zend\Navigation` format to the *global.php* file under the new alias called `'navigation'`.

```
'navigation' => [
    'default' => [
        [
            'label' => 'Home Page',
            'route' => 'home',
            'priority' => '1.0'
        ],
        [
            'label' => 'Users',
            'route' => 'users',
            'pages' => [
                [
                    'label' => 'Add User',
                    'controller' => 'users',
                    'action' => 'add'
                ]
            ],
            'priority' => '0.5'
        ],
        [
            'label' => 'Articles',
            'route' => 'news',
            'priority' => '0.5'
        ],
        [
            'label' => 'Comics',
            'route' => 'comics',
            'priority' => '0.5'
        ],
```

```
[
    'label' => 'Poll',
    'route' => 'polling',
    'pages' => [
        [
            'label' => 'Manage polls',
            'route' => 'polling',
            'action' => 'manage',
            'pages' => [
                [
                    'label' => 'Active poll',
                    'route' => 'polling',
                    'action' => 'view',
                ]
            ]
        ]
    ]
],
[
    'label' => 'Registration',
    'route' => 'register'
],
[
    'label' => 'Login',
    'route' => 'login'
],
[
    'label' => 'My Account',
    'route' => 'user'
],
[
    'label' => 'Logout',
    'route' => 'login',
    'action' => 'logout'
],
[
    'label' => 'Forms',
    'route' => 'forms'
],
]
]
```

Let's note that we have additionally set our first navigation under a key `'default'`, which describes the default container or the navigation. Thanks to that, later we will be able to define further navigations by passing another alias name. Take a look that our element uses a key called 'route', which indicates a place of the page link. Instead of just a 'route' key we can also use a combination of the controller, action and params, so that you can map to the given action of the specific controller with an extra variable passed, as an example:

```
[
    'label' => 'Edit user ID: 4',
    'controller' => 'users',
    'action' => 'edit',
    'params' => ['id' => 4],
]

//would return an address:
users/edit/4
```

We can also define a full WWW address of our site, via a key 'uri':

```
[
    'label' => 'Edit user ID: 4',
    'uri' => 'http://funkcje.net',
]
```

Additionally, each of the pages can contain an unlimited number of the subpages and nesting. In the example above we can easily tell that a Poll section contains a single nested page and another nested page inside the previous ones:

```
[
    'label' => 'Poll',
    'route' => 'polling',
    'pages' => [
        [
            'label' => 'Manage polls',
            'route' => 'polling',
            'action' => 'manage',
            'pages' => [
                [
                    'label' => 'Active poll',
                    'route' => 'polling',
                    'action' => 'view',
                ]
```

```
            ]
          ]
        ]
    ],
```

We can also use a 'controller' definition instead of the 'route' in here, but then our component could get confused by getting the previous parents of the site for the current active page due to the lack of connection with the router definition, called polling.

If we are going to have only a single navigation in our application, then to register it in the Zend environment we need a single line to the key service_manager/factories in the same file, so global.php:

```
'service_manager' => [
    'factories' => [
        ...
        'navigation' =>
Zend\Navigation\Service\DefaultNavigationFactory::class,
    ]
]
```

If however we plan to create other helper navigations in other places, then instead of the key 'factories' we should create a definition in the alias abstract_factories:

```
'service_manager' => [
    'abstract_factories' => [
        Zend\Navigation\Service\NavigationAbstractServiceFactory::class,
    ]
]
```

The only downside of using the abstract factory key is that from now on, whenever we refer to our navigation by a simple 'default' we will need to use Zend\Navigation\Default. It is caused by the additional abilities and generic attitude of the abstract class NavigationAbstractServiceFactory.

To display our newly created navigation as the old one, we just would have to type in the template file:

```
<?= $this->navigation('Zend\Navigation\Default')->menu()
```

```
   ->setMaxDepth(2)
   ->setUIClass('nav navbar-nav')
   ->render()
?>
```

The method `setMaxDepth()` defines what is the maximum level of the nesting, which will be visible in the page heading, however the method `setUiClass()` adds the additional CSS classes to the main menu container. The final `render()` method is responsible for returning the source code of the navigation. An above example is not what we really expected. It however displays all the pages together with the elements like `LoginRegister` or `My Account` and `Logout`. In such case we can either use an integration with `Zend\ACL` via the `setRole()` and `setAcl()` methods, or via extra keys in the configuration navigation called resource:

```
[
    'label' => 'Administrator panel',
    'uri' => '/super_admin',
    'resource' => 'admin',
],
```

We however will use another option, which will reuse our previous `$this->user` variable via our custom view file (partial). For this purpose we will need to modify the menu call in the following way:

```
<?= $this->navigation('Zend\Navigation\Default')->menu()
    ->setMaxDepth(2)
    ->setPartial('application/_shared/menu.phtml')
    ->renderPartialWithParams(
        [
            'user' => $this->user
        ]
    )
?>
```

By the method: `setPartial()` we set a path to a new view, which will begin to generate results. The next execution of the `renderPartialWithParams()` causes the file generation together with the passed variable, in our case the `'user'` variable. Notice that the path to the view must include a module name first, and then the whole rest. Let's create a new view file in the given above location.

```php
<?php $ignoredPages = $user ? ['Registration', 'Login'] : ['My Account',
'Logout']; ?>
<ul class="nav navbar-nav">
    <?php foreach ($this->container as $page) {
        $active = $page->isActive() ? 'class="active"' : '';
        if (in_array($page->getLabel(), $ignoredPages)) {
            continue;
        }
        echo '<li '.$active.'>'.$this->navigation()->menu()->htmlify($page);
        /*if ($page->hasPages()) {
            echo '<ul>';
            foreach ($page->getPages() as $subPage) {
                echo '<li>'.$this->navigation()->menu()->htmlify($subPage).'</li>';
            }
            echo '</ul>';
        }*/
        echo '</li>';
        //echo $page->getRoute();
    } ?>
</ul>
```

By default, we have an access to the property of the page container called
`$this->container` in every view. We iterate these pages, at the same time
generating an `<li>` tag, and we check via a `isActive()` method if that
given page is currently viewed. A variable `$ignoredPages` defines which
navigation elements should not be displayed on the screen. For a logged-in
user we don't want to show links as *Registration* or *Login*, however for
unauthorized guests we don't need to generate links *My Account* and *Logout*.
We use a passed in by `renderPartialWithParams()` 'user' variable,
which holds an object of the currently logged user, if such user exists. To
display the page alias we use a method `htmlify()`, which returns a full link
in the `<a>` tag format an or inactive link in the format of simple `<span>` tag.
Our commented code, beginning from `hasPages()` checks nested pages of
the main elements. We do not want them, in the case of our navigation, to
display in the heading, therefore we passed their sample usage in the
comment. Additionally, each of the `$page` object offers an access to all
defined properties like `getRoute()` or `getAction()`. When we save a view
file after reloading the home page, we should see an unchanged navigation
menu compared to the previous version.

20.2. Adding breadcrumbs and links

Once we have a dynamic menu in the site heading, from now on we will be able to use benefits of `Zend\Navigation`. Let's maybe begin from integrating breadcrumbs, so-called patchway. They are specific links of the given page's parents, usually placed just under the page navigation. Breadcrumbs give us an ability to navigate from the main categories up to the main elements in the page hierarchy. We generate the breadcrumbs in the same way as menu, but with the difference that we call other methods of the primary plugin `breadcrumbs()`:

```
<div class="breadcrumb">
    <?= $this->navigation('Zend\Navigation\Default')->breadcrumbs()
        ->setLinkLast(false)
        ->setMinDepth(0)
        ->setMaxDepth(5)
        ->setSeparator(' / ')
        ->render()
    ?>
</div>
```

We also add the above code to the *layout.phtml*, but in the first lines `<div class="container">` The method `setLinkLast()` determines if the last element of the page links list should be also a link or just a regular text (default behavior). `setMinDepth()` defines when links should be generated, based on the level of nesting. In our example the value set to 0 will force a breadcrumbs plugin to display the links on every page, even on the home page. The `setSeparator()` sets the separator character, which appears between the links; a default setting is a "greater than" character ">". By adding an extra line to the *styles.css*, we can make the distinction of patchway from the rest of the page more visual.

```
.breadcrumb {
    margin-bottom: 7px;
}
```

Finally, on the active poll page our breadcrumbs will look like in the following image:

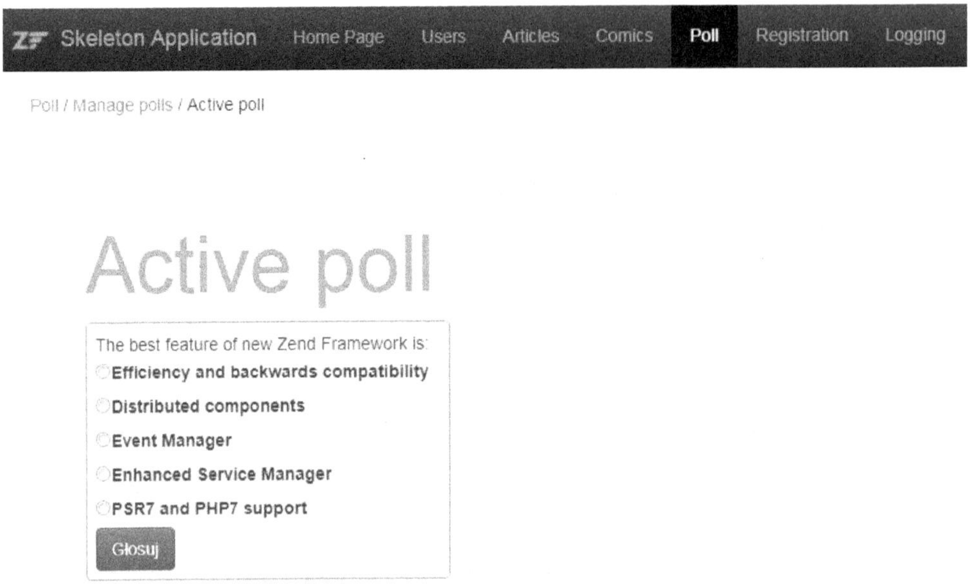
Skeleton Application
Home Page
Users
Articles
Comics
Poll
Registration
Logging
Poll / Manage polls / Active poll
Active poll
The best feature of new Zend Framework is:
Efficiency and backwards compatibility
Distributed components
Event Manager
Enhanced Service Manager
PSR7 and PHP7 support
Głosuj

Image 20.1.

Another step is to add the links to the `HEAD` section of our HTML document. HTML links describe the localization of the previous or next page, previous category or other related categories. The full specification can be found and read at the official W3C website: *https://www.w3.org/TR/html4/struct/↪links.html#h-12-3*. With Zend Navigation, adding such links is really easy to achieve. The only thing we need to do is to modify our template file again by adding the below code inside the `<HEAD>` tag:

```
<?= $this->navigation('Zend\Navigation\Default')->links().PHP_EOL ?>
```

Adding an "end of line" character at the end should improve the readability of our source code, which will look like the following on the active poll page:

```
<link rel="start" href="&#x2F;zend3&#x2F;"
title="Home Page">
<link rel="next" href="&#x2F;zend3&#x2F;polling&#x2F;manage"
title="Manage polls">
<link rel="prev" href="&#x2F;zend3&#x2F;comics" title="Comics">
<link rel="chapter" href="&#x2F;zend3&#x2F;users" title="Users ">
```

```
<link rel="chapter" href="&#x2F;zend3&#x2F;news" title="Articles">
<link rel="chapter" href="&#x2F;zend3&#x2F;comics" title="Comics">
<link rel="chapter" href="&#x2F;zend3&#x2F;register" title="Registration">
<link rel="chapter" href="&#x2F;zend3&#x2F;login" title="Login">
<link rel="chapter" href="&#x2F;zend3&#x2F;user" title="My Account">
<link rel="chapter" href="&#x2F;zend3&#x2F;login&#x2F;logout" title="Logout">
<link rel="chapter" href="&#x2F;zend3&#x2F;forms" title="Forms">
<link rel="section" href="&#x2F;zend3&#x2F;polling&#x2F;manage" title="Manage polls">
```

As we have already mentioned, the links marked as next and prev are the upcoming and previous pages, start describes the starting page, however section is the parent category of current page. Links tagged with the name chapter are the names of the root categories.

20.3. A dynamic sitemap

The culmination of this chapter will be a generated sitemap available under the URL *sitemap.xml*, which does not only contain a list of the pages from of navigation, but also all the articles stored in the database. The sitemap is an informative XML file, which is mostly used by all the Internet web searches in order to specify the list of available pages to index in the search engine. An exemplar element looks like so:

```
<url>
    <loc>http://localhost/zend3/articles/show/test_article</loc>
    <priority>1.0</priority>
</url>
```

A basic information that needs to appear inside the URL tag is obviously a URL address in a `<LOC>` tag, so the full location to the page address. An additional argument can be a `PRIORITY` tag, which describes how important the given site for our webpage is. The available range is between `0.1` and `1.0` for the most important parts.

Our address will be only imitating a XML file – in reality we will create a router of *sitemap.xml* address, which will be redirecting to a newly created controller called `SitemapController` and default index action. Let's take care of the creation of the router in the *module.config.php* file.

```php
'router' => [
    ...
    'sitemap' => [
        'type' => Literal::class,
        'options' => [
            'route' => '/sitemap.xml',
            'defaults' => [
                'controller' => Controller\SitemapController::class,
                'action' => 'index',
            ],
        ],
    ],
],
```

Our new sitemap controller would need an access to the navigation object and `ContentManager`, which we will have to pass in the `controllers` key:

```php
'controllers' => [
    'factories' => [
        ...
        Controller\SitemapController::class => function($sm) {
            return new Controller\SitemapController(
                $sm->get('Zend\Navigation\Default'),
                $sm->get(Model\Admin\ContentManager::class)
            );
        },
    ]
],
```

Our sitemap controller alone will only have a single action index that will be returning only an XML file with the headers of a specific file type.

```php
namespace Application\Controller;

use Zend\View\Model\ViewModel;

class SitemapController extends AbstractController
{
    private $navigation;
    private $cmsModel;
```

```php
public function __construct($navigation, $cmsModel)
{
    $this->navigation = $navigation;
    $this->cmsModel = $cmsModel;
}

public function indexAction()
{
    $cacheKey = 'sitemap';
    $fileCache = \Zend\Cache\StorageFactory::factory(array(
        'adapter' => array(
            'name' => 'filesystem',
            'options' => array(
                    'cacheDir' => 'data/cache',
                    'ttl' => 86400 //24h
            )
        ),
        'plugins' => ['Serializer']
    ));
    $navigationContainer = $this->navigation;
    $cachedArticles = $fileCache->getItem($cacheKey);
    $articles = $cachedArticles ? $cachedArticles : $this->cmsModel->getPages;
    $router = $this->getEvent()->getRouter();
    $plainPages = [];

    foreach ($articles as $article) {
        $page = new \Zend\Navigation\Page\Mvc([
            'route' => 'articles',
            'action' => 'show',
            'params' => ['id' => $article['url']],
            'priority' => '1.0'
        ]);
        $page->setRouter($router);
        $navigationContainer->addPage($page);
        $plainPages[] = $article;
    }
    //we cannot locally parse results from DB PDO,
    //thus we are passing a regular array
    if (!$cachedArticles) {
        $fileCache->setItem($cacheKey, $plainPages);
    }
    $this->getResponse()->getHeaders()->addHeaderLine
↪('Content-Type', 'text/xml');
    $viewModel = new ViewModel();
```

```
        $viewModel->setTerminal(true);
        return $viewModel;
    }
}
```

At the start of the single action, we have defined a Zend\Cache object, so the local memory object, which will be based on the system local files and store that information only for 24 hours. Of course, we don't want to parse and return all of the pages from the database every time, this is why we decided to cache our sitemaps once per 1 day. Furthermore, we serialize all the results before storing them. We set a cache key on sitemap and we check if we don't have any other information in the cache already. If so, then we set a variable $articles on the $cachedArticles; in case of the empty cached results we call a method getPages() on the object $this->cmsModel. Here we also retrieve a default router object, which we will be passing to every page in order to generate a URL address. Before the loop we initiate an empty $plainPages array, which will store results returned from the database to cache. It is required due to the fact that there is no possibility to store those objects of type PDO to any form (not able to store such object to the strings). Inside our foreach loop we create a page of type Zend\Navigation\Page\ ↪Mvc for every article, which sets a router value on articles and action show together with an extra id parameter, which is our URL address stored in the articles table. As we have set the router's label in the still non-existent name articles, in a moment we will create a new rule for such address in the router and the controller class itself. We set a router object for a page by setRouter(), until we finally add this created page to our navigation object via addPage(). Soon after the loop, we store a new cache with returned results and we set the headers for the browser response:

```
$this->getResponse()->getHeaders()->addHeaderLine('Content-Type', 'text/xml');
```

At the end, we specify that we don't want to generate a view template via setTerminal(true) and we return the ViewModel alone. Let's add the missing router to the articles value:

```
'articles' => [
    'type' => Segment::class,
    'options' => [
        'route' => '/articles[/:action][/:id]',
        'defaults' => [
```

```
            'controller' => Controller\ArticlesController::class,
            'action' => 'index',
        ],
    ],
],
```

together with the controller's definition, which will need a CMS object:

```
Controller\ArticlesController::class => function($sm) {
    return new Controller\ArticlesController(
        $sm->get(Model\Admin\ContentManager::class)
    );
},
```

as the short ArticlesController class, so articles controller, in which we implemented only a show method.

```
namespace Application\Controller;

class ArticlesController extends AbstractController
{
    private $cmsObject;

    public function __construct($cmsObject)
    {
        $this->cmsObject = $cmsObject;
    }

    public function indexAction()
    {
        return [];
    }

    public function showAction() {
        $pageDetails = $this->cmsObject->getArticleContentByUrl($this->params()->
↪fromRoute('id'));
        $this->getEvent()->getTarget()->layout()->title = $pageDetails[0]
↪['title'];
        $this->getEvent()->getTarget()->layout()->description =
↪$pageDetails[0]['description'];
        $this->getEvent()->getTarget()->layout()->keywords =
↪$pageDetails[0]['keywords'];
        return [
            'page' => $pageDetails
```

```
        ];
    }
}
```

Let's add a little view file in the *view/application/articles/show.phtml*.

```
<?php foreach ($page as $row): ?>
    <?= $row['content'] ?>
<?php endforeach; ?>
```

I also took the liberty of slightly modifying our navigation configuration by adding a priority parameter to a few root pages in the list. The last thing you should perform is to create a view file *view/application/sitemap/index.phtml*, with the data about the whole generated sitemap.

```
<?= $this->navigation('Zend\Navigation\Default')->sitemap()
    ->setFormatOutput(true)
    ->render()
?>
```

A flag of TRUE set by the setFormatOutput() sets the turned on validations of all sitemap pages and error throwing, if any element does not meet at least one of the standards.

After typing in the address */sitemap.xml,* we should be finally able to see our application sitemap on our screen:

This XML file does not appear to have any style information associated with it. The document tree is shown below

```
▼<urlset xmlns="http://www.sitemaps.org/schemas/sitemap/0.9">
  ▼<url>
      <loc>http://localhost/zend3/</loc>
      <priority>1.0</priority>
    </url>
  ▼<url>
      <loc>http://localhost/zend3/users</loc>
      <priority>0.5</priority>
    </url>
  ▶<url>...</url>
  ▼<url>
      <loc>http://localhost/zend3/news</loc>
      <priority>0.5</priority>
    </url>
  ▶<url>...</url>
  ▼<url>
      <loc>http://localhost/zend3/polling</loc>
    </url>
  ▼<url>
      <loc>http://localhost/zend3/polling/manage</loc>
    </url>
  ▼<url>
      <loc>http://localhost/zend3/polling/view</loc>
    </url>
  ▼<url>
      <loc>http://localhost/zend3/register</loc>
    </url>
  ▼<url>
      <loc>http://localhost/zend3/login</loc>
    </url>
  ▼<url>
      <loc>http://localhost/zend3/user</loc>
    </url>
  ▼<url>
      <loc>http://localhost/zend3/login/logout</loc>
    </url>
  ▼<url>
      <loc>http://localhost/zend3/forms</loc>
    </url>
  ▼<url>
      <loc>http://localhost/zend3/articles/show/stopka</loc>
      <priority>1.0</priority>
    </url>
  ▼<url>
      <loc>http://localhost/zend3/articles/show/test_article</loc>
      <priority>1.0</priority>
    </url>
</urlset>
```

Image 20.2.

395

## CHAPTER 21

Implementing unit tests

In the last chapter of our book (yeah I know, I feel sad too ;)) we are going to test our sample application module. Via the standard PHPUnit library we will learn how to check controllers, test models of rowset type and compare the results returned by base models. We will find out what mocks are and how to use them by a built-in library Prophecy to separate the tested functionality.

21.1. Setting up the environment for tests

PHPUnit is a library inspired by JUnit (JAVA) that, as the definition says, tests a specific unit/section of the code. As an example we could easily test the single class methods like interactions or returned results. Besides, it doesn't limit us at all to test the controller and executed linked codes from different classes. The unit tests improve the code's quality and provide stability of a continued integration of the medium and bigger projects. Thanks to the appropriate tools, their execution is available in the command line on all the platforms like Linux, Windows or Mac. PPHPUnit has many built-in functions for comparing values, imitating other components, or checking for exceptions and errors in the scripts.

Our application's tests are always located in the separate *application/src/test* folder, which also represents the further structure of tested classes. For instance, by default in our skeleton application of Zend Framework 3 we have a class `test\Controller\IndexControllerTest.php`, whose task is to test the controller's class `Controller\IndexController.php`. Our primary goals in this subsection will be a proper setup of the application environment and execution of the default test suite by SHELL window in XAMPP. Let's start a configuration from installing a package responsible for unit testing.

```
composer require --dev zendframework/zend-test
```

Let's also ensure that we have a call in autoloader to our tests location, in the *composer.json* file.

```
"autoload-dev": {
    "psr-4": {
        "ApplicationTest\\": "module/Application/test/"
    }
},
```

Next, we need to copy the file: *config/application.config.php* into a new one with name *application.test.config.php*, in which we will only change a single line to the following one:

```
realpath(__DIR__) . '/autoload/{{,*.}tests,{,*.}local}.php',
```

Given declaration determines from where any additional configuration files with the global and local values should be loaded. We changed the call to the *global.php* file into *tests.php*, so we will have to create that *tests.php* file in the folder `config/autoload` with the given contents:

```
<?php
$global = include __DIR__.'/global.php';
$global['db']['dsn'] = 'mysql:dbname=zend3_tests;host=localhost';
return $global;
```

An action we performed here is getting a standard *global.php* file and overriding the values around the database name, to which we will be referring during the unit tests. A new set database is called `zend3_test`, and the same database we need to create in our phpMyAdmin. The easiest method is to create a copy of previous database is to select a source database, then select Operations at the top menu and enter the name of a new database in the window "*Copy database into:*".

Our unit tests will be controlled by the extra configuration in the XML format from the file called *phpunit.xml.dist* inside the root folder. This file defines what environment variables or constants are available inside each test (as $_SERVER array is unavailable when running form CLI). We can also store the same file under the name *phpunit.xml*, but then this file will be used when running tests. We will however stay with the initial *.dist* file and add two new values into it.

```xml
<?xml version="1.0" encoding="UTF-8"?>
<phpunit colors="true">
    <testsuites>
        <testsuite name="Zend3">
            <directory>./module/Application/test</directory>
        </testsuite>
    </testsuites>
    <php>
        <const name="APPLICATION_PATH"
↪value="D:\RZECZY_ADAM\_XAMPP\xampp-5.6\htdocs\zend3\" />
        <server name="APPLICATION_ENV" value="tests" />
    </php>
</phpunit>
```

Apart from changing the tests package into *Zend3*, we also added a PHP tag, which specifies the configuration of the PHP language. The first new line defines a constant called APPLICATION_PATH and with the value of full absolute path to our application. By default this variable is defined in the *public/index.php*, which unfortunately our tests will not be calling. Next line is creating a variable of name APPLICARION_ENV in the $_SERVER array – it is set by the *.htaccess*, which also is not called when running tests.

The last configuration step is securing the session creation during running the tests. For a moment our tests will not need to use the session during the execution, therefore we will also add a check for environment mode to the *Module.php* file.:

```php
public function onBootstrap($e)
{
```

```
if ($_SERVER['APPLICATION_ENV'] !== 'tests') {
    $this->bootstrapSession($e);
}
```

For the purpose of running the first tests, we should call a phpunit file in the folder *vendor/bin* with the double quotes , by navigating first to our root application folder.

"vendor/bin/phpunit"

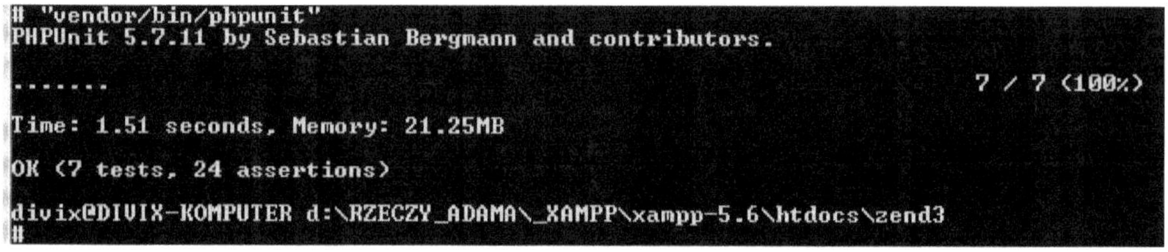

```
# "vendor/bin/phpunit"
PHPUnit 5.7.11 by Sebastian Bergmann and contributors.

.......                                              7 / 7 (100%)

Time: 1.51 seconds, Memory: 21.25MB

OK (7 tests, 24 assertions)

divix@DIVIX-KOMPUTER d:\RZECZY_ADAMA\_XAMPP\xampp-5.6\htdocs\zend3
#
```

Image 21.1.

After typing above code we will get a result similar to the above image. However, if we have made some mistakes or we had an undefined variable or a key, we will get an error message in the same console. By default phpunit is run in error_reporting E_STRICT mode, which means that every NOTCE or WARNING will be displayed and reported as an error during the tests.

21.2. Model Testing – Rowset and Fixtures

Before even writing the tests in our Rowset model, let's update an original file *Rowset\Comics.php*, so that it has its own validation, which later we will check in the tests.

```
namespace Application\Model\Rowset;

use Zend\InputFilter\InputFilter;
use Zend\InputFilter\InputFilterAwareInterface;
use Zend\InputFilter\InputFilterInterface;
```

```php
use Zend\Filter\StringTrim;
use Zend\Filter\StripTags;
use Zend\Filter\ToInt;
use Zend\Validator\StringLength;

class Comics extends AbstractModel implements InputFilterAwareInterface
{
    public $title;
    public $thumb;
    public $gaaw;
    protected $inputFilter;

    ...

    public function setInputFilter(InputFilterInterface $inputFilter)
    {
        $this->inputFilters = $inputFilter;
    }

    public function getInputFilter()
    {
        if ($this->inputFilter) {
            return $this->inputFilter;
        }
        $inputFilter = new InputFilter();
        $inputFilter->add([
            'name' => 'id',
            'required' => true,
            'filters' => [
                ['name' => ToInt::class],
            ],
        ]);

        $inputFilter->add([
            'name' => 'title',
            'required' => true,
            'filters' => [
                ['name' => StripTags::class],
                ['name' => StringTrim::class],
            ],
            'validators' => [
                [
                    'name' => StringLength::class,
                    'options' => [
                        'encoding' => 'UTF-8',
```

```
                    'min' => 1,
                    'max' => 100,
                ],
            ],
        ],
    ]);

    $inputFilter->add([
        'name' => 'thumb',
        //'required' => true,
        'filters' => [
            ['name' => StringTrim::class]
        ],
    ]);
    $this->inputFilter = $inputFilter;

    return $this->inputFilter;
    }
}
```

By the way, we change an access type to the class variable $id in the Rowset\AbstractModel file from protected into public, so that we can refer to it from our test.

Let's create our new first file, which will be testing the easiest model Rowset\Comics – that we will place in the location *test/Model/Rowset/* ↪*ComicsTest.php*.

```
namespace ApplicationTest\Model\Rowset;

use Application\Model\Rowset\Comics;
use Application\Form\ComicsForm;
use PHPUnit_Framework_TestCase as TestCase;

class ComicsTest extends TestCase
{
    public function setup()
    {
        parent::setup();
    }

    public function testInitialComicsValuesAreNull()
    {
        $comics = new Comics();
```

```php
        $this->assertNull($comics->id, 'initial id value
↪should be null');
        $this->assertNull($comics->title, 'initial title value
↪should be null'); $this->assertNull($comics->thumb,
↪'initial thumb value should be null');
    }

    public function testExchangeArraySetsPropertiesCorrectly()
    {
        $comics = new Comics();
        $data = $this->getComicsData();
        //let's check an initial array
        $comics->exchangeArray($data);
        $this->assertSame(
            $data['id'],
            $comics->getId(),
            'id param has not been set properly'
        );

        $this->assertSame(
            $data['title'],
            $comics->getTitle(),
            'title param has not been set properly'
        );

        $this->assertSame(
            $data['thumb'],
            $comics->getThumb(),
            'thumb param has not been set properly'
        );
    }

    private function getComicsData()
    {
        return [
            'id' => 123,
            'title' => 'Testman',
            'thumb' => 'file.jpg'
        ];
    }
```

Each testing class can have its own logic and configuration set in the `setup()` method. The method will be called every time, just before and soon after each test. If we define it, then we need to remember that we also need to call an original `setup()` method from the parent class phpunit: `PHPUnit_Framework_TestCase`. In phpunit, each method that is public and starts from the name `test*`, is marked as a single test. It is assumed that a test name should explain what is mainly tested and with that expected outcome. In our example the first test is called: `testInitialComics` ↪`ValuesAreNull()` and states that it tests the initial values which should be all set to `NULL`. Then we create a `Comics` object, by which we check for every value via an `assertNull()` method. Almost every built-in phpunit method defines the last optional parameter as a message, which will be displayed in case of the unsuccessful test. In the second test `testExchangeArraySetsPropertiesCorrectly()` we perform checks of data filled with dummy called `Comics` object, which we fill with a private method: `getComicsData()` and which will be returning the correct values. Next, by the `assertSame()` call we compare the value of the `$data` variable with the `$copyArray` of `Comics` object as the second parameter, and we pass, the same as in the previous tests, a message about the potential errors.

```
public function testExchangeArraySetsPropertiesToNullIfKeysAreNotPresent()
{
    $comics = new Comics();
    $comics->exchangeArray($this->getComicsData());
    $comics->exchangeArray([]);

    $this->assertNull($comics->id, 'initial id value
↪should be null');
    $this->assertNull($comics->title, 'initial title value
↪should be null');
    $this->assertNull($comics->thumb, 'initial thumb value
↪should be null');
}

public function testGetArrayCopyReturnsAnArrayWithPropertyValues()
{
    $comics = new Comics();
    $data = $this->getComicsData();
    $comics->exchangeArray($data);
    $copyArray = $comics->getArrayCopy();
    $this->assertSame($data['id'], $copyArray['id'], 'id param has not
↪been set properly');

    $this->assertSame($data['title'], $copyArray['title'], 'title param has
↪not been set properly');
```

404

```php
    $this->assertSame($data['thumb'], $copyArray['thumb'], 'thumb param has
↪not been set properly');
}

public function testInputFiltersAreSetCorrectly()
{
    $comics = new Comics();
    $inputFilter = $comics->getInputFilter();
    $this->assertSame(3, $inputFilter->count());
    $this->assertTrue($inputFilter->has('id'));
    $this->assertTrue($inputFilter->has('title'));
    $this->assertTrue($inputFilter->has('thumb'));
}

/**
 * @dataProvider getInvalidComicsData
 * @group inputFilters
 */
public function testInputFiltersIncorrect($row)
{
    $comics = new Comics();
    $comicsForm = new ComicsForm();
    $comicsForm->setInputFilter($comics->getInputFilter());
    $comicsForm->bind($comics);
    $comicsForm->setData($row);
    $this->assertFalse($comicsForm->isValid());
    $this->assertTrue(count($comicsForm->getMessages()) > 0);
}

public function getInvalidComicsData()
{
    return [
        [
            [
                'id' => null,
                'title' => null,
                'thumb' => null
            ],
            [
                'id' => '',
                'title' => 'null',
                'thumb' => 'null'
            ],
            [
```

```
            'id' => 123,
            'title' => '',
            'thumb' => 'file.jpg'
        ]
    ]
  ];
}
```

Next test is `testExchangeArraySetsPropertiesToNullIfKeysAre` ↪`NotPresent`, which checks if the object properties are reset after passing an empty array via method `exchangeArray()`. Another test is `testGetArrayCopyReturnsAnaArrayWithPropertyValues`, which checks the result returned by the method `getArrayCopy()`. However, the last test with name `testInputFiltersAreSetCorrectly` checks a validation array returned by `getInputFilter()`. Finally, a method `testInputFiltersIncorrect` does a check of the comics form called `ComicsForm`. We need to create such class in `Application/src/Form/ComicsForm.php` location; it will be a form of a simple structure with elements as id, title and thumb.

```
namespace Application\Form;

use Zend\Form\Element;

class ComicsForm extends \Zend\Form\Form
{
    public function __construct($name = 'comics')
    {
        parent::__construct($name);
        $this->add([
            'name' => 'id',
            'type' => 'hidden'
        ]);

        $this->add([
            'name' => 'title',
            'type' => 'text',
            'options' => [
                'label' => 'Title'
            ]
        ]);

        $this->add([
```

```
            'name' => 'thumb',
            'type' => Element\Text::class,
            'options' => [
                'label' => 'Thumbnail'
            ],
            'attributes' => array(
                'required' => 'required'
            )
        ]);

        $this->add([
            'name' => 'submit',
            'type' => 'submit',
            'attributes' => [
                'value' => 'Save',
            ]
        ]);
    }
}
```

By using the following form, a test `testInputFiltersIncorrect` connects two objects via the `bind()` command, then it sets the form data into a `$row` variable, which is passed in the parameter of the test, and performs a verification of an unsuccessful outcome of the form and the amount of the error message from the form itself. A magical for us variable from the parameter `$row` is set by using special tags in `docblocks` above the test declaration:

```
/**
 * @dataProvider getInvalidComicsData
 * @group inputFilters
 */
```

Thanks to the `$dataProvider` tag we are able to define which parameters we want to execute a given test with. This tag takes a method name as a value, which exists later in the same file, so the `getInvalidComicsData()`. This method returns three combinations of the same keys with different values inside. These extra methods are used to test the same part of the code via many input values. In our example, we want to make sure that passing all variable set to `NULL` or empty string as title, would also return an information about the validation error of the `Comics` object. The `@group` tag defines a group name, to which our test belongs. In our example where we perform a test of `inputFilter` validation, we set a group into `inputFilters`. Thanks to that by calling phpunit in the command line we will be able to append --group `inputFilter`, which will result in the execution of the tests with linked tag `@group inputFilters` only.

The last two tests of `Rowset Comics` model will test the correct validation of the `ComicsForm` form together with the lack of error message and its correct usage:

```
/**
 * @group inputFilters
 * @author adam.omelak
 */
public function testInputFiltersSuccess()
{
    $comics = new Comics();
    $comicsForm = new ComicsForm();
    $comicsForm->setInputFilter($comics->getInputFilter());
    $comicsForm->bind($comics);
    $comicsForm->setData($this->getComicsData());

    $this->assertTrue($comicsForm->isValid());
    $this->assertCount(0, $comicsForm->getMessages());
}

/**
 * @group inputFilters
 */
public function testInputFiltersFixtureSuccess()
{
    $fixture = include __DIR__ . '/../../Fixtures/Comics.php';
    $counter = 0;

    foreach ($fixture as $comicsData) {
        $comics = new Comics();
        $comicsForm = new ComicsForm();
        $comicsForm->setInputFilter($comics->getInputFilter());
        $comicsForm->bind($comics);
        $comicsForm->setData($comicsData);
        $this->assertTrue($comicsForm->isValid());
        $counter++;
    }
    $this->assertEquals(count($fixture), $counter);
```

```
}
```

The tag @author works the same as just mentioned @group tag, so it defines a group of tests and the category of execution from the command line interface, but it is designed for tagging the main test authors in case the test stops working for unknown reasons. The last test testInputFilters ↪FixturesSuccess gets a sample input data for the Comics object from the external file called *Comics.php* from the folder *Fixtures/*. Then via a foreach loop it fills a form object and checks, the same as in the previous example, the correctness of the filled form based on the validations returned from the Rowset model. However, we will first outline what Fixtures are and why we should use them in bigger projects.

When we work in a team, we often have only some part of a main bigger functionality to do. For instance, our co-worker has a task to build a database and column relations, however we need to implement a part of the view and controller. In such occasions, we need to establish and define a structure, in which the data will be returned from table models. This is where we should use fixtures, so sample structure with a test data, so that we can use all the elements of tested functionality. Fixtures are also often used in unit tests, for those reasons all of our test data we will be placed into a test folder: *module/Application/test/Fixtures* (of course we will have to create ourselves the last folder *Fixtures/*).

Our sample Fixtures file will have three records in the regular PHP array format:

```php
<?php
return [
    [
        'id' => 1,
        'title' => 'Sample Comics',
        'thumb' => 'public/images/comics/test.jpg'
    ],
    [
        'id' => 2,
        'title' => 'Spiderman',
        'thumb' => 'public/images/comics/spiderman.jpg'
    ],
    [
        'id' => 3,
```

```
        'title' => 'Batman',
        'thumb' => 'public/images/comics/batman.jpg'
    ]
];
```

We can now run and verify all our tests or call only those from the new class. A command phpunit gives us an ability to run only a single file via the parameter `--filter [ClassName]`. Here is our current result called by the command "`vendor/bin/phpunit" -filter ComicsTest`:

```
# "vendor/bin/phpunit" --filter ComicsTest
PHPUnit 5.7.11 by Sebastian Bergmann and contributors.

........                                              8 / 8 (100%)

Time: 359 ms, Memory: 5.75MB

OK (8 tests, 24 assertions)
```

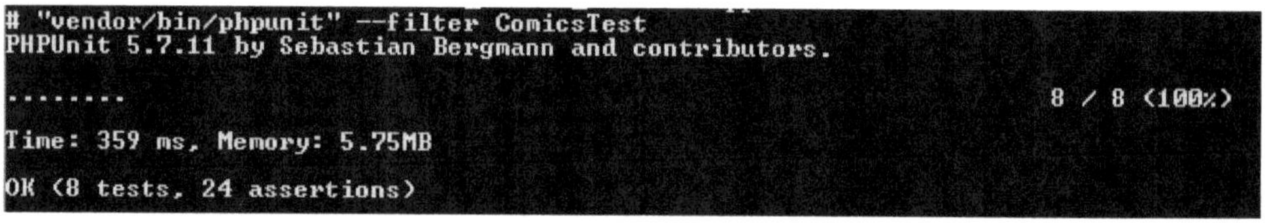

Image 21.2.

21.3. Testing using database

Finally, in this section we will start using our new configuration file *application.test.config.php*, via which we will grant an access to the Service Manager object, and hence other services. In such way we will be able to refer to the objects like ComicsTable or TableGateway, of course under the condition that we append 1 line into *global.php* file:

```
'service_manager' => array(
    'factories' => array(
        'Zend\Db\Adapter\Adapter' => 'Zend\Db\Adapter\AdapterServiceFactory',
        'Zend\Db\TableGateway\TableGateway' => 'Zend\Db\
↪TableGateway\TableGatewayServiceFactory',
```

Let's go back into the tests and file ComicsTable which at the start we will have to update by adding a few additional checks of input parameters here and there:

```
public function patch($id, array $data)
{
```

```php
    if (empty($data)) {
        throw new \Exception('missing data to update');
    }
    $passedData = [];

    if (!empty($data['title'])) {
        $passedData['title'] = $data['title'];
    }

    if (!empty($data['thumb'])) {
        $passedData['thumb'] = $data['thumb'];
    }
    $this->tableGateway->update($passedData, ['id' => $id]);
}

public function save(Rowset\Comics $comicsModel)
{
    return parent::saveRow($comicsModel);
}

public function delete($id)
{
    if (empty($id)) {
        throw new \Exception('missing comics id to delete');
    }
    parent::deleteRow($id);
}
```

and to the *Model/AbstractTable.php* file, which we will replace so that it would accept a `TableGateway` interface and contains an option to remove the cache of paginator results:

```php
use Zend\Db\TableGateway\TableGatewayInterface;

use Application\Model\Rowset\AbstractModel;
use DivixUtils\Zend\Paginator\Paginator as CustomPaginator;
use Zend\Paginator\Adapter\DbSelect;
use Zend\Cache\StorageFactory;

class AbstractTable
{
    protected $tableGateway;
    public static $paginatorCache;
    public static $paginatorCacheEnabled = true;
```

```
    public function __construct(TableGatewayInterface $tableGateway)
    {
```

Later in the same file, we add a line for setting up a cache:

```
$paginator = new CustomPaginator($paginatorAdapter);
$paginator->setCacheEnabled(self::$paginatorCacheEnabled);
```

and the method allowing to change the cache behavior of an object:

```
public function disableCache()
{
    self::$paginatorCache = 'disabled';
    self::$paginatorCacheEnabled = false;
}
```

For such well-prepared base class, we will begin to create a new unit tests file in the folder *test/Model/ComicsTableTest.php*.

```
namespace ApplicationTest\Model;

use Application\Model\ComicsTable;
use Application\Model\Rowset\Comics;
use Zend\Db\ResultSet\ResultSetInterface;
use Zend\Db\Adapter\Adapter;

class ComicsTableTest extends
\Zend\Test\PHPUnit\Controller\AbstractHttpControllerTestCase
{
    protected $tableGateway;
    protected $comicsTable;
    protected $traceError = true;
    protected $usersTable;
    protected $baseUrl;

    protected function setup()
    {
        $this->setApplicationConfig(include APPLICATION_PATH .
↪'/config/application.test.config.php');
        $this->tableGateway = $this->prophesize(TableGatewayInterface::class);
        $this->comicsTable = $this->getApplicationServiceLocator()->
↪get(ComicsTable::class);
        //let's disable cache from paginator results
        $this->comicsTable->disableCache();
```

```
$config = $this->getApplicationServiceLocator()->get('Config');
$this->baseUrl = $config['view_manager']['base_url'];

//let's remove data from tested tables
$this->getApplicationServiceLocator()->get(Adapter::class)->
↳query('TRUNCATE TABLE comics')->execute();
    parent::setup();
}
```

The beginning of the file is obviously an initial configuration and an extension of the PHPUnit class. However, in this example we extend `Zend\Test\Controller\AbstractHttpsControllertestCase`, so we get an access to the `setApplicationConfig()` method, which is called in the `setup()` method. We also set a `$traceError` variable on `TRUE` to display the fully explained reasons of the occurred errors. Otherwise, we only get messages about the errors without the extra details attached. A class variable `$this->tableGateway` only shows how to retrieve an object of `TableGateway` used in other services, however it is not later used in the test file. It appears only for the informational reasons here. On the other hand, `$this->comicsTable` gets an access to the full Service Manager and a service with alias `ComicsTable::class` via the `$this->getApplication` ↳`ServiceLocator()`. Another line is just disabling the cache and gets a service from the main configuration, thanks to which we will get a value of `base_url`. We will use it later for creating a `Comics` object. Because in the testing class we will be using a physical database, we also have to prepare an environment for the tested data. Every test in this class should await the complete database structure like tables and columns, however there shouldn't be any records. This is why we are doing a call to the database adapter to run a query of `TRUNCATE`, so deleting all records from the table comics. Of course, there are also developers who would start to complain about the usage of the actual database in our unit tests. However, they cannot argue with the fact that it is the most realistic simulation of the operation of the whole system at once. Such testing is also called a functional testing or integration testing, as it tests the full integration of all linked components. There also exists a concept of using mocks, which imitates the whole lot of linked, but not necessary testable system components. They are also important and will be described in the next section, in which we will test an operation of the controller itself.

```
public function testGetByIdNotFound()
{
    $resultSet = $this->prophesize(ResultSetInterface::class);
    $resultSet->current()->willReturn(null);
    $id = 1;
    $this->setExpectedException(
        \Exception::class,
        'comics with id: '.$id.' has not been found'
    );
    $this->comicsTable->getById($id);
}

public function testGetBySuccess()
{
    $rowset1 = new Comics($this->baseUrl);
    $rowset1->exchangeArray(['title' => 'abc', 'thumb' => 'file.gif']);
    $rowset2 = new Comics($this->baseUrl);
    $rowset2->exchangeArray(['title' => 'abc2', 'thumb' => 'file.jpg']);
    $rowsetId1 = $this->comicsTable->save($rowset1);
    $rowsetId2 = $this->comicsTable->save($rowset2);
    $rowset1->setId($rowsetId1);
    $rowset2->setId($rowsetId2);
    $this->assertEquals([$rowset1, $rowset2], iterator_to_array($this->
↪comicsTable->getBy()->getCurrentItems()));
}
```

Our two first tests in the class `ComicstableTest` are `testGetByIdNotFound()` and `testGetBySuccess()`. First one, as the name suggests, expects the exception being thrown with a specific message, when we pass an id that does not exists. A second test is responsible for testing the whole `getBy()` method, under the condition that there are 2 results returned in an array by the iterator `getCurrentItems()`. We execute of course a call to the `save()` method, then we get and assign such added `ID` into our objects `$rowset1` and `$rowset2`.

```
public function testPatchInvalidData()
{
    $id = 1;
    $this->setExpectedException(
        \Exception::class,
        'no params sent to update'
    );
    $this->comicsTable->patch($id, []);
```

```php
}

public function testPatchSuccess()
{
    $rowset1 = new Comics($this->baseUrl);
    $rowset1->exchangeArray(['title' => 'abc2', 'thumb' => 'file.jpg']);
    $updatedData = [
        'thumb' => 'updated_file.jpg',
        'title' => 'updated_title'
    ];

    $rowsetId1 = $this->comicsTable->save($rowset1);
    $this->comicsTable->patch($rowsetId1, $updatedData);
    //let's check a result after new Comics object
    $expected = new Comics($this->baseUrl);
    $expected->exchangeArray($updatedData);
    $expected->setId($rowsetId1);
    $this->assertEquals([$expected], iterator_to_array($this->comicsTable->getBy()->
↪getCurrentItems()));
}

public function testDeleteInvalidId()
{
    $this->setExpectedException(
        \Exception::class,
        'missing comics id to delete'
    );
    $this->comicsTable->delete('');
}

public function testDeleteSuccess()
{
    $rowset1 = new Comics($this->baseUrl);
    $rowset1->exchangeArray(['title' => 'delete_title', 'thumb' => 'delete.jpg']);
    $rowset2 = new Comics($this->baseUrl);
    $rowset2->exchangeArray(['title' => 'normal_title', 'thumb' => 'normal.jpg']);

    //let's add two comics
    $rowsetId1 = $this->comicsTable->save($rowset1);
    $rowsetId2 = $this->comicsTable->save($rowset2);

    //let's delete only 1 comics
    $this->comicsTable->delete($rowsetId1);
```

```
//let's check a result after new Comics object
$rowset2->setId($rowsetId2);
$this->assertEquals([$rowset2], iterator_to_array($this->comicsTable->getBy()->
↳getCurrentItems()));
}
```

Another methods perform analogical checks such as `patch()`, responsible for updating the data, and `delete()` that removes records. Of course, firstly inside each of them we verify an invalid input data, and after that their successful execution. It is worth to notice that we are comparing the results returned by the `getBy()`, which are the iterator objects here. In order to convert them into an array, we use a built-in function `iterator_to`
↳`_array()`.

21.4. Controller tests and mocks

All our tests presented in this subsection, in contrast to the previous ones, will be using `Mocks` objects to imitate the dependencies and define the boundaries of the tested code. Let's begin from changing the name of *IndexControllerTest.php* into *NewsControllerTest.php*, so that we can start testing more things than just a static home page.

```
namespace ApplicationTest\Controller;

use Application\Controller\NewsController;
use Zend\Stdlib\ArrayUtils;
use Zend\Test\PHPUnit\Controller\AbstractHttpControllerTestCase;

class NewsControllerTest extends AbstractHttpControllerTestCase
{
    protected $traceError = true;

    public function setUp()
    {
        $configOverrides = [];
        $this->setApplicationConfig(ArrayUtils::merge(
            include __DIR__ . '/../../../../config/application.config.php',
            $configOverrides
```

```php
    ));
    parent::setUp();
}

public function testIndexActionCanBeAccessed()
{
    $this->dispatch('/news', 'GET');
    $this->assertResponseStatusCode(200);
    $this->assertModuleName('application');
    $this->assertControllerName(NewsController::class);
    $this->assertControllerClass('NewsController');
    $this->assertMatchedRouteName('news');
}

public function testIndexActionViewModelTemplateRenderedWithinLayout()
{
    $this->dispatch('/news', 'GET');
    $selector = '.jumbotron .zf-green';
    $this->assertQuery($selector);
    $this->assertQueryCount($selector, 1);
    $this->assertQueryContentContains($selector, 'Articles');
    //xpath
    $this->assertXpathQuery("//span[@class='zf-green']");
}

public function testInvalidRouteDoesNotCrash()
{
    $this->dispatch('/invalid/route', 'GET');
    $this->assertResponseStatusCode(404);
}
}
```

Apart from changing the address into *news* and updating the expected controller into ComicsController, we perform here a new usage of the methods responsible for checking the related data of the returned HTTP request. A method assertQuery() uses a Zend\Dom package, which is used to extract the data from the HTML/XML files using a standard format of CSS type. Example usages would be .class_name, #id_name or tag_name. This is exactly why we have defined our selector in the variable $selector, which with combination with assertQuery() method, does a check if results returned from the query are found there, after calling the method dispatch(). A method assertQueryCount(), however, checks the number of occurrences of a given result, and at the end `assertQueryContentContains()` gives us an ability to verify the content of the returned result. Alternatively to the standard CSS format, we can also use selectors of type Xpath. `Zend\Dom` also supports all linked methods with query in name, but they should be prefixed with xpath instead. Therefore, we can use methods as `assertXpathQueryCount` or `assertXpathQuery`, whose usage we have just showed in the code above.

A class `NewsControllerTest`, however, did not show us mocks nor their usage. This is why we will create another class for testing `UsersControllerTest` controller, which will test adding, saving and deleting the users without even touching the `UsersTable` model.

```
namespace ApplicationTest\Controller;

use Application\Model\UsersTable;
use Application\Model\UserHobbiesTable;
use Application\Model\Rowset\User;
use Zend\ServiceManager\ServiceManager;
use Prophecy\Argument;

class UsersControllerTest extends
\Zend\Test\PHPUnit\Controller\AbstractHttpControllerTestCase
{
    protected $tableGateway;
    protected $comicsTable;
    protected $traceError = true;
    protected $usersTable;
    protected $userHobbiesTable;

    protected function setup()
    {
        $this->setApplicationConfig(
            include APPLICATION_PATH . '/config/application.test.config.php'
        );
        parent::setup();
    }
```

Similarly as in the previous section, we extend an `AbstractHttp`↪`ControllerTestCase` class, which provides an access to the MVC methods such as `dispatch()` or `getResponse()`. This time in an initial method `setup()` we will set only an application configuration into a newly created one: *application.config.test.php*. We do that only because in the `configureServiceManager()` method, which we will call in the specific tests, we override a single service with mocks. Let's represent then how does the setup look in class imitating database together with `UsersTable` and `UserHobbiesTable`, which are called from the controller: `UsersController` in all actions.

```php
protected function configureServiceManager(ServiceManager $services)
{
    $services->setAllowOverride(true);
    $services->setService('config', $this->updateConfig($services->get('config')));
    $services->setService(UsersTable::class, $this->mockUsersTable()->reveal());
    $services->setService(UserHobbiesTable::class, $this->mockUserHobbiesTable()->
↪reveal());
    $services->setAllowOverride(false);
}

protected function updateConfig($config)
{
    $config['db'] = [];
    return $config;
}

protected function mockUsersTable()
{
    $this->usersTable = $this->prophesize(UsersTable::class);
    return $this->usersTable;
}

protected function mockUserHobbiesTable()
{
    $this->userHobbiesTable = $this->prophesize(UserHobbiesTable::class);
    return $this->userHobbiesTable;
}
```

Overriding services methods are located inside `configureConfig` ↪`Manager()`, but we get an access to this change only after calling `setAllowOverride(true)` method. After making an appropriate "replacements", we call this method at the very beginning, but with the Boolean flag set to FALSE, to secure the tests from overriding the services. Initially, we override the database configuration, which we reset into an empty table, to make sure that our tests of `UsersController`, will not be using a database connection. A method `mockUsersTable()` reuses the helper method of the mocks library: Prophecy `prophesize()`, which clones a class passed as argument and clears the logic of each method. Exactly the same applies to another helper method `mockUserHobbiesTable()`, with an exception that we imitate here the `UserHobbiesTable` class.

Finally, let's have a look at our first test, which will perform a check if the controller has called an `UsersTable` model properly.

```
/**
 * @group users.save
 */
public function testAddActionSuccess()
{
    $this->configureServiceManager($this->getApplicationServiceLocator());
    $this->usersTable
        ->save(Argument::type(User::class))
        ->shouldBeCalled();
    $postData = [
        'username' => 'new_user'
    ];
    $this->dispatch('/users/add', 'POST', $postData);
    $this->assertResponseStatusCode(302);
    $this->assertRedirectTo('/users');
}
```

Obviously, we have grouped our tests to the `users.save` group and we called a method of overriding the services in Service Manager at the beginning. The next line invokes an appropriate `save()` method in the prophecy object `$this->usersTable()`, which marks as executed with the given parameter of `Rowset\User` type thanks to the appended method `shouldByCalled()`. In this example we test a case where at the end of the test `testAddActionSuccess()` we check if an expected Prophecy object assumptions have been met. In our instance we prepare the data to send to */users/add* in POST format, then we check if the controller has redirected us by a heading (302) into a */users* page. After the test execution, there is another check by the mocks library if the method `save()` from the `$this->usersTable` was performed, and how many times. If we have not added the user successfully, then the `save()` method is not called, and the test returns an error with the following information:

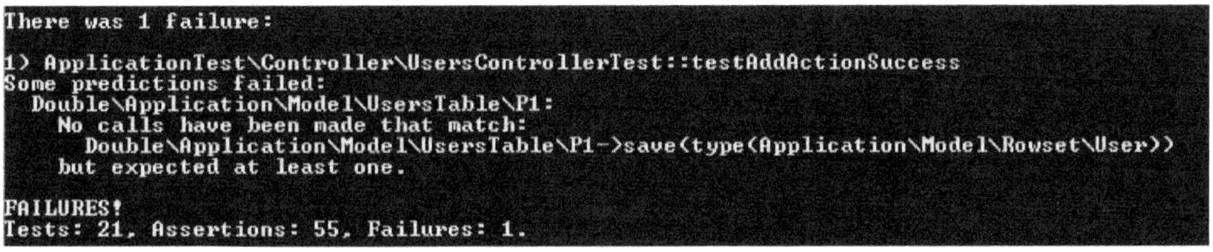

```
There was 1 failure:

1> ApplicationTest\Controller\UsersControllerTest::testAddActionSuccess
Some predictions failed:
  Double\Application\Model\UsersTable\P1:
    No calls have been made that match:
      Double\Application\Model\UsersTable\P1->save(type(Application\Model\Rowset\User))
    but expected at least one.

FAILURES!
Tests: 21, Assertions: 55, Failures: 1.
```

Image 21.3.

Another test will pass more data via the POST method to the address */users/edit* to display an information about the user on the edit page.

```
/**
 * @group users.update
 */
public function testUpdateActionValidate()
{
    $this->configureServiceManager($this->getApplicationServiceLocator());
    $id = 1;
    $editData = [
        'username' => 'new_user_updated',
        'email' => 'abc@funkcje.net',
        'user_info' => [
            'hobby' => ['books'],
            'gender' => 'male',
            'education' => 'primary',
            'comments' => 'test comment'
        ],
        'id' => $id
    ];

    $rowset = new User();
    $rowset->exchangeArray($editData);
    $this->usersTable->getById($id)->willReturn($rowset);
    $this->dispatch('/users/edit/'.$id, 'GET');
    $this->assertResponseStatusCode(200);
    $dom = new \Zend\Dom\Query($this->getResponse());
    $results = $dom->execute('input[name="username"]');
    $this->assertEquals($editData['username'], $results[0]->getAttribute
('value'));
    $this->assertQueryContentContains('.jumbotron .zf-green',
'Editing User id: '.$editData['id']);
```

```
    //we check if when we pass unexisting user id, controller would redirect us to the index
↪page
    $this->dispatch('/users/edit/9999', 'GET');
    $this->assertResponseStatusCode(302);
    $this->assertRedirectTo('/users');
}
```

The beginning of our `testUpdateActionValidate()` test is creating a sample `User` object with the specified data. We imitate a `getById()` method with a passed argument as `$id = 1`, into which we append a method `willReturn($rowset)`. As the name already points, it always returns an object `$rowset` when calling a `getById()` with parameter equal to `1`. Thanks to that, from now on we can display a user edit page */users/edit/1* and verify if the input field like `name="username"` have the same value as the data from `$editData` array. Then a check `assertQueryContent` ↪Contains() verifies if in the HTML header a text of *Editing User id: 1* exists. The last check is a call to the same edit page, but this time with an incorrect user id number. In such case our controller should redirect the user back to the `indexAction` page.

The penultimate test is a check if the user edit action was run successfully and if the data was stored correctly in the `UsersTable` and `UserHobbiesTable` objects.

```
/**
 * @group users.update
 */
public function testUpdateActionSuccess()
{
    $this->configureServiceManager($this->getApplicationServiceLocator());
    $id = 1;
    $editData = [
        'username' => 'new_user_updated',
        'email' => 'abc@funkcje.net',
        'user_info' => [
            'hobby' => ['books'],
            'gender' => 'male',
            'education' => 'primary',
            'comments' => 'test comment'
        ],
        'id' => $id
    ];
```

```
$rowset = new User();
$rowset->exchangeArray($editData);
$this->usersTable->getById($id)->willReturn($rowset);
$this->usersTable->save($rowset, $editData)->willReturn(true);
$this->userHobbiesTable->getPlainHobbies($id)->
↪willReturn($editData['user_info']['hobby']);

//let's try to edit the just created user
$this->usersTable
    ->save(Argument::type(User::class), Argument::type('array'))
    ->shouldBeCalled();
$this->userHobbiesTable
    ->save(Argument::type('int'), Argument::type('array'))
    ->shouldBeCalled();
$this->dispatch('/users/edit/'.$id, 'POST', $editData);
$this->assertResponseStatusCode(302);
$this->assertRedirectTo('/users');
}
```

The same as in the previous test, we prepare all the user data together with the hobbies. One more time we imitate a result for `getById(1)`, but additionally we also mock a `save()` method for the parameters: `$rowset` and `$editData`; a method result should now be returning TRUE. Next, we use `UserHobbiesTable` to get a list of all user's hobbies with id 1, thus we also imitate a method `getPlainHobbies($id)`, which returns a stored in our example array list of the hobbies: `$editData['user_info']` ↪`['hobby']`. For such crafted services we determine that our mocks will be called by specific arguments, so `Rowset\User` and `Array` for the first one and then `Integer` and `Array` for the second model. A final check will be an execution of the request POST to the address */users/edit/1*, which should save the new user data for the id: 1.

```
/**
 * @group users.delete
 */
public function testDeleteActionSuccess()
{
    $this->configureServiceManager($this->getApplicationServiceLocator());
    $id = 1;
    $editData = [
        'username' => 'new_user_updated',
        'email' => 'abc@funckje.net',
```

```
            'gender' => 'male',
            'education' => 'primary',
            'id' => $id
        ];

        $rowset = new User();
        $rowset->exchangeArray($editData);
        $this->usersTable->getById($id)->willReturn($rowset);
        $this->dispatch('/users/delete/'.$id, 'POST', $editData);
        $this->assertResponseStatusCode(302);
        $this->assertRedirectTo('/users');
    }
```

The last test in this chapter will be a check for a removed user from the
system. We repeat the steps for setting an initial user, simulate the
`getById()` method as before, but in this case instead of the user edit we call
a removal action of such user by the */users/delete/1*. Of course, later we also
test the behavior of the controller in such case, that is if the `index` action
redirect has been made.

At the end we can see if all of our tests function as expected, and if we don't
have any errors. If we have done everything as we were supposed to, then we
should get a result of 21 tests and 57 assertions, as below:

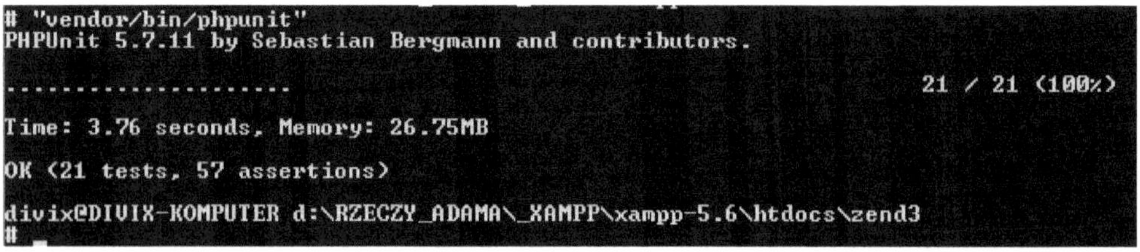

```
# "vendor/bin/phpunit"
PHPUnit 5.7.11 by Sebastian Bergmann and contributors.

.....................                                    21 / 21 (100%)

Time: 3.76 seconds, Memory: 26.75MB

OK (21 tests, 57 assertions)

divix@DIVIX-KOMPUTER d:\RZECZY_ADAMA\_XAMPP\xampp-5.6\htdocs\zend3
#
```

Image 21.4.

www.ingramcontent.com/pod-product-compliance
Lightning Source LLC
LaVergne TN
LVHW080111070326
832902LV00015B/2519